THE ARTS AND CRAFTS MOVEMENT

THE ARTS AND CRAFTS MOVEMENT
ROSALIND P BLAKESLEY

Φ

Phaidon Press Limited
Regent's Wharf
All Saints Street
London N1 9PA

Phaidon Press Inc.
180 Varick Street
New York, NY 10014

www.phaidon.com

First published 2006
Reprinted in paperback 2009
© 2006 Phaidon Press Limited

ISBN: 978 0 7148 4967 6

A CIP catalogue record for this book
is available from the British Library

Typeset in Eric Gill's Golden Cockerel type
designed in 1929 for Robert Gibbings's
Golden Cockerel Press

Designed by Webb & Webb Design Limited
Printed in China

Frontispiece: Philip Webb and William Morris
Saint George Cabinet, 1861–2 (fig. 25)

CONTENTS

Charles Robert Ashbee
Muffin Dish, *c.*1900 (fig. 60)

INTRODUCTION

THE ARTS AND CRAFTS MOVEMENT WAS ONE OF ENORMOUS INTELLECTUAL AMBITION AND OFTEN SUPERLATIVE ARTISTIC SKILL, ENCOMPASSING EVERYTHING FROM ENAMELLED BROOCHES TO CHURCHES, IN PLACES AS DIVERSE AS CALIFORNIA AND BUDAPEST.

Born of thinkers and practitioners in Victorian England who despaired of the ornate clutter which seemed to be pervading architecture and design, it was a movement about integrity. It was about respecting your materials, and the way you used them. It was about showing how things were constructed, so that they never looked different from what they really were. Equally, it was about respecting the maker. Against a background of the filth and degradation of industrialization, the Arts and Crafts Movement wanted people to work in happy, healthy surroundings, and to take pleasure in what they made.

One of the vital corollaries of this focus on environment was a new concern with the domestic and the commonplace. While there are important Arts and Crafts churches and public buildings, it was houses and their contents that mattered most – convenient, comfortable and functional spaces which met the demands of the modern inhabitant, and enhanced his or her quality of life. From the very first exploration of Arts and Crafts ideas – which this book argues came in the 1860s, long before the term was coined with the establishment of the Arts and Crafts Exhibition Society in London in 1887 – the need to produce furnishings and household goods which were both practical and aesthetically pleasing took centre stage. In the words of the architect and designer Charles Robert Ashbee, 'The Arts and Crafts Movement began with the object of making useful things, of making them well and of making them beautiful; goodness and beauty were to the leaders of the movement synonymous terms'.[1] Particularly strident was the call to dissolve the artistic hierarchy which had been in operation since the Renaissance, and which prioritized architecture, painting and sculpture above the so-called 'minor' arts. While never denying the importance of painting and sculpture, Arts and Crafts artists accorded new value to the decorative and applied arts and insisted that these become an integral part of any larger design. It was no longer enough to rely on serendipity or personal whim for the choice of armchairs in a sitting room, or the hanging of a tapestry in a church. Rather – reflecting the notion of the 'total work of art', or *Gesamtkunstwerk*, which the composer Richard Wagner had described as the aim of his operatic productions in the mid-nineteenth century – every element had to be designed as part of a single, organic whole.

The first half of this book explores the development of these ideas, and their offshoots and transmutations, in England, Scotland and Ireland. It does so chronologically, not only to provide a narrative to what can be a disparate set of buildings and objects, but also to capture the sense of community which is one of the most endearing aspects of the Arts and Crafts Movement. Its practitioners were not isolated artists united by stylistic similarities: they were masters and pupils, colleagues and rivals, lovers and friends who often conversed and collaborated in their efforts to raise standards of everyday design. There is, however, little visual coherence to their work. While some developed a rich, medievalizing imagery as part of their emulation of the social and artistic values of the Middle Ages, others strove for simplified forms whose decorative language depended on the natural properties of the materials. Indeed, the Arts and Crafts Movement derives its identity from a set of shared principles, rather than from any uniform visual code. As a result, it demands great intellectual agility from its students, who have to accept both its stylistic multiformity, and the diversions which its adherents often made from the Movement's theoretical framework. Famously, the elevation of the handicrafts, which were invested with a regenerative power in modern society, and the attendant distaste for the mechanical processes of industrialization, inspired many of the Movement's acolytes to focus on beautiful, hand-crafted products. But such was the expense of producing these that they had to be sold at prices beyond the pocket of the average household which Arts and Crafts practitioners were so anxious to reach. Rather than being irksome side issues, these, and other contradictions fundamental to the Movement, are tackled here when we negotiate the transition from theory to practice at the beginning of Chapter 2.

The second half of the book addresses the development of the Arts and Crafts Movement in continental Europe, before crossing the Atlantic to consider the great expansion in the United States of America. At this point the structure of the book becomes geographical rather than chronological, as the histories in different areas are dealt with in turn. The need to acknowledge patterns and themes means that national borders are not always respected. Finland, for example, is discussed alongside the Scandinavian countries, despite being part of Russia during the period in question, while developments in Poland and Hungary merit their own chapter, even though both nations were subsumed into neighbouring empires at the time. Nor are those countries which witnessed Arts and Crafts developments given equal attention: Belgium is considered in more detail than Holland, and a much fuller picture of the Movement in Finland is given than of that in Denmark. This is a reflection of the decision not to attempt to mention every artist or organization involved in the Arts and Crafts Movement. Rather, the aim has been to illustrate its complexity and richness by focusing on seminal figures and works of art.

The Movement developed different characteristics in the countries in which it appeared. On the whole, artists and designers in continental Europe and America did not share the anti-industrial sentiment which had motivated their British colleagues. In Austria and Germany, architects and designers emerging from the Arts and Crafts tradition embraced modernity to such an extent that the urban environment and industrial design became major concerns in their work. In contrast, in Europe's peripheralized nations such as Hungary, Poland and Finland, the Arts and Crafts evolved out of the broader political landscape of national resurrection and resistance to the oppression of foreign rule. In the arts, these concerns gave rise to a movement known as National Romanticism, in which vernacular and folk traditions, both real and invented, were appropriated and reworked to serve the cause of national definition. With its focus on folk art as a repository of 'pure' national forms, its interest in the recovery of minority cultures, and its concern with the revival of handicraft skills, National Romanticism has significant overlap with the Arts and Crafts. But this was not just a case of promoting vernacular art and architecture as expressions of nationhood and cultural identity. Rather, it involved artists and intellectuals, the majority of whom came from middle-class, urban backgrounds, drawing on vernacular examples in order to develop sophisticated languages of design which could compete in the modern world.

This brings us to the thorny question of class. The desire to make good design available to all sectors of society lay at the very heart of the Arts and Crafts Movement. As the renowned designer William Morris proclaimed in a famous *cri de cœur* in his first public lecture in 1877: 'I do not want art for a few, any more than education for a few, or freedom for a few.'[2] At the same time, many Arts and Crafts figures believed fervently that the working classes should be encouraged to realize their potential as producers, as well as consumers, of art. Yet in practice, this often resulted in educated designers and design theorists telling the lower classes what to produce, and what to like. In Eastern Europe, Russia and Norway, for example, it was through the intervention of largely middle-class artists that the traditional crafts of the peasantry were translated into modern, saleable works of art. As far as patronage is concerned, the Arts and Crafts had their aristocratic supporters (notably in Russia and Ireland), but here too the Movement was predominantly middle-class, embracing the range of financial and social status implied by that term. While families of comfortable but not abundant means welcomed the lack of pretension in the smaller Arts and Crafts houses, and culturally aware urbanites delighted in the decorative objects, self-made men who had earned fortunes in commerce and industry tended to be those financing the Movement's more ambitious buildings and designs.

One contentious aspect of the Arts and Crafts Movement is its relationship to other developments in the fine and decorative arts, notably Art Nouveau. It is not for one movement to claim exclusive ownership of an artist, group of artists or their creative output, and there are architects and designers in this book who also produced Art Nouveau work. Equally, works of art can carry multiple meanings which lead to different readings, with the result that individual designs can be associated with more than one artistic trajectory. Nevertheless, there are countries in which the term Art Nouveau has been used as a general moniker for a range of artistic expression at the turn of the century,

Finland being a prime example. Conversely, in the United States, there are objects treated as part of the Arts and Crafts Movement whose visual stylistics accord with the European understanding of Art Nouveau. The aim here is to offer a sensitive and nuanced account which acknowledges the common ground, but where necessary draws a distinction between the two movements. On occasion, this has meant unashamedly claiming or reclaiming a particular work for the Arts and Crafts.

The Arts and Crafts Movement had its fault lines. How did traditional craftsmen, particularly those of peasant origin, view the activities of those who came to tell them how to weave their tapestries or throw their pots? In those houses in which the architect designed everything from the furniture to the doorknobs, where were the inhabitants meant to keep the paraphernalia which they had accumulated in their previous lives? For a venture predicated on the need to cross class divisions, the Arts and Crafts Movement could be highly elitist, and its laudable aim of improving the lot of the common man could be the target of ridicule. As a character called Hamlin barked in Vernon Lee's novel, *Miss Brown* (1884), 'Any one is free to give the lower classes that taste of beauty, as long as I am not required to see or speak to the noble workmen [...] I hate all that democratic bosh.'[3] Today, many people on their first encounter with the Arts and Crafts Movement can even be put off by its name, conjuring up as it does images of worthy women doing clever things with fir cones. In certain circles, the word 'craft' is met with at best benign tolerance, and at worst derision: it is the world of smock dresses, macramé and slightly wonky pots. Yet, the Arts and Crafts Movement produced works of extraordinary vibrancy and intellectual rigour. It opposed vulgarity, pretension and shoddy workmanship. It championed the maker and the process of making, as much as the object made. And it created a new understanding of the need for local and national expression in art and design. The Movement itself came to an end shortly after the First World War, but these values have proved to be ones of lasting appeal.

A W N Pugin
Jardinière, c.1850 (fig. 5)

ESCAPING THE 'INEXHAUSTIBLE MINES OF BAD TASTE'

IN LATE-EIGHTEENTH-CENTURY BRITAIN, A HANDLOOM WEAVER WITH ANY IDEA OF WHAT FATE AWAITED HIS FAMILY MIGHT WELL HAVE CHOSEN TO EMIGRATE TO THE NEWLY INDEPENDENT UNITED STATES OF AMERICA.

A worker based in a textile centre such as Bolton in Lancashire was able to earn about thirty-three shillings a week in 1795, but twenty years later, as factory owners introduced wage-cutting and machine labour to increase profits, his son would be struggling on less than half that sum. By the time his grandson took up the family profession in the 1830s, wages as low as five shillings and sixpence a week would have forced the young man's wife and children to seek employment as well. In the cotton mills, where the cheap labour of women and children sometimes constituted three-quarters of the factory workforce, a boy of seven might work a fifteen-hour day. Alternatively, the family income could be supplemented with work down the mines, where the Children's Employment Commission of 1842 found children as young as four, 'so young they go in their bed-gowns'. While the weaver's children pushed wagons of coal along seams too narrow for adults or ponies, their mother would pull heavier loads attached to chains between her legs, even when pregnant, and would probably suffer a couple of miscarriages as a result. At the end of the day, the family would return to slum accommodation which they shared with rats, sewage, cholera, and several other families. Britain's

textile industry flourished, with the country's output of cloth growing from 40 million yards a year in 1785 to 2,025 million yards by 1850. During the same period, half a million handloom weavers starved.

This potted history of three generations of textile workers gives an insight into the dramatic social impact of the Industrial Revolution in Britain. A revolution on many fronts, industrialization had transformed everything from the economy to the country's landscape and the life expectancy of its inhabitants. It was against this background, which saw unheard-of fortunes in the railway and textile industries coexist with acute child mortality, that the social, cultural and intellectual debates which were to form the Arts and Crafts ethos began to evolve.

One of the first men to tackle the social consequences of industrialization was Robert Owen (1771–1858), who was arguably the most unorthodox and enlightened industrialist of his day. Owen made his fortune in the cotton manufactures of Manchester, and in 1799 acquired the New Lanark Mills, which still exist in an idyllic valley of the River Clyde, south-east of Glasgow. There, he vowed to find an alternative to the dehumanizing working practices which he had witnessed elsewhere and which, in his view, damaged man's moral as well as his physical state. 'I had to change these evil conditions for good ones', he later wrote, '[...] to supersede the inferior and bad characters, created by inferior and bad conditions, by superior and good characters to be created by superior and good conditions'. He therefore established a model village at New Lanark Mills which, for the first time, paid attention to living and working conditions, with a well-ventilated mill which enjoyed picturesque views, and special accommodation for the employees. Owen also campaigned tirelessly to improve the conditions of child labour in factories, arguing for a limit to the number of hours children could work, a minimum age at which they could be hired, and an educational test as a prerequisite to employment. The last point was particularly close to Owen's heart: New Lanark boasted two schools, including Britain's first infants' school, where children were taught from the age of two in an innovative educational system that won national acclaim. On occasion, Owen's good intentions backfired. One factory in Glasgow claimed that it recruited a stream of New Lanark workers, who found Owen's supposedly beneficial drills and dancing classes more exhausting than the longer working day elsewhere. His attempts to encourage good behaviour among his workers could also be patronizing and authoritarian. A piece of wood, for example, was suspended near the work station of each employee; its four sides were painted different colours and the colour displayed at the front indicated the worker's level of conduct the previous day.[2] Nevertheless, Owen made an enormous contribution to the campaign for industrial reform, not least by insisting that man's character is moulded by his environment. Half a century later, this connection between environment and morality became a cornerstone of Arts and Crafts debate.

In the 1820s, Britain began to awaken to the different ways in which public opinion could be channelled. In 1824, William Pitt's Combination Acts, which had outlawed trade unions at the beginning of the century, were repealed. This had the significant effect of removing the revolutionary undertones to working-class gatherings, and allowing lawful agitation by and on behalf of the socially disadvantaged. Major reform initiatives followed, including William Wilberforce's anti-slavery campaign, and the Earl of Shaftesbury's attempts to curb the exploitation of women and children in the factories and mines. Slavery in the British Empire was abolished in 1833 (a month after Wilberforce died), and in the same year the Factory Act established an

eight-hour working day for children between the ages of nine and thirteen. The battle to reform conditions in Britain's industrial centres was far from won. There were still abysmal standards of hygiene, and outbreaks of disease (31,000 people died of cholera in 1832, followed by a second epidemic in 1848–9). Moreover, children continued to be accidentally maimed or deliberately punished (sometimes with pickaxes) down the mines, and factory proprietors found loopholes in the new legislation, responding to the Factory Act by simply lengthening the adult working day. However, by the 1830s, steps were being taken to bring about social improvement at the expense of capitalist profit. At this point, a more cultural critique of the rationalist mentality of early-nineteenth-century capitalism began to emerge, as various thinkers and writers turned to the effect of industrialization on moral virtues and the creative drive.

The most powerful early analysis of the relationship between industry and morality came from the historian and political philosopher Thomas Carlyle (1795–1881) (fig. 1). The son of a Scottish stonemason, Carlyle was expected by his devout Calvinist family to enter the Church but instead threw himself into academic pursuits, teaching mathematics, translating from German, and writing acclaimed texts on historical subjects. In 1834, with his wife Jane Baillie Welsh (a long-suffering if neurotic consort whose erratic behaviour later included pasting photographs of murderers into an album), Carlyle moved to London, where his home in Chelsea became a centre of intellectual debate. Luminaries ranging from the poet Alfred Lord Tennyson to the Russian novelist Ivan Turgenev would pay their respects, gingerly picking their way through Jane's menagerie of assorted pets. It was in London, a metropolis whose population quadrupled in the course of the nineteenth century, that Carlyle focused his attention on the moral degradation in urban society. He saw the inhabitants of Britain's smog-bound cities as economically and spiritually destitute, and endeavoured to find out why.

Even before he moved to London, Carlyle had noted that craftsmen were marginalized and demoralized by mechanized production. 'The living artisan', he wrote, 'is driven from his workshop, to make room for a speedier inanimate one. The shuttle drops from the fingers of the weaver, and falls into iron fingers that ply it faster.'[3] As a result, 'Men are grown mechanical in head and in heart, as well as in hand. They have lost faith in individual endeavour, and in natural force, of any kind'.[4] In other words, man's mental and spiritual growth was being sacrificed in the name of technical

1. John Linnell
Thomas Carlyle, c.1837
Oil on canvas, 70 x 55 cm (27 ½ x 21 ½ in)
Scottish National Portrait Gallery, Edinburgh

progress. In Carlyle's view, a major factor in this was the *laissez-faire* policy at the heart of capitalism, whereby a self-regulating economy is allowed to develop independently of any governmental control. The policy enabled factory owners to enforce long hours, minimal wages and crippling working conditions with impunity, while slum landlords turned a blind eye to problems of drainage, sewage management and overcrowding. The poor and disadvantaged, it was argued, existed anyway, and it was not the job of industry to concern itself with issues of welfare.

Laissez-faire politics lay behind the Poor Law Amendment Act of 1834, which claimed that an able-bodied pauper was to blame for his plight, and offered him or her no alternative but the workhouse. Carlyle reacted with eloquent indignation in 1839: 'To believe practically that the poor and luckless are here only as a nuisance to be abraded and abated, and in some permissible manner made away with, and swept out of sight, is not an amiable faith.'[5] It was a long time before Carlyle's denunciation of *laissez-faire* politics bore fruit. Almost a decade later, *The Economist* magazine still maintained that 'suffering and evil are nature's admonitions; they cannot be got rid of; and the impatient attempts of benevolence to

banish them from the world by legislation [...] have always been more productive of evil than good.'[6] However, Carlyle's concept of progress meaning the moral development of an individual, as opposed to financial gain or industrial improvement, greatly stimulated social debate. He never relented in his castigation of the Industrial Revolution's reduction of life to material profit and loss. 'British industrial experience', he fulminated in 1850, 'seems fast becoming one huge poison-swamp of reeking pestilence physical and moral; a hideous *living* Golgotha of souls and bodies buried alive.'[7] This belief that the industrial impetus was a cause of moral decay awakened a public conscience which was to influence the ideology, if not always the practice, of the Arts and Crafts.

While Carlyle and his peers were considering the interaction between social virtues and a healthy environment, others had turned their attention to a very different problem: the apparent decline in standards of taste, in particular in the decorative arts. Attempts to reverse this decline had been made in the 1820s, in new initiatives to improve the education of the urban workforce. Thus the Mechanics' Institutes, established in Scotland in 1823, included the 'drawing of ornament' in their curriculum. The Institutes were so popular that in 1824 a tailor called Francis Place described 'from 800 to 900 clean respectable-looking mechanics paying most marked attention to a lecture on chemistry', and the same year the *Mechanics' Magazine* (1823–58), which advised on issues of design as well as on practical matters, reached a circulation of 16,000.[8] However, the distrust of mechanization in many design reform circles, coupled with simple class discrimination, prevented Britain's intellectuals from accepting that the Mechanics' Institutes could make any serious contribution to aesthetic standards. Instead, in 1835, the Government established the first of several inquiries, 'the Select Committee of Arts and their connection with Manufactures', to promote the study of art and design, in particular in Britain's growing manufacturing communities.

The Select Committee had two overriding concerns. First, why was Britain, the world's leading industrial nation, patently inferior to the Continent in terms of industrial design? Second, why was she failing to provide any relevant training? France had systematized the education of craftsmen ever since the seventeenth century, and the French Government now supported the École Royale de Dessin (later the École des Arts Décoratifs), industrial art schools in provincial cities such as Lyon, and even a school for women artisans. The German states also outclassed Britain in design

2. J R Herbert
Augustus Welby Northmore Pugin, 1845
Oil on canvas, 90 x 70 cm (35 ½ x 27 ½ in)
Palace of Westminster, London

education: Prussia boasted five schools (the *Gewerbeschule*) serving manufacturing communities, where pupils even had their fees paid by the state. In Britain, by contrast, the only institutions that taught the applied arts were the Mechanics' Institutes and the military colleges of Woolwich and Sandhurst, and these offered no more than an elementary training. Faced with evidence that British designers often copied foreign models, and that manufacturers in search of original designs imported work from abroad, the Select Committee recommended that Britain should follow the French and German precedent and establish state-funded institutes to teach communicable rules of good design. The result was the foundation in 1837 of London's School of Design, which for the first time in Britain attempted to provide a systematic training in the applied arts. Sixteen provincial schools followed, including one in Newcastle upon Tyne, a quintessential industrial centre of the Victorian age. The schools were beset with problems, and by 1846 were accused of failing to meet the needs of manufacturers by still leaning towards a fine art training. However, they did place the question of design education firmly in the public arena.

In the meantime, a new voice had begun to address the problematic web of industry, art and morality in the form of Augustus Welby Northmore Pugin (1812–52) (fig. 2). Pugin came from an artistic family (his father was a leading designer of Gothic detail for the architect John Nash) and by the age of fifteen he was designing silverware for the Royal Goldsmiths, and furniture for Windsor Castle. Most importantly, he inherited his father's love of medieval architecture and became a leading proponent of the Gothic Revival, a vast movement in the eighteenth and nineteenth centuries which drew on Gothic sources and imagery in the design of buildings and interiors, in literature, and in the fine and applied arts. The culture of the Middle Ages was admired for many reasons in the nineteenth century: there was a general feeling that art had been better appreciated then, and that individual ways of working had been encouraged, with devout artists pouring their souls into rich, colourful illumination and good, solid craftsmanship; the different polities of the medieval past could be interpreted to suit various social and political ends; and the structural principles of Gothic architecture were thought to offer a rational framework for modern design. At a time of aesthetic disquiet in Britain, these ideas held great appeal, and the Gothic Revival became the pre-eminent style for hundreds of Anglican buildings which followed the Church Building Act of 1818, and for Catholic churches which accompanied the increasing tolerance of Catholicism. It was also used extensively for private houses and public buildings, most famously Sir Charles Barry's New Palace of Westminster (1835–60), home of the Houses of Parliament, in which the Tudor Gothic's powerful messages of patriotism, liberty and legitimate authority perfectly suited the political constitution that the building housed. With its medievalizing attitudes, its quest for rational form, and its revival of craft skills, the Gothic Revival was a vital breeding ground for Arts and Crafts artists, many of whom trained with leading Gothic Revivalists (see Chapter 2). Pugin himself, a devout Roman Catholic from 1835, indulged his love of Gothic in designs ranging from jewellery and ceramics to his celebrated interiors for the Palace of Westminster. Such was his enthusiasm for the Gothic that when he married for the third time, in 1848, he wrote to a friend: 'I am married, I have got a first-rate Gothic woman at last'.⁹

In 1836, Pugin elaborated on his enthusiasm for the Gothic in his book *Contrasts; Or a Parallel between the Noble Edifices of the Fourteenth and Fifteenth Centuries, and Similar*

Buildings of the Present Day; Shewing the Present Decay of Taste.
In this work he developed a novel method of discussing
architecture, drawing on political cartoons and the visual
conceits of the popular press to launch a scathing attack on
modern buildings by contrasting them with Gothic design.
The book also promoted the social organization and working
practices of the Middle Ages, the implication being that these
could serve as a panacea for the evils of modern industrial
life. Thus in 'Contrasted Residences for the Poor' (fig. 3), the
poor in the medieval example are fed and housed in a
monastery, taught discipline from the pulpit and given a
dignified Christian burial. In contrast, the master of the
modern poorhouse administers a diet of gruel and enforces
discipline with a whip and handcuffs, while dead bodies,
wryly captioned as 'a variety of subjects always ready for
medical students,'[10] are carried off for dissection. Underlying
it all was Pugin's identification of Gothic architecture as
'moral' because its builders and craftsmen had shared a
common Christian faith. Both this and Pugin's idealization of
medieval society are questionable: he had no proof that every
Gothic architect was Christian; he gave no explanation for
his assumption that the work of Christian architects would
by association be 'good'; and he ignored the social problems
of medieval times. But his belief that a work of art reflected
the ethical values of its creator, and his insistence on a
cross-current between morality, creativity and environment,
were to make a singular impact on future critiques of art
and design.

If *Contrasts* championed Gothic design as moral,
Pugin's second book, *The True Principles of Pointed or Christian
Architecture* of 1841, attempted to explain its stylistic and
practical superiority. For Pugin, the Gothic embodied certain
'true principles' which were essential to all good architecture.
First, a building should show truth to purpose by
demonstrating the use for which it is intended. Thus the
religious purpose of a church should be evident in every
aspect of its design. Second, an architect must demonstrate
structural honesty, so that the methods of construction are
visible, and any details should be appropriate to the
architecture. Finally, Pugin insisted that an artisan stay true to
his material by drawing on its inherent properties, rather than
adopting methods better suited to another medium.

In Pugin's elucidation of the 'true principles' we
encounter what was to become a keyword in Arts and Crafts
debate – the notion of 'honesty'. For Pugin, both the architect
and his architecture had to be honest, the former by keeping

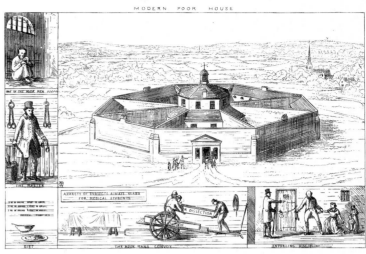
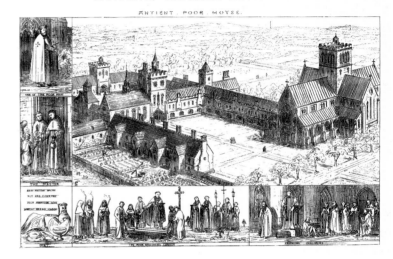

3. 'Contrasted Residences for the Poor'
from A W N Pugin, *Contrasts*, 1836

a pious Christian faith, and the latter by demonstrating structural fitness and propriety. 'Honesty' therefore became an unusual critical and analytical method, employed to determine the aesthetic and the social merits of a work of art. Moreover, Pugin also demanded 'honesty' of its interim methodology: the very process by which architecture was made had to be 'honest', by involving the designer or craftsman at every stage. Conversely, the division of labour, a key practice on which the profitability of industry rested, was *dis*honest: it denied the craftsman any intellectual or creative contribution, and was therefore debasing for the individual concerned. If one accepted Pugin's correlation between spiritual well-being and standards of design, it followed that a man reduced to being just part of a fragmented production line would produce substandard work.

Pugin's condemnation of the division of labour was not new. Gustav Waagen (1795–1868), the German art historian and museum director, had told the Select Committee of 1835 that a prime objective of the design schools in Prussia was to restore the artistic integrity of the High Renaissance, when 'the artists were more workmen and the workmen were more artists',[11] confirming that the need to integrate craftsmen into the creative process had been recognized on the Continent. But Pugin took the importance of unity in production further, and translated it into the need for unity in design: only by restoring a synergy between architect, designer and craftsman would each find joy in his labour, and be inspired to produce good, 'honest' work. Pugin endeavoured to revive several crafts of the Middle Ages to prove his point, producing hundreds of designs for church furniture, memorial brasses, textiles and stained glass. (A surge in church building inspired by the rise of Catholicism in England and by Tractarianism, an intellectual appeal to promote Anglican tradition, had intensified the demand for church craftsmanship.) His magnificent *Glossary of Ecclesiastical Ornament and Costume, Compiled and Illustrated from Antient Authorities and Examples* (1844) also helped to revive the production of ecclesiastical vestments and furnishings which had fallen into disuse. Craftsmen who carried out Pugin's designs for thousands of square feet of carving for the Palace of Westminster were trained in medieval techniques, and designers of woodwork, metalwork, tiles and painted glass were encouraged to study medieval models. Thus the Middle Ages became a repository of moral and 'honest' methods of production which, Pugin insisted, would result in good design.

In 1851, Pugin's zealous promotion of the Middle Ages was rewarded when he was asked to design a room called the Medieval Court at the world's first international exhibition, the Great Exhibition in London (fig. 4). He responded with a stunning array of Gothic-inspired designs which were made by the renowned craftsmen George Myers, John Hardman, Herbert Minton and John Gregory Crace. With their superior craftsmanship and relative restraint, the artefacts designed for the Medieval Court stood in stark contrast to other more fussy objects in the exhibition. Particularly telling is the comparison between Pugin's jardinière (fig. 5) and an ornate urn by Watherston and Brogden whose handles are barely visible under seated bishops and helmeted knights (fig. 6). All those involved in the Medieval Court were awarded medals, including the highest prize, the Council Medal, for Minton and Hardman, and Pugin won several commissions on the strength of the display. Sadly he died before he could fulfil these, at the age of forty in September 1852. Nevertheless, Pugin left an abiding legacy by expanding the appreciation of, and market for, high-quality craftsmanship, and by reviving the methods of medieval art and architecture in contemporary British construction and design. Five years after his death, medieval artefacts figured prominently at the Art Treasures Exhibition in Manchester, confirming the valued position which the Middle Ages now occupied in the British artistic consciousness.

The Great Exhibition of 1851 signalled a transitional point in the history of design. England was now a thoroughly industrialized society. Although the car manufacturer Henry Ford was not to perfect the production line until the early twentieth century, the American Oliver Evans had invented an assembly line for transporting grain as early as 1783, and mechanical assembly lines had become commonplace in Britain, starting with one for biscuit manufacturing in Deptford, London, in 1833. By 1849, £223.6 million had been invested in the railways, and the 1851 census revealed that mainland Britain's urban population exceeded its rural population for the first time. Urban degradation was still acute (the average life span for 'mechanics, labourers and their families' in Manchester was just seventeen, as opposed to thirty-eight in rural Rutlandshire).[12] But the Great Exhibition was designed to celebrate the positive aspects of the age of steam, and to advertise Britain's supremacy in industry and trade by providing a forum in which British products could be compared with those of its foreign rivals. In many respects it succeeded. Joseph Paxton's Crystal Palace, which housed the

4. Louis Haghe
Chromolithograph of the Medieval Court at the Great Exhibition
from *Dickinson's Comprehensive Pictures of the Great Exhibition of 1851*, 1854

5. AWN Pugin
Jardinière, *c.*1850
Printed earthenware, mounted in gilt cast iron
44.5 x 37.6 x 37.6 cm (17 ½ x 14 x 14 in)
Victoria and Albert Museum, London

6. Plate of an Urn by Watherston and Brogden, London,
from *The Art-Illustrated Catalogue for the Great Exhibition*, 1851

17

Exhibition, was acclaimed as a triumph of modern engineering, opening its doors just nine months after its site was secured in Hyde Park (fig. 7). The public came in droves, and countries as remote as Russia gave the exhibition extensive coverage in the periodical newspapers. George Cruikshank was one of many to comment on its popularity in an etching of crowds running after one of the special exhibition omnibuses, umbrellas raised to hook themselves on, while a woman on the front seat looks with disdain at those who might attempt to displace her (fig. 8). As the *Illustrated Catalogue* proudly stated:

> *The experiment of an Exhibition of the Industry of all the civilized Nations of the World [...] has succeeded beyond the most sanguine expectations of its projectors. [...] Other nations have devised means for the display and encouragement of their own arts and manu-factures; but it has been reserved for England to provide an arena for the exhibition of the industrial triumphs of the whole world. She has offered an hospitable invitation to surrounding nations to bring the choicest products of their industry to her capital, and there to enter into an amicable competition with each other and with herself.* [13]

The exhibition's aim of highlighting British pre-eminence, however, backfired. Despite a general consensus that British heavy industry led the field, the comparison of British decorative arts with their continental counterparts revealed the weakness of British design to an alarming extent, and a drop in standards was perceived across the board. 'It appears to us that the art-manufactures of the whole of Europe are thoroughly demoralized, and destitute for the most part of correct principles,'[14] wrote one critic. Even the exhibition's *Illustrated Catalogue* included an essay by Ralph Wornum ominously entitled 'The Exhibition as a Lesson in Taste'. Wornum, a lecturer at the School of Design and later Keeper of the National Gallery, made explicit both the general low standards, and Britain's subservience to France in matters of design, concluding 'that there is nothing new in the Exhibition in ornamental design; [...] that the taste of the producers generally is uneducated, and that in nearly all cases where this is not so, the influence of France is paramount in the European productions.'[15] Wornum spared Pugin's work from his invective, writing that 'the few Greek, or so-called Etruscan specimens, and the Gothic examples, in the

8. George Cruikshank
Etching of the 'Omnibus to the Great Exhibition'
from Henry Mayhew and George Cruikshank, *1851: Or The Adventures of Mr and Mrs Sandboys and Family*, 1851

7. (opposite) Chromolithograph of the 'View Across the Transept of the Crystal Palace from South to North'
from *Dickinson's Comprehensive Pictures of the Great Exhibition of 1851*, 1854

9. Portrait of Henry Cole from
The Illustrated London News, July 1873

singularly styled Medieval Court, are almost the only exceptions as regards European design'.[16] Nevertheless, the official aim of the exhibition, which had been 'exhibition, competition and encouragement',[17] had failed dramatically on the last point. It had supplied 'sources of after-education to manufacturers and artisans of all classes, and of all countries,[18] as the *Illustrated Catalogue* had hoped, but primarily as examples of what *not* to do. Instead, the majority of exhibits demonstrated what the designer and critic Owen Jones (1809–74) called 'novelty without beauty, or beauty without intelligence'.[19] Many commentators blamed industrialization for the fall in standards which, as the design historian Paul Greenhalgh has noted, was illogical: it is more likely that detailed ornamentation symbolized affluence to the upper working and lower middle classes, who were entering the art market and created a demand for lavishly decorated work. But this does not alter the fact that in the minds of many reviewers, industrial practices were associated with the deterioration in taste and design.

Practical measures were immediately taken to remedy this state of affairs. A Government grant of £5,000 was used to purchase objects from the exhibition which, coupled with collections from the Schools of Design, opened as the Museum of Manufactures in Marlborough House in 1852. With its aim of 'the improvement of taste in design, and the application of fine art to objects of utility',[20] the Museum reaffirmed Pugin's belief that the distinction between the fine and the decorative arts had to be removed if standards in design were to rise. At the insistence of Prince Albert, Queen Victoria's husband and the driving force behind the Great Exhibition, profits from the event, totalling over £180,000, were used to buy eighty-seven acres of land in South Kensington for new museums and university institutions. These included the South Kensington Museum (now the Victoria and Albert Museum), whose original purpose was to assemble examples of applied and decorative art to serve as teaching models for the Schools of Design. The London School of Design moved from its original home in Somerset House to Marlborough House when the Museum of Manufactures opened there in 1852 and then to South Kensington in 1863, where it eventually became the Royal College of Art.

A key figure in these developments was Sir Henry Cole (1808–82), Prince Albert's right-hand man in the organization of the Great Exhibition (fig. 9). Cole was a splendidly whiskered bureaucrat of meddlesome inclination, and from an early age his impatience with bad managerial practice compelled him to push for institutional reform: his complaints about inefficiency at the Record Commission (where he worked from the age of fifteen) led to its reorganization as the Public Record Office, and to Cole's appointment as its Assistant Keeper in 1838. This pattern of Cole rising in the ranks after campaigning for an institution's reform was to recur, thanks to his prodigious organizational skills, his ruthless self-promotion, and his thick skin. So high was his own opinion of his career that he later called his autobiography *Fifty Years of Public Work* (1884).

In the 1840s, Cole focused his irrepressible energy on the arts, writing children's literature under the pseudonym of Felix Summerly, and commissioning Britain's first commercial Christmas card. In 1847, he also established Felix Summerly's Art-Manufacturers, buoyed by the success of a tea service which he had submitted the previous year to a competition for 'objects of everyday use'[21] organized by the Society of Arts. The Felix Summerly Art-Manufacturers aimed to improve aesthetic standards by commissioning household objects from well-known artists (some of them Royal Academicians), establishing a novel system which harked back to medieval and Renaissance systems of working and did not distinguish between the fine and decorative arts. Cole's persuasive tactics enlisted the support of eminent manufacturers such as the Coalbrookdale Iron Company, Hollands the cabinet-makers, and the Minton and Wedgwood potteries. He summarized the venture's objective as 'to produce in each article superior utility, which is not to be sacrificed to ornament; to select pure forms; to decorate each article with appropriate details relating to its use, and to obtain these details as directly as possible from nature. These principles [...] may be adhered to advantageously in most articles of use, and may possibly contain the germs of a style which England in the nineteenth century may call its own.'[22] Thus Cole shared Pugin's insistence on appropriate ornament and on truth to purpose, as well as the growing, pan-European preoccupation with national identity in art and design.

By the 1850s Cole had become positively evangelical about design standards, and elbowed his way into numerous reform initiatives. His triumph as chief organizer of the Great Exhibition led to his appointment as General Superintendent of the Government's new Department of Practical Art in 1852, under whose auspices he ran the Museum of Manufactures. The Museum contained examples of what designers should emulate, as well as the so-called Chamber of Horrors, stocked with objects which Cole deigned to class as bad design. During his tenure at the Department, the number of art schools in the provinces increased from thirty-six in 1852 to ninety-one in 1861, and drawing skills were promoted to such an extent that by the mid-1860s they were being taught to over ninety per cent of the nation's schoolchildren. Cole was also instrumental in the appointment of a Select Committee to investigate the Schools of Design. He appeared as a witness, wrote three of the Committee's reports, and wheedled his way into the job of secretary to the reformed schools from 1852 until 1873. His fervent hopes of improving industrial design were never fully realized: new classes in applied arts, including textiles, pottery and metalwork, were short-lived and ineffectual, and the Schools of Design never found a sustainable balance between their arts-based teaching and the demands of industry. But Cole, whose formal artistic training had comprised little more than lessons in watercolour painting and perspective drawing, was without question one of the most efficient arts administrators of the century, and an inexhaustible catalyst in attempts to define and regulate good industrial design.

By the middle of the century, standards of design were being debated in a number of new periodicals. These included *The Art Union* (renamed *The Art Journal* in 1849); *The Builder* (1843–1966); *The Decorator's Assistant* (succeeded by *The Universal Decorator* in 1858); and Cole's own *Journal of Design and Manufactures* (1849–52). A dense and bulky publication, this last journal adopted the innovative practice of gluing to its pages samples of textiles and wallpaper provided by manufacturers, and rehearsed many arguments which had underpinned Cole's practical initiatives, such as the need to improve the interface between designers and producers. It also asserted the paramountcy of function over form, insisting 'that until the form best adapted for the required purpose has been obtained, and that refined to its most graceful line, ornament had better not be added'.[23] The periodicals were joined by important monographs, notably Owen Jones's *The Grammar of Ornament* (1856: fig. 10), an exquisite volume of 100 colour plates which illustrate patterns in styles ranging from Egyptian to Hindu, and in categories from Arabian to 'Savage Tribes' (fig. 11). In this work, Jones urged artists to study both nature and historical precedent, arguing that 'the future progress of Ornamental Art may be best secured by engrafting on the experience of the past the knowledge we may obtain by a return to Nature for fresh inspiration.'[24] This concept of nature and the past as key

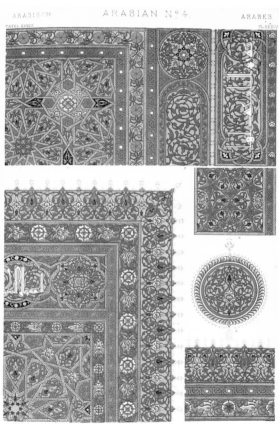

10, 11. Owen Jones
Frontispiece and plate from *The Grammar of Ornament*, 1856

stimuli to artistic creativity was shared by many Arts and Crafts artists (William Morris, for one, read Jones's work in detail) and *The Grammar of Ornament* became the classic Victorian reference book of ornamental design. The most influential of all the mid-century publications, however, were those of John Ruskin (1819–1900), whose writing became a mainstay of the Arts and Crafts Movement.

Ruskin (fig. 12) was the greatly over-protected child of a prosperous sherry merchant and his fanatically religious wife, who famously moved to Oxford when her son matriculated at the university in order to safeguard his Christian faith. His passion for art was aroused on his thirteenth birthday when he was given the 1830 edition of Samuel Rogers's *Italy*, which included vignettes by the English landscape artist J M W Turner. Ruskin's ensuing passion for Turner led to his own first book, *Modern Painters*, which appeared in five volumes between 1843 and 1860. However, it is Ruskin's writing on architecture, begun as an undergraduate in articles for the *Architectural Magazine* and later developed in his seminal books *The Seven Lamps of Architecture* (1849) and *The Stones of Venice* (1851–3), which is of importance here. *The Seven Lamps* develops a series of architectural axioms or 'lamps', which set out what Ruskin deemed the essential requirements of good architecture. *The Stones of Venice*, in contrast, is a detailed, if peculiar, architectural history of Venice, but in a central chapter in the second volume, entitled 'The Nature of Gothic', Ruskin deviates to discuss questions of industry and work. It is this chapter which was to prove particularly determinant on the Arts and Crafts.

In his early writing, Ruskin agreed with Pugin, Cole and Jones that nature was the foremost artistic source: in *The Seven Lamps*, the 'Lamp of Beauty' required architectural decoration to be based on natural motifs, as 'all most lovely forms and thoughts are directly taken from natural objects [...] forms which are *not* taken from natural objects *must* be ugly.'[25] Ruskin's religious upbringing was a mainspring to this argument, as is evident in the first volume of *The Stones of Venice*: 'all noble ornamentation is the expression of man's delight in God's work.'[26] Ruskin's practical work supported his view that nature alone inspired good art. He produced superbly detailed drawings of plants, mountains and the contours of rock formations (fig. 13), and then abstracted from these simple diagrams to demonstrate how decoration could be derived from natural forms. He also contributed designs for the ornamentation of the University Museum in Oxford (1855–61), a remarkable engineering structure adorned with intricate stone carvings of birds, animals and plant motifs. Although Ruskin later rejected the primacy of natural forms, based on his bizarre argument that nature herself had somehow deteriorated, his early emphasis on truth to nature greatly influenced Arts and Crafts design. It also led to Ruskin's theory of 'organic architecture', which was to become a major part of the Arts and Crafts vocabulary.

Ruskin's notion of 'organic architecture' demanded that architecture should evolve like a living organism, revealing the ground in which it developed, and relating every part harmoniously to the whole. Thus the 'Lamp of Memory' required buildings to reveal their historical as well as their formal associations, and the 'Lamp of Truth' required honest workmanship and truth to materials to ensure an organic synthesis of craftsmanship, media and design. The architect should avoid 'the suggestion of a mode of structure or support, other than the true one', and 'the painting of surfaces to represent some other material than that of which they actually consist (as in the marbling of wood), or the deceptive representation of sculptured ornament upon them'.[27] Many of these ideas echo those of Pugin and, like him, Ruskin identified the Gothic as the most honest or 'organic' style. There was, however, one crucial point on which Ruskin differed from Pugin: he saw no viable relationship between industry and art. Pugin may have loathed the modern metropolis – he dismissed Birmingham and Sheffield as 'inexhaustible mines of bad taste'[28] – and he associated industrialization with deterioration in design, but he did not condemn mechanical innovation *per se*. Rather, Pugin wanted to monitor the *application* of industrial techniques: 'we do not want to arrest the course of inventions, but to confine these inventions to their legitimate uses'.[29] Ruskin was never to show such tolerance, insisting that evidence of handwork was the most important barometer of a work's success. Thus his 'Lamp of Life' demanded signs of the human hand, rather than the monotonous perfection achieved by machine. By the time Ruskin wrote 'The Nature of Gothic' in *The Stones of Venice*, his abhorrence of industrial labour was absolute:

> Men may be beaten, chained, tormented, yoked like cattle,
> slaughtered like summer flies, and yet remain in one sense,
> and the best sense, free. But to smother their souls within them,
> to blight and hew into rotting pollards the suckling branches of
> their human intelligence, to make the flesh and skin which,
> after the worm's work on it, is to see God, into leathern thongs to
> yoke machinery with – this is to be slave-masters indeed.[30]

12. John Ruskin
Self-Portrait in Blue Neckcloth
Watercolour and gouache, 35.3 x 25.3 cm (13 7/8 x 10 in)
The Pierpont Morgan Library, New York

13. John Ruskin
Gneiss Rock, Glenfinlas, 1853
Ink wash and gouache on paper, 47.7 x 32.7 cm (18 3/4 x 12 3/4 in)
Ashmolean Museum, Oxford

This vitriolic attack on industry was fundamental to those Arts and Crafts designers who never even considered reconciling art and industrial design.

'The Nature of Gothic' weaves the arguments of earlier design theorists into a lucid, compelling whole. The idea that the division of labour led to moral and artistic collapse, for example, was hammered home with ironic hyperbole: 'We have much studied and much perfected, of late, the great civilized invention of the division of labour; only we give it a false name. It is not, truly speaking, the labour that is divided; but the men: – Divided into mere segments of men – broken into small fragments and crumbs of life; so that all the little piece of intelligence that is left in a man is not enough to make a pin, or a nail, but exhausts itself in making the point of a pin or the head of a nail.'[31] While an impressive number of pins could be made in a day, their points had been polished with the sand of the 'human soul'. Never before had the well-being of the worker been quoted so convincingly as a criterion of good art. For Ruskin, there was one, incontrovertible way in which art and design could be morally uplifting, and that was by ensuring that a craftsman controlled every stage of production, from design to execution. 'It is only by labour that thought can be made healthy, and only by thought that labour can be made happy, and the two cannot be separated with impunity. [...] The painter should grind his own colours; the architect work in the mason's yard with his men; the master-manufacturer be himself a more skilful operative than any man in his mills.'[32] With its condensation of this key issue, 'The Nature of Gothic' became a central creed of the Arts and Crafts Movement.

In the 1850s, Ruskin began a friendship with Carlyle, just five years his senior, and became increasingly involved in practical social initiatives. In 1854, he assisted in organizing relief after a cholera epidemic, and his interest in education made him an early supporter of the Working Men's College, which opened in London the same year. In 1857, he began a lecture on art in Manchester with a controversial disquisition on poverty, and in 1860 he abandoned his mantle of artistic sage completely and contributed four essays on political economy to the *Cornhill Magazine*. This growing concern with the conditions under which art might prosper, rather than with art itself, was of importance to Arts and Crafts practitioners, who themselves questioned the relationship between society and design. It also placed Ruskin at the heart of European socio-economic debate. His belief that a person's

intellectual life depended on social factors, for example, reflects the Marxist relation between superstructure and base. As Karl Marx (1818–83) wrote in *A Contribution to the Critique of Political Economy* (1859), 'It is not the consciousness of men that determines their existence, but (on the contrary) their social existence that determines their consciousness.'[33] The French critic and philosopher Pierre Joseph Proudhon (1809–65) also examined the dynamic between art, politics and social ideals in *Philosophie du progrès* of 1853, the year in which the final volume of *The Stones of Venice* appeared. Proudhon's social thought, based on the Utopian theories of earlier French thinkers such as Fourier and Saint-Simon, was more controlled than the inspired but chaotic brilliance of Ruskin's political diatribes, and should not be ignored in the history of British design. It was Proudhon, for example, who advocated rural co-operatives and *atelier* communities as an antidote to the inequality and squalor of industrial life, anticipating a path taken by many later Arts and Crafts collectives.

In the 1870s, Ruskin's concern with social and economic conditions intensified. Was it not, he wondered in 1870, 'the vainest of affectations to try to put beauty into shadows while all real things that cast them are left in deformity and pain?' Anxious to make a practical impact, he attempted to address the working class directly in *Fors Clavigera*, a series of monthly letters published at his own expense between 1870 and 1884. He embarked on a number of projects to 'benefit' society, including street-sweeping in the London slums and, in 1874, recruiting strapping young undergraduates at the University of Oxford to mend roads at Hinksey, a small village on the outskirts of the city. In 1871, Ruskin also founded the Guild of St George, an organization which had the immediate objective of buying land for impoverished townspeople to reclaim and cultivate in accordance with idealistic, anti-industrial principles, and the ultimate aim of creating a new, rural society. Ruskin envisaged the Guild running a network of schools, museums and libraries across the country, starting with the Museum of St George which he founded in Sheffield in 1875. The Guild was unable to achieve these aims, with few sources of income other than Ruskin's private donations (though it does still exist as an educational charitable trust). Ruskin's attempt to create a self-governing rural collective nevertheless set a precedent for many Arts and Crafts societies which appeared from the 1880s onwards.

Ruskin died in 1900, by then a deranged man who had endured severe depression, repeated disappointments in love, paedophiliac tendencies and, in 1854, acute betrayal when his wife Effie, after a marriage that had never been consummated, left him for his friend, the Pre-Raphaelite artist John Everett Millais. But despite his personal unhappiness, Ruskin left an unrivalled body of work of enormous intellectual ambition, which was to tax the interpretative powers of design theorists, among others, for decades. He would readily devote his energies to explaining what he saw as a simple truth to an unusual audience, as when arguing in his lectures to the Bradford Mechanics' Institute in 1859 that only people surrounded by beautiful objects will produce beautiful things. He could also write with remarkable clarity, as when he claimed in *The Seven Lamps* that 'the right question to ask, respecting all ornament, is simply this: Was it done with enjoyment – was the carver happy while he was about it?'[34] On other occasions his argument is so convoluted and meandering that it becomes unintelligible. However, periods of madness apart, Ruskin never lost sight of the need to integrate the *entire* human personality in the production of art: 'all art is great, and good, and true, only so far as it is distinctively the work of *manhood* in its entire and highest sense; that is to say, not the work of limbs and fingers, but of the soul'. Introspective Victorian society had the inclination to address this problem as never before, and Ruskin's social and moral principles assumed a central role in cultural debate. It was time to see the extent to which they could be put into practice.

Dante Gabriel Rossetti
'Music' from *King René's Honeymoon, c.*1863 (detail of fig. 24)

FIRST EXPLORATIONS: WILLIAM MORRIS AND HIS CIRCLE

THE 1860s AND 1870s SAW THE EMERGENCE OF A GENERATION OF ARCHITECTS AND DESIGNERS IN BRITAIN WHO WERE DETERMINED TO RAISE THE STATUS OF CRAFTSMEN, AND TO RESTORE SOCIAL AND MORAL MEANING TO THE ARTS.

Britain was now a very different place from that which had galvanized reformers like the Earl of Shaftesbury and provoked the ire of Thomas Carlyle. The country's population had soared (that in England and Wales doubled, to 20 million, in the period 1811–61 alone), and sixty-five per cent of it now lived in cities, a proportion two and a half times larger than that in Germany or France. At the same time, Britain was riding the crest of a wave as the world's leading industrial power. She produced half of the world's coal, more than half its iron and steel, and owned over a third of its merchant shipping. The national product more than doubled between 1851 and 1881, and exports rose from £100 million in the decade 1850–9, to £218 million in the decade 1870–9. In the words of Benjamin Disraeli, the Prime Minister in 1868 and again from 1874 to 1880, the country was enjoying a 'convulsion of prosperity'. If we add to Britain's ascendancy in commerce and manufacturing the fact that she could boast of a stable government, a renowned parliamentary system, the absence of any significant foreign aggressor, and a vast empire, we can appreciate why the Victorian boom of the 1860s and 1870s engendered considerable national pride.

Britain's social structure had also developed from the polarization between canny factory owners and underpaid textile workers with which this book began. While there was still extreme poverty and exploitation, being born into the working classes no longer preordained a life of unmitigated toil. Instead, the latest generation of our original textile family might secure white-collar work in factories now managed by a new class of professional administrator. They might find clerical work in banks, offices or the civil service; they might serve in the growing number of shops; or they might turn to the teaching profession, which expanded rapidly after the Elementary Education Act of 1870. The Act required Education Boards to establish board schools where there was no other provision for primary education, creating a demand for new teachers. The schools, for their part, aimed to provide the levels of literacy and numeracy necessary to secure a white-collar job. These and other professional opportunities contributed to the expansion of the middle classes, the more entrepreneurial of whom enjoyed a rapid social ascent. Boundaries between the upper middle classes and the lower gentry became fluid and negotiable, as the sons of factory owners mixed with young aristocrats at public schools and at the universities of Oxford and Cambridge, while their fathers took advantage of falling land values to purchase a country estate. From the 1860s wealthy businessmen began to exceed rich landowners in number, if not in size of fortune, and middle-class politicians gained ministerial rank in a Parliament long dominated by aristocratic status and wealth. One of the most striking stories is that of Mr W H Smith, whose early career as a newsagent led to an empire of shops which still carry his name across Britain: he entered Parliament in 1868, became First Lord of the Admiralty in 1877, and was leader of the Commons by 1886. Other self-made men began to have their achievements rewarded with national honours: whereas few members of the middle classes were ennobled before 1880, by the end of the century they accounted for over forty per cent of new peerages. Their route to ennoblement lay not in the inheritance of land and title, but in their perseverance in trade: while Lord Armstrong gained a peerage thanks to his armaments empire, Lord Leverhulme owed his rise to phenomenal sales of one-penny bars of Lifebuoy soap.

The consolidation and gentrification of the middle classes is important not only in illustrating the increasing diversity of Britain's demographic framework. Educated, enriched, and on occasion ennobled, they began to celebrate their status and success by improving their domestic surroundings. As the introduction to the 1851 census recognized: 'the possession of an entire house is strongly desired by every Englishman, for it throws a sharp, well defined circle round his family and hearth.' The design, construction and decoration of these houses provided both financial and intellectual stimulus to the practical realization of Arts and Crafts ideals.

But it is when we begin to address the ways in which the ideas of Pugin, Ruskin and their fellow thinkers were put into practice that we have to grasp the nettle that is the Arts and Crafts. The ideas outlined in Chapter 1 are vital in that they motivated and provoked the artists of the day and provided them with the language which they sometimes needed to explain the relationships between themselves, their art and the world at large. But they are not blueprints, and letting them dominate can distort our understanding of the work which Arts and Crafts artists went on to create. Instead, we need to give the objects, as well as the ideas, authority, so that the Movement is understood as protean and multifaceted, rather than confusing and confused. It is a question of balancing the ideas and the objects, the principles

and the practice, and three particular dualities need to be explored from the start.

The first of these lies in the patronage of the upper middle classes. Theirs was the wealth which galvanized new ideas in architecture and design, but their riches often stemmed from industrial practices – the division of labour, the substitution of man by machine – which the artists and designers opposed. The question of whether to address the social implications of artistic production, or to accept the patronage of those who could actually afford good craftsmanship, became an infuriating and ultimately insoluble dilemma for those attempting to strike a balance between the moral tenets of Pugin and Ruskin and the concern to elevate standards in design. Thus architects and designers found themselves negotiating hazardous intellectual territory as they tried to accommodate both the vital financial input of a social elite, and the more democratic concerns from which the Arts and Crafts Movement stemmed. Ultimately, the democratic impetus of the Movement has to be weighed up against the middle- and upper-class patronage on which both artists and workshops came to depend.

The second area of conflict is that between the advocacy of handwork and the vilification of the machine. The problem here lies in the propensity – both then and now – to use the words 'machine' and 'mechanization' as if they had one meaning. In reality, mechanized production denotes a variety of processes, and while some alienate the worker from the product or disenfranchise the human operator, others demand creative thought and intellectual involvement – surely satisfying Ruskin's demands of ennobling work? Certain types of mechanization even release the operator from monotonous tasks, so that he or she is free to engage in more fulfilling pursuits. Moreover, in industrialized societies, mechanization of some description is often essential to make products commercially viable, while working by hand is expensive and an impractical way of popularizing good design. We must therefore be circumspect about the loose dismissal of the 'machine', and the supposed primacy of the handmade.

The final problem concerns the much-vaunted notion of integrated labour, which insisted that a craftsman realize his own designs. This was deemed essential to his self-esteem and well-being and, by association, to the success and status of his work. But the division of labour was not necessarily pernicious. Would a needlewoman really recoil from embroidering somebody else's pattern, or a joiner feel slighted at being given a design for a table? When others praised their skill, would they resent the fact that they had not originated the design, and as a result take less delight in the finished work? Similarly, would an ambitious workshop jeopardize its commercial viability simply to ensure that every object it produced had been the work of just one person? Reduced to these blunt, human terms, the argument seems shaky, and we realize that integrated labour was not always feasible in the workplace, nor was it essential for good, enjoyable work. Indeed, dividing production according to skill and technique could *flatter* the individual by recognizing his or her expertise.

These, then, are the three main paradoxes of the Arts and Crafts. They do not have to be approached as obstacles to understanding, which we must resolve into statements of seamless logic. We can instead acknowledge the richness and diversity which they bring, and welcome the interpretative challenge which they present. It is by avoiding over-literal readings of the discourses in Chapter 1 that we can understand what shaped the artists and designers, and how they in turn shaped the Movement as a whole.

The most important of the first generation of Arts and Crafts designers was William Morris (1834–96). Master of half a dozen crafts and practitioner of several more, Morris was in addition a writer and translator of international recognition, a poet so highly esteemed that he was offered the Professorship of Poetry at Oxford University and, for the last two decades of his life, one of Britain's leading socialists. His own versatility led him to develop high expectations of others: 'If a chap can't compose an epic poem while he's weaving a tapestry, he had better shut up, he'll never do any good at all.'[1] Bearded, rotund, indefatigable, and given to frightening rages now thought to be a form of epilepsy, Morris was the most charismatic and influential British designer of his age. It was he and his friends and colleagues who, in the 1860s and 1870s, effected the transition from the abstract ideas of the first half of the century to a vibrant web of objects, people and places which gave tangible form to Arts and Crafts concerns.

Morris was the third child and first son of a broker in the City of London, who had made his fortune by speculating in copper mining in the West Country. He grew up in Walthamstow, then a rural area to the north-east of London, and in 1840 his father's considerable income enabled the family to move to Woodford Hall, an impressive Georgian mansion with its own fifty-acre park, brewery, bakery and buttery. In 1847, however, the peaceful and prosperous existence of the Morris family was shattered when Morris's father died suddenly and, seven days later, the firm in which he had been a partner suspended business. The family moved to a smaller, though still substantial, property, Water House in Walthamstow (now the William Morris Gallery), where Morris's mother managed to put their finances back on an even keel and they lived comfortably enough on dividends from the copper-mining shares. However, Morris, now the eldest male in a one-parent family of nine, had had an abrupt and early taste of the value of money. He was later to develop a keen business sense, not least when he saw sources of income drying up and had to support a family of his own. This commercial acumen was to play a significant role in his success as a designer.

In 1852 Morris matriculated at Exeter College in Oxford, where his tutor remembered him as 'a rather rough and unpolished youth, who exhibited no special literary tastes or capacity, but had no difficulty in mastering the usual subjects of examination'.[2] The assessment suggests an uninspiring student, but outside the formal teaching of the university, Morris found a milieu in which he thrived. He became firm friends with the future painter and designer Edward Burne-Jones (1833–98), and the two developed the custom of Morris reading aloud to Burne-Jones from favourite works including Sir Thomas Malory's *Le Morte d'Arthur* and Ruskin's *The Stones of Venice* (fig. 14). While Burne-Jones, who was from Birmingham, had been exposed to the industrial world, Morris's privileged upbringing had isolated him from urban reality, and it was through Ruskin that he began to consider the social implications of the modern age. He came to loathe railways – 'verily railways are ABOMINATIONS'[3] – and later condemned Victorian industrialization as impersonal and degrading, claiming that 'Apart from the desire to produce beautiful things, the leading passion of my life has been and is hatred of modern civilization.'[4] Ruskin also fuelled Morris's interest in the arts. By the time he graduated he had decided to train as an architect, and entered the Oxford practice of George Edmund Street (1824–81) – architects then learning their profession as pupils to established architects, rather than by following an academic course.

Street was a dedicated exponent of the Gothic Revival: 'We are medievalists and rejoice in the name; to us it implies a belief in all that is best, purest, truest, in our art.'[5] Passionate about the uses and abuses of decoration, he adopted a distinctly holistic approach, considering it so architectural drawings in the 1870s and 1880s, and was extremely skilful in working in a number of styles. John Dando Sedding (1838–91), the Gothic Revival architect, also worked in Street's office from 1858 to 1863, and in many ways prepared the ground for the Arts and Crafts, with his enthusiasm for Ruskin and decorative carving, his strong sense of locality at times, and his keen interest in the actual process of building, as opposed to architectural design alone. 'It was not what he did that should command our greatest admiration', Sedding's chief assistant Henry Wilson (1864–1934) later declared, 'but what he made others do [...] He was a radiant centre of artistic activity; a focus of creative fire; a node of magnetic force.'[8] Morris himself did not take to the architectural profession: such was his frustration at the drawing board that Webb recalled him beating his head with his fists, adding with delightful understatement, '[Morris] was out of place in an office.'[9] But he and Street's other protégés – Webb, with his principled reserve, Shaw, with his famous versatility, and the sociable and enthusiastic Sedding – were to play a major role in exploring and developing the meanings of the Arts and Crafts.

Soon after Morris joined Street's firm, the architect moved to London and took his young pupil with him. Morris rented lodgings with Burne-Jones at 17 Red Lion Square, where the two lived a boisterous, bachelor existence in the company of a long-suffering housekeeper known as Red Lion Mary, and a pet owl. They attended life-drawing classes, and met their hero Ruskin. Finding nothing suitable to furnish their rooms, Morris also produced his first designs for furniture, which were made by a local cabinet-maker. Comprising little more than planks pinned together, the furniture embodied Pugin's dictum of 'honesty of construction', with two surviving chairs revealing the crude method of construction (fig. 15). The notion of truth to purpose, however, did not enter the equation at this stage: when Morris's friends complained that the furniture was uncomfortable, he retorted that if they wanted to be comfortable they should go to bed. The furniture was painted with chevron motifs, stylized flowers and medieval scenes from the tales of King Arthur and the Knights of the Round Table. This was executed by Burne-Jones and – a newcomer to Morris's circle – Dante Gabriel Rossetti (1828–82).

Rossetti was already a painter of repute, having in 1848 co-founded the Pre-Raphaelite Brotherhood, a group of seven artists and writers who rejected the contrived history painting of their peers and the idealized beauty supposedly perfected by the sixteenth-century artist Raphael, and instead

14. Edward Burne-Jones
William Morris Reading Poetry to Ned
Mid-nineteenth century

important that an architect should understand every element of a building that he learnt ironwork and joinery, and even constructed a staircase in one of his houses to ensure that he knew how it was made. His office became a crucible of Arts and Crafts talent. When Morris joined the practice, Street's chief assistant was Philip Webb (1831–1915), a lanky young man who had been articled to an architect in Reading before starting work as an architect's clerk in Wolverhampton in 1854. Appalled at the squalor and degradation of the slums there – the 'rows of infernal dog holes'[6] as Webb called them – he stayed just four weeks before gratefully accepting a job with Street in Oxford. Quiet and withdrawn, Webb was a private man who rarely published his architectural designs. But he had a sunny demeanour – what Morris's daughter May (1862–1938) later called 'that look on his face that isn't a smile but a "state" of smiling beneath the skin'.[7] Morris took to him immediately, and Webb was one of the few to remain friends with the irascible Morris throughout his life.

In 1859 Webb was succeeded as Street's chief assistant by Richard Norman Shaw (1831–1912), who was a very different character. While Webb shunned publicity and tried to avoid working in any fixed idiom, Shaw published countless

15. William Morris, Edward Burne-Jones and Dante Gabriel Rossetti
Chair from 17 Red Lion Square, c.1857
Wood and oil paint, 90 x 40 x 40 cm (36 x 16 x 16 in)
Christie's, London

16. Lewis Carroll (Charles Lutwidge Dodgson)
Dante Gabriel Rossetti, 1863
Albumen print, 14.6 x 12.1 cm (5 3/4 x 4 3/4 in)
National Portrait Gallery, London

advocated a more naturalistic style. Burne-Jones and Morris had long admired Rossetti, and the self-assured artist, with his wide forehead and dark, penetrating eyes (fig. 16), was to become a key figure in Morris's life. It was with his encouragement that Morris abandoned architecture to become a painter: 'Rossetti says I ought to paint, he says I shall be able; now as he is a very great man, and speaks with authority and not as the scribes, I *must* try.'[10] In 1857, Rossetti also invited Morris and Burne-Jones to take part in a communal painting project, the commission to decorate the Debating Chamber of the Oxford Union (the university's student debating society), giving the young friends their first taste of practical collaboration in the visual arts.

The Oxford Union project brought together seven artists, who painted the upper walls of the Debating Chamber (now the library) with scenes from *Le Morte d'Arthur*, their dense, medievalizing imagery in jewel colours causing a visitor in 1857 to compare it to 'the margin of a highly-illuminated manuscript.'[11] Morris also decorated the ceiling with mythical creatures in a web of vegetation, and affectionate portraits of him, presumably by his friends, appeared in the crannies of the intersecting beams (this was

17. Edward Burne-Jones and Philip Webb
The Prioress's Tale Wardrobe, 1858
Oak, deal and oil paint, 200 x 130 x 60 cm (79 x 51 x 23 ¹/₂ in)
Ashmolean Museum, Oxford

hidden by a new foliage design which Morris executed in the 1870s). Such was Morris's enthusiasm that he commissioned a smithy to make a sword and a suit of armour which he had designed as props, and was so delighted with the result that he wore the mail coat to dinner one night, and on another occasion got stuck inside the helmet. Burne-Jones, painting on the scaffolding, saw Morris 'embedded in iron, dancing with rage and roaring inside'.[12] Unfortunately, the artists' ambition outweighed their technical expertise. Criticism was levelled at the proportions of the figures and animals, and Morris later found his own contribution 'extremely ludicrous in many ways'.[13] Each bay was pierced with two foliated windows, which meant that the frescoes could not be seen against the light. Most damagingly, none of the artists had experience of fresco painting, and they painted in distemper on bare brick, before the mortar had been allowed to dry, with the result that the frescos faded within months and are barely visible today. Nevertheless, the Oxford Union project was of enormous significance, as its development of medieval imagery and communal practice became characteristic of the Arts and Crafts. Morris loved the social aspect of working in a group and from then on endeavoured to reconcile work and pleasure, claiming that one of the reasons why he admired Ruskin was for Ruskin's 'lesson' that 'art is the expression of man's pleasure in labour; that it is possible for man to rejoice in his work'.[14] The Union project was also vital to Morris on a personal level, as it was while working on it that he met his future wife, Jane or 'Janey' Burden, whom he married in 1859.

Morris and Janey initially rented lodgings in London, surrounded by bits of furniture from Red Lion Square and a magnificent wardrobe which Burne-Jones had decorated with scenes from Chaucer's *Prioress's Tale* and given the newly-weds as a wedding present (fig. 17). The wardrobe exemplifies the junction between Pre-Raphaelite painting and Arts and Crafts design: its medieval subject, languid figures, rich colouring and attention to detail, from the turreted houses to the heavy-headed dandelions and wilting poppies, were all characteristic of the Pre-Raphaelites, while the artist's attention to a household object of solid construction brings it within the purview of the Arts and Crafts. The lodgings were only temporary though, as Morris had already commissioned his first proper marital home – Red House in Bexleyheath, ten miles to the east of London. Designed by Philip Webb, who had now set up his own practice, Red House is often seen as the first Arts and Crafts house, and at this point we must leave Morris and his circle for a while to address the characteristics of Arts and Crafts architecture, and the reasons why Red House holds the significance which it does.

Fundamental to the development of Arts and Crafts architecture was the railway, a key component of the Industrial Age which had, paradoxically, been rejected by early Arts and Crafts thinkers as an acceptable way of life. By the 1860s, Britain was covered by a railway network which had transformed patterns of work and leisure. It was now possible to live at some distance from the workplace and commute on a daily basis, and it soon became fashionable to maintain weekend or holiday homes in more remote parts of the country as well. The upper middle classes took advantage of this and began to commission houses in areas well served by a railway line. Thus Morris's site for Red House, while now a walled haven in deepest suburbia, was at the time set in Kentish orchards, close enough to a railway station to be accessible from London, but remote enough to give a feeling of escape.

The new, mobile client who took advantage of the railway to live further afield required a new sort of house. In the first place, emphasis was placed on a comfortable and functional building which could accommodate the latest in domestic amenities. To achieve this, the interior and the exterior had to be planned organically, rather than fitting the furnishings in as an afterthought, and materials were chosen and used with great care, developing ideas of truth to purpose, good craftsmanship and unity of design. In that improvements in transport allowed the patron more choice of where he lived, the house also had to maximize the beauties and benefits of its location, encouraging the use of local materials, the incorporation of site-specific peculiarities, and a new respect for traditional buildings. The result was a move away from the Gothic Revival mansions of the 1850s and 1860s, and the rise of Arts and Crafts houses which, based on small manor houses or large cottages, took their cue from local construction methods and materials, harmonized with existing buildings, and suited the geography and climate of the site. Some of these ideas had surfaced in the work of mid-century Gothic Revival architects such as Street, William Butterfield (1814–1900) and George Devey (1820–86). In the schools and parsonages they designed, both Butterfield and Street employed local brick to convey the character of an area; and Devey showed great sensitivity to local traditions when he extended a group of ancient cottages in Penshurst, Kent, from 1848 to 1850 (Devey's extension was so skilful that it is now difficult to distinguish the old from the new). But it was Webb whose work provided the bridge to Arts and Crafts design.

18. Philip Webb
Red House, Bexleyheath, Kent, 1859

Webb believed that architecture was an ambitious discipline which had to confront the needs of each individual building. He therefore opposed the formulaic revival of past styles, which not only prevented architects from considering the requirements of their own age, but also deprived a building of the spirit of its creators which Webb, like Ruskin, believed essential to good design. This was not to say that architects should work in a void: but rather than blindly appropriating a style which could be historically and geographically distant, they should concentrate on good, simple building practices which demonstrated common sense and intelligent use of the form, colour and texture of vernacular materials and motifs. These ideas are explored at Red House, which is a transitional building between the Gothic Revival and the Arts and Crafts (figs 18–21). The building has obvious Gothic qualities in its steeply pitched roofs and pointed arches, reflecting the work of Street and other Gothic Revivalists. At the same time, Webb allowed the needs of the interior to dictate the form of the exterior, leading to irregular massing and fenestration, and the conical roof of the well-house reflects the oast house vernacular of Kent (though we cannot be sure that this last point was Webb's

specific intent). Inside, a newel post in the form of a miniature Gothic spire and pointed arches of exposed brick again revealed Gothic affinities, but there was a new sense of space and light (fig. 19). The plan, for its part, was L-shaped and just one room and a corridor wide: indebted to Pugin and Butterfield, it became famous for its practicality, and spawned a host of L-shaped room-and-passage plans. A couple of years after Red House was completed, Morris considered extending the L-shaped building to form a quadrangle around a central courtyard, with the corridor running around all four sides like an enclosed cloister. The plan, which aimed to provide living and working accommodation for the Burne-Jones family as well, was eventually abandoned, but it gives a sense of the way in which Morris saw Red House as an embodiment of some medieval, monastic ideal.

Red House was completed in 1860. Later, as Webb distanced himself from any form of revivalism, he rejected it as of his 'Gothic days'. But Morris was delighted with it and, unimpressed by what was available in the shops, decided that he and his friends should decorate and furnish the house themselves. They all rallied round. Morris hauled himself up ladders to paint the ceilings, and supervised the production of stained glass and furniture, most of which was designed and decorated by Burne-Jones and Webb. A vast settle which Morris had designed for Red Lion Square was also moved, with unimaginable difficulty, to the first-floor drawing room, where Rossetti painted its doors with *The Salutation of Beatrice* and Webb added a ladder and a minstrels' gallery, providing ingenious access to the storage space in the roof (fig. 20). Wives and sisters embroidered Morris's designs for wall hangings, and Burne-Jones began a set of wall paintings depicting the wedding of Sir Degrevaunt, from the medieval story by Froissart. Even the trellises and walkways in the garden, and a 'Gothic' cart designed by Webb to collect excited guests from the local railway station, were conceived as part of an integrated whole. The result, said Rossetti, was 'more a poem than a house'.[15]

The decoration for Red House was never completed. However, such was its success that the painter Ford Madox Brown (1821–93), who had been introduced to Morris and his circle by Rossetti, suggested that they establish a decorating firm. The idea made commercial sense, as Burne-Jones, Webb and Brown were already designing furniture and stained glass for individual commissions, and for companies such as the glass-makers James Powell & Sons of Whitefriars. The year 1861 therefore saw the establishment of Morris, Marshall, Faulkner & Co., which in 1875 was reorganized as Morris & Co. and which here will be referred to by the shorter name. The firm numbered seven partners: Morris, Burne-Jones, Rossetti, Webb, Brown, the engineer and amateur painter Peter Paul Marshall, and Charles Faulkner, a maths don at Oxford University who had been Morris's best man. It was financed by £1 from each partner and by a loan of £100 from Morris's mother (one of several occasions when Morris's affluent background was to subsidize his artistic activities). Space was leased at 8 Red Lion Square in London for workshops, a showroom and a small office, and a prospectus was issued which began:

> Morris, Marshall, Faulkner and Company, *Fine Art Workmen in Painting, Carving, Furniture and the Metals. The growth of Decorative Art in this country, owing to the effort of English Architects, has now reached a point at which it seems desirable that Artists of reputation should devote their time to it.*[16]

Thus from its very inception, Morris & Co. gave the decorative arts a status previously reserved for the fine arts.

Many of Morris & Co's earliest goods were designed for friends and family. Thus Webb designed brass and copper

19. Stairwell at Red House, 1859

candlesticks in a simple Gothic style for Red House (fig. 22), one of which was carefully balanced on a door so that it would topple on to the hapless Morris the moment he walked in. Decorated tiles were also popular and had the advantage of being produced in a small kiln on the firm's premises, rather than being subcontracted to outside manufacturers. These were often painted by Burne-Jones's wife Georgiana and by Faulkner's sisters Lucy and Kate, demonstrating how much of the firm's initial activity remained an in-house, family affair. Most important of all was the firm's early production of stained glass. Members of Morris & Co. already had experience in this – Burne-Jones had produced outstanding work for James Powell & Sons – and in 1861 the Gothic Revival architect George Frederick Bodley (1827–1907), a friend of Webb, commissioned the firm to design the windows for his church of St Michael and All Angels in Brighton. Bodley went on to commission stained glass from Morris & Co. for many of his churches, and demand grew so quickly that as early as 1862 the firm was employing a professional glass painter, an experienced glazier, and twelve workers recruited from the Industrial Home for Destitute Boys in Euston Road. The firm used the medieval

20. Drawing Room at Red House

21. Hall at Red House

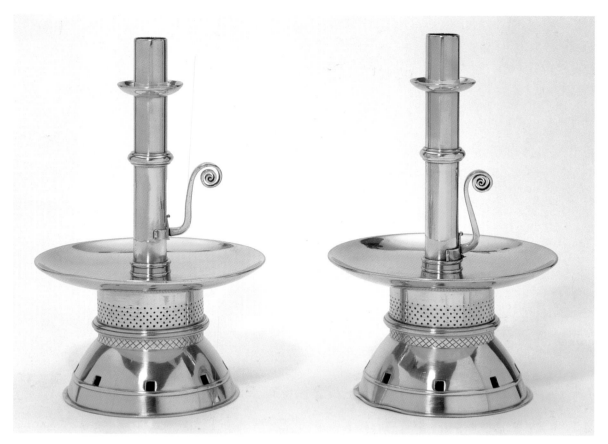

22. Philip Webb
Candlesticks designed for Red House, 1861–3
Copper, each 26.7 x 17.8 cm (10 ½ x 7 in)
Victoria and Albert Museum, London

mosaic technique of assembling pieces of pre-coloured glass which had been popular in Victorian stained-glass manufacture since the 1840s, fuelled by Gothic Revival interests and by the research and publications of Charles Winston (1814–64). Morris & Co. was not, therefore, a pioneer in reviving the technique, but its windows excelled among nineteenth-century stained-glass firms in the quality and originality of their colour.

Morris & Co.'s early stained-glass work was a truly collaborative endeavour. Burne-Jones or, less frequently, Brown and Rossetti tended to design the central figures; Webb designed the quarries, canopies, upper lights and lettering, and dealt with composition and with aspects of the windows' architectural setting; and Morris took responsibility for the colour schemes. This was no easy task. For a start, Morris was a perfectionist who would have parts of the windows remade if they did not meet his standards. Moreover, the only way he could view the larger windows before installation was by passing them section by section in front of the workshop light, which can only have given a fragmented impression of the finished effect. Nevertheless, Morris & Co.'s stained-glass designs (which were often

repeated) are among the firm's greatest legacies, not least for their astonishing human detail. Thus, in Burne-Jones's window, *Hope, Charity, Faith* (fig. 23) in St Martin's Church in Brampton, Cumbria (a building which Webb designed), the boys remind us of any shy child entering the public gaze in the reassuring presence of a parent. Morris & Co. also designed stained glass for domestic settings, notably the *King René's Honeymoon* series which the firm produced for the home of the painter Myles Birket Foster (1825–99) in 1863, based on earlier Morris & Co. designs for the painted panels of a desk. In the 'Music' panel (fig. 24), Rossetti shows his prowess at evocative detail, from the wood grain of the organ and the silk and fur of the robes, to the gentleness with which the king holds the chin of his queen. Rossetti did not take the medium particularly seriously, telling Brown that 'anything will do for stained glass.'[17] But the vibrant colour and authentic appearance of Morris & Co.'s stained glass attracted attention – so much so that when it was exhibited at the 1862 International Exhibition in South Kensington, London, the firm was accused of touching up original medieval work.

Stained glass was not the only Morris & Co. product to feature at the 1862 exhibition. The firm also exhibited

23. Edward Burne-Jones
Hope, Charity, Faith, 1889
Stained-glass window,
St Martin's Church, Brampton

embroideries and furniture, much of which was expensive
and richly decorated. The *Saint George* cabinet (fig. 25) designed
by Webb and painted by Morris, for example, typified some
of the ornate furniture of medieval inspiration which the
firm was producing at the time. As the 1860s progressed,
however, Morris & Co. diversified into less elaborate objects
such as smaller embroideries and simpler furniture, from the
adjustable Morris armchair (so popular in America that it
featured in a Bing Crosby song) (fig. 26), to the rush-seated
range of chairs, inspired by vernacular furniture in Sussex,
which became the firm's most commercially successful line
(fig. 27). The firm also began to undertake high-profile
commissions such as that to decorate the Green Dining
Room (fig. 28), one of three new refreshment rooms at the
South Kensington Museum, in 1865. As it was a novelty to
provide refreshment areas in public galleries, the Green
Dining Room (still extant, in what is now the Victoria and
Albert Museum) was guaranteed an inquisitive audience, and
became something of a flagship for the firm. With stained-
glass windows and figurative panels by Burne-Jones, and fruit
and foliage designs by Morris and Webb, the project made the
most of individual talents: but these are sublated into a

24. Dante Gabriel Rossetti
'Music' from *King René's Honeymoon*, c.1863
Stained and painted glass
64.2 x 54.7 cm (25 ¼ x 21 ½ in)
Victoria and Albert Museum, London

scheme of subaqueous intensity, tempered only by the floral and sunburst motifs which explode like fireworks on the ceiling above.

For Morris, with the early excitement of the firm and the birth of two daughters, the first half of the 1860s was a happy time. His contentment was noted ironically by a friend who wrote just before Christmas in 1863: 'I grieve to say [Morris] has only kicked one panel out of a door for this twelve-month past.'[18] By 1865, however, the commute from Bexleyheath was proving arduous, and, with great sadness, Morris returned to live in London, prompted by Burne-Jones's announcement that he and his family would never move to Red House. 'I cried', Morris wrote on hearing Burne-Jones's news, his love of his home almost palpable in those two simple words, 'but I have got over it now.'[19] Morris & Co. moved to more spacious premises at 26 Queen Square in Bloomsbury, and Morris and his family lodged in rooms above the 'shop'. The contented existence of Red House – which Morris sold, and to which he could never bring himself to return – was not to continue, not least because Janey and Rossetti began their long and public affair at about this time. Moreover, towards the end of the decade, Morris &

Co. began to see business decline. The intense church building of the previous few decades was beginning to wane, leading to a fall in demand for stained glass and ecclesiastical furnishings, which were still among the firm's main earners. While the resulting drop in profits did not matter for some of the partners, Morris was beginning to rely on his earnings from the firm. He now had to support a family, and his share dividends were drying up as the West Country copper-mining industry collapsed, falling from £819 in 1857 to £187 in 1870. His great friend Burne-Jones also needed his income from Morris & Co., and in 1867 drew so much from his partnership account that he ended the year £91 in debt.

At this point we see evidence of Morris's shrewd business sense as, aware that he had to adapt to changes in the market, he expanded his work in wallpaper and textile designs. Morris is renowned for the brilliance of his repeats, which are often so well disguised that we can only decipher them by looking at his original design (fig. 29). The *Jasmine* wallpaper of 1872 is also revealing of how Morris developed a pattern, for while dark swirling tendrils have an unstabilizing effect in a working drawing (fig. 30), these were later absorbed into a more limited colour scheme, which is

25. Philip Webb and William Morris
Saint George Cabinet, 1861–2
Painted and gilded mahogany, pine and oak,
with copper mounts
59.5 x 178 x 43 cm (23 ½ x 70 x 17 in)
Victoria and Albert Museum, London

26. Morris, Marshall, Faulkner & Co.
Adjustable Back Armchair, c.1866
Ebonized mahogany, upholstered in Utrecht velvet
96.5 x 73.7 x 83.8 cm (38 x 29 x 33 in)
Victoria and Albert Museum, London

27. Advertisement for the Sussex Range, c.1860
Illustrated in the Morris & Co. Catalogue, c.1915

28. Morris, Marshall, Faulkner & Co.
The Green Dining Room at the South Kensington Museum
(now the Victoria and Albert Museum), London, 1865–7

easier on the eye (fig. 31). Morris initially tried to cut the woodblocks and print the wallpapers himself, but this proved too taxing. Instead, the blocks were cut by Alfred and later James Barrett of 489 Bethnal Green Road, London, while the hand-printing of Morris & Co. wallpapers was undertaken by Jeffrey & Co. in Islington from 1864 until as late as 1930. With hand-printing, each colour is printed from separate blocks, which allows for sufficient drying time between the different stages. This has the advantage over machine printing, where the colours are printed together, necessitating quick-drying colours which tend to be thin and liable to fade. However, the process of hand-printing is tedious and repetitive, particularly with Morris's designs which often used up to twenty blocks, and on one occasion required as many as sixty-eight. The production of wallpaper therefore signals one of the tensions between theory and practice, for while Morris advocated an enjoyable, Ruskinian work process, he was happy to sanction tiresome, demeaning labour when his designs required it, and rarely allowed craftsmen working under him the luxury of carrying out their own designs.

Morris's textile designs, for their part, were first printed in Lancashire with synthetic aniline dyes, which were then used almost without exception in textile factories. However, Morris found the resulting colours crude and garish, and began to investigate natural, vegetable-based dyes, first experimenting at Queen Square, and then travelling to Leek in Staffordshire to study the dyeing and printing practice of Thomas Wardle, brother-in-law of the firm's manager George. Living happily with fingers dyed blue, Morris attempted to master the difficult indigo discharge process, whereby areas of the pattern were bleached out of blue cloth before printing the other colours of the design. His efforts eventually paid off, with designs such as *Medway* (fig. 32) showing the delicate white lines which this process allowed. Despite Morris's rapid pre-eminence in two-dimensional patterns, he was not working in a vacuum, for at times his patterns drew on Jones's *The Grammar of Ornament* and on the work of Jones's pupil Christopher Dresser (1834–1904), whose designs included wallpapers for Jeffrey & Co., and who lectured and published extensively on the applied arts. Dresser argued that plant forms in pattern design should be what he termed 'conventionalized', a practice of abstraction which Morris also adopted, and though Morris never mentioned Dresser, he must have been familiar with such a prominent figure in contemporary British design.

Morris had now acquired fame as a designer and as a writer, having published the final volume of his epic poem *The Earthly Paradise* to acclaim in 1870. However, domestic happiness continued to elude him, with Rossetti and Janey's affair at a peak. In 1871, in what may have been the generous gesture of a man resigned to his wife's infidelity, Morris took out a joint tenancy with Rossetti on Kelmscott Manor, a large Elizabethan house in the village of Kelmscott in Gloucestershire. Despite the unusual domestic arrangements, Morris found peace at Kelmscott, boating and fishing on the Thames (he was suspicious of men who did not fish), and the house remained his country retreat for the rest of his life. Of all its furnishings, most striking are the bedhangings for Morris's four-poster bed, which his daughter May, an accomplished needlewoman who ran the embroidery division of Morris & Co. from 1885 to 1896, embroidered with brightly plumed birds and flowers entwined in a pomegranate tree (fig. 33). On the valance, May embroidered a poem composed by Morris, while Janey decorated the coverlet with flowers, kingfishers, caterpillars, fish, frogs, and a tiny vignette of Kelmscott Manor itself on the bank of the Thames. In this May was helped by two Morris & Co. embroiderers, Ellen Wright and Lily Yeats, the sister of the poet, while Mary De Morgan, sister of the ceramic artist William, assisted Janey. With their beautiful, hand-worked decoration, collaboration between friends and family, and an overwhelming sense of the pleasure taken in creative work, the bedhangings embody some of the Arts and Crafts Movement's most cherished ideals.

By the time Morris acquired Kelmscott Manor, the Arts and Crafts Movement was expanding beyond the practice of his immediate circle. In the first place, other workshops had begun to appear, starting with that of the brilliant ceramicist William De Morgan (1839–1917) who had been decorating pottery for Morris & Co. since 1863. De Morgan's earliest venture in ceramic production was not a success, for his explosive experiments in a home-made kiln set fire to his first workshop at 40 Fitzroy Square. Undeterred, he founded a new workshop in Chelsea in the early 1870s, where he continued to research new glazes and pigments, alternative kiln designs, and lost techniques of firing pottery, sharing Morris's compulsion to master the intricacies of his craft. De Morgan had originally worked as a stained-glass designer, and was intrigued by the incandescence caused in stained glass when streaks of silver were over-fired. This interest led to his revival of lustre, a form of glaze with an iridescent, metallic sheen which was made by adding metal

tim drush

yellow

3 block
White
brown
yellow

29. (previous page) William Morris
Design for *Windrush* Wallpaper, 1881–3
Pencil, ink and watercolour on Whatman paper, 131.5 x 99.6 cm (52 x 39 in)
Kelmscott House, London

30. (above) William Morris
Design for *Jasmine* Wallpaper, c.1872
Pencil, ink and watercolour on paper, 90.3 x 64.1 cm (35 ½ x 25 in)
Kelmscott House, London

oxides to the decoration before the final firing of his pots and plates (fig. 34). De Morgan also produced quirky tiles of birds and animals, such as his *Dodo* (fig. 35), which waddles on ungainly feet, fixing the viewer with his comic, knowing stare. De Morgan's work was enormously popular: Lewis Carroll bought his tiles to decorate the rooms in Oxford where he wrote *Alice's Adventures in Wonderland*; the Tsar of Russia commissioned tiled panels for his yacht; and De Morgan's ceramics featured in many of Morris & Co's interiors. His was no doctrinaire approach to Arts and Crafts thinking, though: the ceramic painters in his pottery had to carry out his designs, rather than creating works of their own. 'I don't pay you to think!' De Morgan apparently once snapped at an employee who had altered the design. 'If you think again, you must think elsewhere!'

Just as important as the workshops of the 1870s were developments in domestic architecture. Britain was enjoying marked advances in welfare at the time: housing and diets were improving, with food testing implemented by legislation in 1860, 1872 and 1875; cheap soap was becoming widely available, raising standards in hygiene; from 1870, the horse-drawn tram enabled more people to live in the suburbs; and in the early years of their government, from 1874 to 1880, the Conservatives launched a series of social reforms which addressed everything from artisans' dwellings and river pollution to factories, education and public health. A growing number of people were also enjoying leisure time, not least after public holidays were introduced with the Bank Holiday Act of 1871, and the railway began to be used for recreational purposes. In line with this burgeoning culture of consumption and relaxation, the middle and upper classes spent increasing amounts of money on heightening their domestic comforts, and their patronage gave a vital injection of energy to the Arts and Crafts.

The most successful architect to respond to these opportunities was Richard Norman Shaw, who by the late 1880s was earning the enormous sum of £8,000 per annum, compared to Webb's average of £562. Shaw had begun his career with an interest in the Gothic Revival, and used the Gothic for almost all his church designs (eighteen in total, of which sixteen were built). After leaving Street's office in 1862, however, he and his first partner, William Eden Nesfield (1835–88), had turned away from French Gothic and towards English vernacular prototypes for their domestic work, taking off with their sketchbooks to study the Tudor manor houses and farm buildings of Sussex and Kent, as well as

31. William Morris
Jasmine Wallpaper, 1872
Block-printed in distemper colours on paper, 68.6 x 50 cm (27 x 19 ½ in)
Victoria and Albert Museum, London

32. William Morris
Detail of *Medway* Furnishing Fabric, 1885
Indigo-discharged, block-printed cotton
165 x 92 cm (65 x 36 ¼ in)
Victoria and Albert Museum, London

sympathetic new work such as Devey's Penshurst cottages. The result was Shaw's first professional trademark – the Old English style, which is also referred to as his vernacular revival work. Old English buildings often include a masonry ground floor, half-timbering or tile-hanging on the upper storeys, and a picturesque roofscape of chimneys and gables. Inside, bay windows, inglenook fireplaces and alcoves provide a note of intimacy. Alternatively, the inclusion of a great hall might create a medieval air. The style did not wholly endorse the principles of the Arts and Crafts: it frequently disregarded the site, and at times the half-timbering and even the gables were false, which would have made Pugin turn in his grave. But the mix of vernacular materials such as tile, stone and half-timbering proved highly influential, and the reference to a native English idiom created an architecture truly national in character, which increasingly became a keynote of the Arts and Crafts.

One of Shaw's earliest buildings in the Old English style was Leys Wood (1867–9) in Groombridge, Kent. With its half-timbered gables, leaded-light windows, and imposing chimneys, Leys Wood was highly acclaimed, not least because of the flattering perspective drawings which Shaw exhibited at the Royal Academy in 1870 and published in *Building News* in 1871. But Leys Wood is now greatly altered, and the best place today to appreciate Shaw's ingenuity is Cragside, near Rothbury, which negotiates a delicate balance between creative ambition and practical good sense. Cragside was commissioned by Sir William Armstrong (1810–1900), later 1st Lord Armstrong, who was one of the great polymaths of the Victorian age – lawyer, engineer, inventor, arms manufacturer, and a seminal figure in the industrial and cultural advancement of the North East. Armstrong's great passion was for hydraulics (his family used to say that 'William had water on the brain'[20]), and such was his success in developing water power that his firm supplied Tower Bridge in London with its original hydraulic lifting gear. In 1863, Armstrong had commissioned a small weekend retreat from an unknown architect in the spectacular landscape of Coquetdale, north-west of Newcastle upon Tyne, where his business was based. With an expanding profile in the region and a rising fortune to match, he soon outgrew the original premises and, encouraged by a railway extension from Newcastle to Rothbury, he decided to make Cragside his principal home. Thus in 1869, just as Leys Wood was completed, Armstrong requested Shaw to transform his small lodge into a large country house.

33. (opposite) May Morris, Ellen Wright and Lily Yeats
William Morris's Bed Hangings at Kelmscott Manor, Gloucestershire

34. (above) William De Morgan
Vase and Cover, 1888–98
Earthenware, painted in lustre on a blue background, 30.4 x 23.2 x 9.5 cm (12 x 9 x 3 3/4 in)
Victoria and Albert Museum, London

35. William De Morgan
Dodo Tile, c.1873–6
Glazed earthenware, 15.2 x 15.2 cm (6 x 6 in)
Private collection

36. Richard Norman Shaw
Perspective Drawing of the Proposed Changes to the West Front of Cragside House, 1872
Ink on paper, 64 x 86 cm (25 x 33 ½ in)
Cragside House, Northumberland

The location which Armstrong had chosen for Cragside, with its rocky outcrops and dark, mysterious valleys, evokes the eighteenth-century aesthetic of 'the sublime', which described the sensations of terror and awe produced by dramatic natural landscapes. As had been the case at Leys Wood, Shaw chose to dominate, rather than pander to, the rugged terrain, and the house rises out of its spectacular projection like a majestic bird of prey (fig. 36). Shaw was constrained by the fragmented nature of the commission, which comprised an extension to the north of the house in 1869, enlargements in the 1870s, and finally the south-east wing of rooms completed in 1884. As a result, Cragside is a maverick of gables, towers, battlements and bays, and embodies 'changefulness', a word which Ruskin had coined in *The Stones of Venice* to commend variety in architectural design. Inside, characteristic features of the Old English style include the oak panelling and coffered ceilings, and many of the rooms have furniture by Shaw, furnishings by Morris & Co., and ceramics by De Morgan. The dining-room inglenook, for example, has Morris & Co. stained-glass windows, with fire irons and settles probably designed by Shaw, all of which feature in H H Emmerson's painting of *Sir William Armstrong* (fig. 37) – an image which speaks eloquently of the priority given to the comfort of the client. Armstrong used his hydraulic and engineering expertise to introduce novel domestic conveniences. The first house in the world to be lit by hydroelectricity, Cragside also boasted a hydraulic system which turned spits, raised lifts, churned silage, and was for years the driving force behind the property's farm machinery. 'The palace of a modern magician',[21] as a visitor called it, Cragside both typifies aspects of the Old English style, and develops themes which were to become characteristic of the Arts and Crafts. It was built for an upwardly mobile patron in an exciting setting; it provided cosy, functional interiors, with features such as panelling and inglenook fireplaces; and it laid great emphasis on the studied inclusion of furnishings and decorative art.

By the time Morris & Co. was commissioned to provide furnishings for Cragside, the firm was beginning to effect a revolution in public taste. It had carried out decorative schemes for several Cambridge colleges; it had been employed to design two interiors at St James's Palace in London; and its private clients included aristocrats as illustrious as the Hon. George Howard, who in 1889 was to become the 9th Earl of Carlisle. Morris, however, was never a man to rest on his laurels, and in 1877 his activities took a new direction when, motivated by his indignation at recent cases of over-restoration, he set up the Society for the Protection of Ancient Buildings, known by its initials SPAB or, more affectionately, as 'Anti-Scrape'. SPAB's membership included many Arts and Crafts designers and supporters, notably Webb, De Morgan, Thomas Wardle, and Emery Walker (1851–1933), a gifted and influential typographer whom we will meet in Chapter 3. After the weekly committee meetings they would gather to share ideas during convivial meals at Gatti's restaurant in the Strand. SPAB also had ramifications for Morris & Co. as Morris felt compelled to follow its policy in practice as well as in theory, and in April 1877 announced that the firm would 'undertake no more commissions for windows in ancient buildings. We have so concluded on the grounds that glazing ancient windows with modern (ornamental) glass must necessarily produce an incongruity, whatever may be the merits of the glass itself'.[22] Exceptions would be made for churches which already had Morris & Co. glass, or those not considered 'monuments of ancient art'.[23]

This stance probably explains the fall in stained-glass commissions from twenty-one in 1877 to only eleven in 1880, and may be one of the reasons why Morris again expanded his practice at this point. In the first place, he endeavoured to attract affluent new clients, placing advertisements in well-chosen publications and in 1877 opening a showroom in Oxford Street, in the heart of London's fashionable West End. His efforts paid off; from the late 1870s the firm received lucrative commissions from a new clientele. On a practical level, Morris turned his hand to weaving, assisted by Louis Bazin, 'Our Froggy weaver',[24] who installed a mechanical Jacquard loom at Queen Square. Morris began to study high-warp tapestries and hand-knotted carpets and rugs. Taking his usual methodical approach, he bought and scrutinized Persian carpets and dismantled medieval tapestries to examine their structure, before putting them back together again. A carpet frame was set up in the attic at Queen Square, and then in the coach house and stables of Kelmscott House, the five-storeyed Georgian house which Morris leased in Hammersmith in 1878 (now the headquarters of the William Morris Society). Morris also set up a loom in his bedroom, and in 1879 embarked on his first tapestry, the *Vine and Acanthus*, which, as he recorded in his diary, took him 516 hours over the course of six months. *Vine and Acanthus* is an ungainly piece of work (Morris himself compared the acanthus leaves to cabbages, and it is often referred to as the 'Cabbage and Vine'), but tapestry production was added to

37. H H Emmerson
Sir William Armstrong, 1880
Oil on canvas, 105 x 92 cm (41 x 36 in)
Cragside House, Northumberland

Morris & Co.'s repertoire to great effect. Most famous of all are the Holy Grail tapestries which Burne-Jones designed from 1890–3 for William Knox d'Arcy's home of Stanmore Hall in Middlesex. This is decorative art at its most ambitious – skilled, monumental, and with all the narrative potency of an Old Master painting (its source was again *Le Morte d'Arthur*). The series took almost four years to complete and cost £3,500, of which £1,000 was given to Burne-Jones for his designs, and it became the model for later versions which were adapted to suit their respective sites (fig. 38).

By 1880, the expanding business of Morris & Co. needed larger premises, and Morris determined to find it a country base. After an extensive search he settled on Merton Abbey, a disused eighteenth-century silk-weaving factory on the River Wandle, near Wimbledon. Tests were carried out on the river water to check that it was suitable for dyeing and, satisfied with the results, Morris moved his company there in 1881. Workshops for chintz printing, weaving and stained glass were set up and dye vats, printing tables, and carpet and tapestry looms were installed (fig. 39), so that all but the wallpaper and furniture production could now take place on the firm's premises. Morris endeavoured to provide a healthy

38. Edward Burne-Jones, William Morris and John Henry Dearle
'The Knights of the Round Table Summoned to the Quest by the Strange Damsel'
from *The Holy Grail Series*, designed *c.*1890–3, made *c.*1898–9
Tapestry wool and silk weft on cotton warp, 245 x 535 cm (96 ¹/₂ x 210 ¹/₂ in)
Birmingham Museum and Art Gallery

39. Jacquard Looms at Merton Abbey, *c.*1881

working environment: as an American visitor of 1886 recalled, 'Scrupulous neatness and order reigned everywhere in the establishment; pleasant smells as of dried herbs exhaled from clean vegetable dyes, blent with the wholesome odors of grass and flowers and sunny summer warmth that freely circulated through open doors and windows. Nowhere was one conscious of the depressing sense of confinement that usually pervades a factory.'[25] Morris continued to pay close attention to marketing and publicity. In 1882 he showed the firm's goods at the Fine Art and Industrial Exhibition in Manchester, a city which had a reputation for patronizing the applied arts, and he rented a shop in Manchester's prosperous commercial district around Albert Square. He also sent his manager, George Wardle, to America with letters of introduction to like-minded design enthusiasts, and Wardle was charged with exhibiting the firm's wares at the Boston Foreign Fair in 1883–4. Morris clearly appreciated the potential of the American market, and took pains to appoint reliable and effective agents there.

The irony is that while Morris wanted to propagate good design, it was only the middle and upper classes who could afford the beautiful, time-consuming furnishings which his firm produced. Thus C R Ashbee, a key Arts and Crafts figure in the 1880s, later wrote in his memoirs, 'We have made of a great social movement, a narrow and tiresome little aristocracy working with great skill for the very rich.'[26] This was a paradox which Morris was never to resolve. He complained bitterly that he spent his time 'ministering to the swinish luxury of the rich,'[27] and his career is full of

ambiguities. The man who railed against the division of labour instituted it in his stained-glass workshops. The man who declared that he hated 'commerce and money making more than ever'[28] rescued his firm from the brink of bankruptcy by taking sharp, commercial decisions. The man who loathed mechanization admitted that he could not carry out 'certain kinds of weaving I should like to do because my capital can't compass a power-loom.'[29] Finally, the man who was to become one of the great socialists of his age did not set up a system of profit-sharing at his workshops at Merton Abbey. Morris's frustration at the contradiction between the commercial and the ideological aims of his business may therefore be rather disingenuous. Was he instead an astute early scholar of material culture and the mechanics of its consumption?

Whatever the case, by the late 1880s Morris was so famous that he had to ration his time and introduced a system of fees for visiting clients' homes, writing that these were not to apply to 'well known and useful customers', but were 'to stop fools and impertinents.'[30] Anxious not to alienate good customers, Morris nevertheless had a firm appreciation of his value as the figurehead of a thrusting and profitable firm. His transformation from the genial host at Red House, who had been happy to use his private income to support the convivial artistic collaboration of his friends, to a successful businessman in the increasingly competitive Victorian era, symbolizes the gradual transition of the Arts and Crafts Movement from an endearing theoretical proposition to a viable commercial concern.

Thomas James Cobden-Sanderson
Cover of William Morris's Copy of *Le Capital*, 1884 (fig. 57)

CRAFT AND COMRADESHIP IN THE METROPOLIS

IN THE 1860s AND 1870s THE ARTS AND CRAFTS HAD BEEN CHARACTERIZED BY AN INTERLACING WEB OF THEMES. IN THE 1880s AND 1890s, HOWEVER, ONE STRAND CAME TO THE FORE – THAT OF FELLOWSHIP.

This was linked to the rise of socialism, with its agenda of shifting systems of power and means of production from private hands to the community as a whole. Many members of the Arts and Crafts Movement in Britain became committed socialists, its byword of social inclusion matching their concern to democratize the arts. Fellowship as a form of empowerment also developed in other walks of life, from welfare and science to education and philanthropy, and while some of the groups which resulted were little more than clubs for hard drinking and gluttonous dining, others, such as the Institution of Civil Engineers, were committed to a specific cause. There was a rise in the membership of Friendly Societies, a network of working-class clubs which stemmed from trade-related associations of the eighteenth century, and offered subsidies such as sickness and funeral benefit (by 1880, membership had reached approximately 2.2 million). From the middle of the century trade unionism was also on the increase, and in 1884 the Fabian Society was established with the aim of engaging in non-revolutionary reform along socialist lines. On a less political level, there was everything from the literary and philosophical societies, which increased rapidly from the 1820s, to the intriguing Society for the Suppression of Vice.

Whatever their size or purpose, these groups all shared a fundamental sense of community. This had featured strongly in the rhetoric of Pugin, Ruskin and Morris, and in the 1880s was to become a defining characteristic of the British Arts and Crafts Movement. As Morris asserted in his socialist story, *A Dream of John Ball*, which was published in instalments from 1886 to 1887: 'Fellowship is heaven, and lack of fellowship is hell: fellowship is life, and lack of fellowship is death.'[1] Reflecting this sentiment, a succession of craft guilds, workshops and societies began to develop throughout Britain, in city centres and rural retreats, with formal manifestos or simple bonds of friendship, each realizing to varying degrees the social, creative and, on occasion, philanthropic aims of the Arts and Crafts. If, up until now, the Movement had been a set of ideas and aspirations shared by a few assertive and charismatic individuals, in the 1880s it acquired a wide support base, a coherent identity and, in 1887, a name, when the writer and bookbinder Thomas James Cobden-Sanderson (1840–1922) coined the phrase 'the Arts and Crafts'.

Some of the earliest craft associations of the period were run by women, for whom the applied arts had long been an acceptable form of activity. In 1879 Elizabeth Wardle,

40. Arthur Heygate Mackmurdo
Single Flower Fabric, c.1882
Printed cretonne, 59 cm (23 in) repeat
William Morris Gallery, London

and became involved in occupational therapy, while groups in agricultural areas aimed to alleviate seasonal unemployment and sustain the fabric of rural life. It attracted influential backers, not least the artist George Frederick Watts (1817–1904), who wrote to a possible donor in 1894: 'In the operations of this society we may have potentialities hardly to be overestimated, and which in view of the industrial competition with other nations, prudence alone would prompt us to seize upon, while in awakening the worker's pleasure in his work, we have an element of a still nobler nature.'[2]

In many ways these craft associations enforced traditional gender divides, as their social concerns were in keeping with a woman's caring, nurturing role. They suited the Victorian concept of 'separate spheres', whereby men worked and participated in public life, while women were confined to maternal, wifely and domestic duties in the home. But the rising profile of female craft industries also reflected developments in gender politics, as the women's campaign for education, equality for married women, the parliamentary vote, and the right to engage in the professions got under way. From 1869, women's university colleges were founded in Oxford, Cambridge, London and Glasgow; the Married Women's Property Acts of 1870 and 1882 ensured that a wife's property remained hers after she married (previously it had passed to her husband); a network of suffrage societies appeared from 1870 to 1890, coalescing as the National Union of Women's Suffrage Societies in 1897; and a wider range of employment opportunities for women became available, including work in the expanding service sector as shop assistants, typists, telegraphists, teachers, nurses and even doctors (women first carried out surgery as early as 1871). In line with these advances, women who engaged in the applied arts became increasingly proactive, and set up craft initiatives which gave vital momentum to the Arts and Crafts.

In the meantime, in London (on which this chapter will focus), a very different craft association was developing under the architect and designer Arthur Heygate Mackmurdo (1851–1942). Mackmurdo was a determined young man who in 1873 had persuaded the architect James Brooks (1825–1901) to take him on as an apprentice: Brooks put Mackmurdo in charge of the decorative details of his church designs, impressing on his trainee the need for unity in the arts. Mackmurdo also studied drawing with Ruskin, and in 1874 travelled with the critic to Italy. Ruskin's theoretical arguments were highly compelling at this time, having the

whose husband Thomas had taught Morris the rudiments of the dyeing industry, founded a School of Embroidery in Leek which included both amateur and professional embroideresses, and specialized in ecclesiastical textiles coloured with Wardle and Morris's organic dyes. On a more ambitious scale, in 1884 Mrs Eglantyne Jebb and others founded the Home Arts and Industries Association which set up handicraft classes in cities and villages, stemming in part from earlier initiatives on the west coast of Ireland. The Association inherited about 120 classes from a predecessor, the Cottage Arts Association, which Jebb had founded in Shropshire in the 1870s, and at its height managed some 500 courses throughout England and Ireland, including one at Sandringham, where the Princess of Wales fashioned a log basket. It also ran a series of exhibitions at the Royal Albert Hall, the last of which took place in 1933. The purpose of the Home Arts classes varied from place to place. While some endeavoured to revive local skills and craft industries, such as lace-making in Buckinghamshire, others were more concerned with keeping people out of the pubs by providing some improving leisure activity to occupy their time. The Association also fostered links with schools for the disabled wisdom of experience but none of the inconsistencies and diversions which appeared as his mind deteriorated during the 1880s and 1890s, and he must have been a formidable travelling companion. Inspired, Mackmurdo determined that his work should play a social role, and later taught at the Working Men's College, whose teachers and supporters included Ruskin, Rossetti, Burne-Jones and Brown. Mackmurdo doubtless also heard of Ruskin's ambitions for the Guild of St George, fuelling his interest in the potential of collaborative work.

On his return to England, Mackmurdo established an architectural practice in London. Possibly inspired by Morris, whom he met, he also taught himself carving, embroidery and cabinet-making, and in 1882, with Herbert Horne (1864–1916), founded the Century Guild of Artists. The Guild's aim was 'to render all branches of Art no longer the sphere of the tradesman but of the artist. It would restore building, decoration, glass-painting, pottery, wood carving and metal to their right place beside painting and sculpture. [...] In other words, the Century Guild seeks to emphasize the Unity of Art'.[3] Mackmurdo and Horne were probably the only formal members (they alone used the initials MCG, which seem to mean 'Member of the Century Guild', after their names), but the Guild advertised the services of about twenty independent craftsmen and designers and acted as an agent for other firms, notably the Royal School of Art Needlework and Morris & Co. Thus it was not an exclusive enterprise, but a loose partnership of designers, with a workshop and showroom in Mackmurdo's architectural office, which promoted and exhibited a range of crafts – in Mackmurdo's words, fostering 'an union by which we each anticipate having better chance of success in the exercise of our especial arts'.[4] Some of Mackmurdo's early designs for the Guild owe a debt to Morris and Ruskin. His *Single Flower* cretonne print (fig. 40), for example, uses the regular, naturalistic imagery and intricate repeat of Morris's patterns, while the organic motifs stem from the studies from nature which Mackmurdo had made under Ruskin's direction in Italy. But in *Cromer Bird* (fig. 41), a printed cotton cretonne employing a vibrant palette of amber, ochre and yellow, which Morris rarely used, Mackmurdo suggests sweeping motion in a windswept setting, anticipating the liquid whiplash curves and stylized, fluid forms of Art Nouveau.

In 1884 the Century Guild began to publish a quarterly magazine, *The Century Guild Hobby Horse*, heralding a wave of art-oriented journals in Britain in the 1880s and

1890s. Its chief editor was Herbert Horne, the versatile young aesthete who became a partner of Mackmurdo's architectural firm, designed textiles, furnishings, title pages and typefaces and later established a career as a notable art historian, collector and connoisseur. Horne was only twenty when *The Hobby Horse* was launched, but managed to persuade established and upcoming artists and writers to contribute, including Ruskin, Burne-Jones, Oscar Wilde, Rossetti's sister Christina, and Morris's daughter May. However, *The Hobby Horse* is best remembered for its overall design, rather than for the contributions of individuals, as for the first time the look of a magazine was deemed as important as what it had to say. Advised by the great typographer Emery Walker, the editors took pride in the size and design of the typeface and headings, the relationship of the illustrations to the text, and the overall distribution of the copy on the page. Walker's influence first becomes evident in the layout and typeface of the January issue of 1888: from then on, *The Hobby Horse* became the first magazine in Britain to see itself as a work of art, spawning a host of similarly self-conscious publications and establishing graphics and book production as an important part of Arts

41. Arthur Heygate Mackmurdo
Detail of *Cromer Bird* Fabric, c.1882
Printed cretonne, 40 cm (15 ½ in) repeat
Victoria and Albert Museum, London

42. Selwyn Image
Front Cover of *The Century Guild Hobby Horse*, 1886

43. The Century Guild
'The Drawing Room' for Pownall Hall, Cheshire, from *The Art Journal*, 1891

and Crafts design. Its most famous individual design is the front cover by Selwyn Image (1849–1930), who had been educated at Oxford and ordained as a priest, but who in 1882 resigned from his church post to devote himself to poetry and the visual arts. In this (fig. 42), we see echoes of Morris's passion for birds and foliage coupled with Mackmurdo's more abstract, sinuous forms. There is also an attempt to integrate image and text, with the words 'The Century Guild' highlighted by the superimposed shield, enforcing the synthetic aims of the publication as a whole.

In 1886 the Century Guild won its only substantial commission, when the brewer Henry Boddington asked it to re-furnish the dining and drawing rooms of Pownall Hall in Cheshire, and provide fittings for other parts of the house. Today, only individual furnishings and fragments of the decoration survive, but an illustrated review of Pownall Hall in *The Art Journal* in 1891 gives an idea of the overall scheme. In the drawing room (fig. 43), a frieze by Image depicted a classical landscape with draped female figures representing the different arts, while the lower section of the wall was covered with a gathered cretonne printed with Horne's *Angel with Trumpet* design. The fireplace was tiled with De Morgan's whimsical birds and animals, while the square panels of the ceiling were decorated with fruit, snipes and hares to Horne's design. The drawing room's Arts and Crafts credentials lie in its integration of painting, textiles and ceramics to achieve a balance of colour, media and design. The Guild's exuberant metalwork for the main door, on the other hand, is Arts and Crafts in its evident truth to materials (fig. 44): the sinuous, vegetal relief of the peephole grille and the hinges – three irrepressible bunches of thistles which splay out across the woodwork – demonstrate beautifully the malleable quality of iron.

The work of the Century Guild was displayed both in its own shows in London, and at the major exhibitions of the 1880s, where the Guild set an important precedent by naming each craftsman who had been involved in a design. The Royal Jubilee Exhibition in Manchester in 1887, for example, included Mackmurdo's magnificent cabinet with panels designed and painted by Horne, which was made by the Manchester firm of E Goodall and Co. (fig. 45). From 1888, the Guild stopped holding its own exhibitions and exhibited with the Arts and Crafts Exhibition Society (see p. 61). It entered a new phase in 1890 when Mackmurdo moved his office and home to 20 Fitzroy Street (just around the corner from De Morgan's first, incinerated workshop), where the first floor

44. The Century Guild
Main Door at Pownall Hall, Cheshire, 1886

46. Charles Robert Ashbee
Design for the 'Procession of the Fair Cities' at the Art Workers' Guild Masque, 1899
Ink and watercolour, 8.9 x 15.2 cm (3 ½ x 6 in)
In the Possession of the Ashbee Family

became an exhibition and performance space, the basement served as a communal dining area, and residential and studio space was let to other artists. As a visitor later recalled: 'They all had meals together at an ancient oak table, without a cloth, of course; in the middle stood a plaster figure, and four bowls of bay which, I noticed, were covered with dust. Mackmurdo believed in the simple life.'[5] This continued until 1892, when the Guild members went their separate ways: Image to new Arts and Crafts endeavours; Mackmurdo to focus on social economics and elaborate but unrealized community projects; and Horne to pursue his art historical studies in Italy. *The Century Guild Hobby Horse* ceased publication the same year (although four issues of a successor title, *The Hobby Horse*, edited by Horne, came out in 1893–4). The Century Guild may not have had any sustained or far-reaching output but, with its exhibitions and a total of seven volumes of *The Hobby Horse*, it demonstrated the unity of effect which could be achieved through collaborative work in art and design.

The Century Guild was far from alone in promoting the applied and decorative arts. In January 1882 a group of friends, stranded by a storm in the house of the writer and designer Lewis F Day (1845–1910), formed a group called The

Fifteen which, led by Day and Walter Crane (1845–1915), met regularly to debate the revival of the decorative arts. In 1883 the young architects Ernest Newton (1856–1922), Edward S Prior (1852–1932), Gerald C Horsley (1862–1917), Mervyn Macartney (1853–1932) and William Richard Lethaby (1857–1931), all of whom trained under Shaw, also formed a discussion group, called the St George's Art Society, which met monthly in rooms in Bloomsbury Square to debate the role of architecture, and to voice concerns about the increasing separation between architecture and art. Realizing that they hewed to similar ideals, in 1884 The Fifteen and the St George's Art Society joined forces to form the Art Workers' Guild, a professional debating society which met in the Century Club in Pall Mall, with the aim of fostering collaboration between different branches of the arts. Its members were initially united by a common reaction against narrow-minded attitudes in the Royal Academy of Arts and the Royal Institute of British Architects, and the Guild's original intention was to promote architecture, painting and sculpture on equal terms, a fine arts bias evident in the membership at the first annual meeting (twenty-six painters, fifteen architects, four sculptors, and only eleven people

45. Arthur Heygate Mackmurdo and Herbert Horne
Cabinet, 1887
Satinwood, with mahogany door panels painted in oils, brass handles and key plates
201 x 259 x 86.4 cm (78 ¹/₂ x 101 x 33 ³/₄ in)
William Morris Gallery, London

47. The Third Exhibition of the Arts and Crafts Exhibition Society,
New Gallery, Regent Street, London, 1890

involved to some extent with the 'lesser' arts). But the Guild's focus gradually shifted to the decorative arts, and it became committed to establishing craftsmen, architects and artists as equals, and promoting the creative marriage of architecture, art and design.

The Guild met regularly to achieve this aim, encouraging frank and informal discussion among its members and professional collaboration between them, and hosting demonstrations, lectures, social gatherings and debates. These were not all solemn and worthy occasions, not least in 1899 when, after months of rehearsing and bickering, the Guild staged a masque entitled *Beauty's Awakening* at the Guildhall in the City of London. In the presence of an astonished Lord Mayor and Aldermen, Guild members enacted a series of allegorical scenes alluding to the event's twin themes of the revival of the arts and the revival of the City. In one scene, the demons of London with names as absurd as Bumblebeadalus and Slumdum merrily cavorted, while in another female embodiments of the 'Fair Cities' – played by the wives and sisters of members – processed across the stage. Versatility was the order of the day: the architect and designer Henry Wilson acted as stage designer; Lethaby,

Crane, Ashbee and the stained-glass artist Christopher Whall (1849–1924) designed props and costumes, many of them medieval in tone (fig. 46); and artists and craftsmen took to the stage. The project was not an unqualified success: an architect staying with Ashbee found it odd that talented men should be so underemployed, and Image delivered a prologue so irredeemable that the design historian Fiona MacCarthy has commented: 'The mise-en-scène, one hopes, was rather better than the verse.'[6] But the masque as a whole, a flamboyant pageant of collaboration and merriment, epitomized not only the comradeship, but also the humour of the Arts and Crafts.

Although the *Beauty's Awakening* masque followed in the Morrisian tradition of rumbustious camaraderie, the Art Workers' Guild was primarily committed to serious polemical debate. It was particularly exercised by the conservatism of the Royal Academy of Arts, which ignored many progressive developments in painting and sculpture, and refused to exhibit the decorative arts at all. The Guild was not alone in its concern: the 1870s and 1880s had seen the rise of numerous exhibiting organizations which challenged the oligarchic nature of the Academy, including the Grosvenor Gallery of 1877, the New English Art Club of 1886, and the New Gallery of 1887. In 1884 Morris reported with characteristic candour that he had gone to the summer exhibition at the Academy looking for 'traditional workmanlike skill', but instead had found works which were 'dashing, clever and – useless'.[7] Crane and others added their views, often in the *Pall Mall Gazette*, and in 1886 the *Gazette* called for a royal commission to investigate whether the Academy was violating its original aim. 'The Academy', it declared, 'was founded to promote the "arts of design"', but had instead become 'a mere society of painters in oil colours'.[8]

Spurred by such declarations, some of the Academy's most outspoken opponents began to meet in Chelsea in 1886, going by the name of the 'Chelsea Conspirators' and calling for wider recognition of all types of art. Within months they had 399 signatories, including founder members of the Art Workers' Guild; key Arts and Crafts practitioners such as Voysey, Lethaby and Day; and Mackmurdo, Image and Horne from the Century Guild. They were joined by the metalworker and furniture designer William Arthur Smith Benson (1854–1924), who proposed creating a new exhibition forum under the provisional title of 'The Combined Arts'. A split soon divided the 'Conspirators' into those who believed that they should co-operate with existing institutions, and those who wanted complete independence. In March 1887 the latter group broke away to establish an entirely new exhibiting platform, which Cobden-Sanderson suggested calling the Arts and Crafts Exhibition Society (the point at which he coined the term 'the Arts and Crafts').

The Society gradually took shape with Crane as its president and Benson as its secretary. They were an unusual pair: the committed socialist Crane, who had made his name illustrating children's stories before turning to wallpaper and pottery design, and the Oxford-educated Benson, who had trained as an architect but found fame as a designer of lamps in copper and brass. Crane was later described by Ashbee's wife, Janet, as 'the worst chairman of a meeting imaginable,'[9] but he and Benson (or 'Mr Brass Benson', as Morris called him[10]) made a formidable team, chivvying and cajoling their busy colleagues to serve on the Society's committees. By 1888 they were ready to issue a call for submissions for the first exhibition and this opened on 4 October in the New Gallery on Regent Street, so enabling competition and comparison which would not have been possible elsewhere. While the Society's membership was fairly small, its exhibitions were open to anyone whose work satisfied the selection committee

and at times exhibitors numbered in their hundreds, making these events a prominent public platform for the display of the Arts and Crafts. Importantly, many of the exhibitors also hoped to influence relevant manufacturing industries, debunking the idea that the Movement as a whole was unconcerned with the exigencies of the commercial world.

Nowhere is the impact of that inaugural exhibition more evident than in the effusive reminiscences of one of the visitors:

> *when the New Gallery opened its doors, a thrill of pleasure and surprise ran through the spectators. Many of us remember the beautiful effect of the Central Court – the pyramid of De Morgan tiles glowing with the ruby lustre of old Gubbio ware, with Persian and Rhodian blues, Mr Benson's luminous copper fountain, Mr Sumner's* sgraffito *designs and gesso roundels, the glorious tapestries from Merton Abbey, and all the lovely colour and pattern in silk embroideries and exquisitely tooled morocco, that met the eye.*

The exhibition received equally favourable notices in the press. The incorrigible playwright George Bernard Shaw, who

48. Walter Crane
Allegorical Design for the Arts and Crafts Exhibition Society, 1888
Ink on paper, 12.1 x 41.1 cm (4 3/4 x 16 1/4 in)
Victoria and Albert Museum, London

49. William Arthur Smith Benson and George Heywood Sumner
Charm of Orpheus Music Cabinet, 1880s
Mahogany and birch, 190 x 84.5 x 45 cm (74 ¾ x 33 ¼ x 17 ¾ in)
National Museum, Stockholm

for years flirted outrageously with May Morris, wrote two days after the exhibition opened: 'It has been for a long time past evident that the first step towards making our picture-galleries endurable is to get rid of the pictures [...] signboards all of them of the wasted and perverted ambition of men who might have been passably useful as architects, engineers, potters, cabinet-makers, smiths or bookbinders.'[11] He went on to praise the Arts and Crafts Exhibition Society for taking that first step. Another enthusiastic reporter from the *Pall Mall Gazette* interviewed Crane to mark the occasion, and commented that the Society 'will become accepted as an authority on all matters of ornament'. 'I hope so', was Crane's laconic reply.[12]

As a photograph of the third Arts and Crafts Exhibition in 1890 demonstrates (fig. 47), the New Gallery was an imposing venue, with curved skylights in a barrel vault and first-floor galleries, all of which gave a seductive variation in light and shadow. The visitor would have walked in wonder from space to space, dazzled by the reflections in a polished piece of copper, or examining the painstaking workmanship in a delicate textile hung in the shade. While some visitors marvelled at De Morgan's glistening lustreware or Whall's richly coloured stained glass, others examined the stitches in Morris's tapestries, admired his hand-knotted *Hammersmith* rug, or tried to work out the repeat in his chintzes and silks. Morris also exhibited samples of his calligraphy, while Benson showed his lamps, every weld and screw-joint visible in the Arts and Crafts tradition of showing how an object was made. The Century Guild exhibited thirty-four works, alongside silks by Thomas Wardle, George Heywood Sumner's (1853–1940) celebrated *sgraffito* work, which involved cutting a design from layers of coloured plaster, and bold, vibrant wallpapers by Crane and Day. Unlike the Art Workers' Guild, which did not admit women until 1966, the Arts and Crafts Exhibition Society welcomed female members: May Morris and De Morgan's wife Evelyn were among those who joined, and the exhibition included embroideries by May and by members of the Leek School of Embroidery. Crane produced an allegorical design for the Society (fig. 48), in which two classical figures symbolizing the handicrafts and design hold hands under the initials 'ACES'. To the left, a putto works at an anvil, while his friend on the right draws a circle with a pair of dividers, a palette and paintbrushes lying at his feet. Even a poorly informed visitor to the exhibition could not fail to appreciate Crane's message of unity in the arts.

The impact of the Art Workers' Guild and the Exhibition Society was immediately evident in new collaborative ventures. These might concern a couple of artists joining forces on one object, as when Benson exhibited the exquisite *Charm of Orpheus* music cabinet with decoration by Sumner at the second Arts and Crafts Exhibition in 1889 (fig. 49). Alternatively, it might involve a whole posse of designers working on a more ambitious project such as Holy Trinity Church in Sloane Street, London, which was designed by John Dando Sedding in 1888, and completed by Henry Wilson after Sedding's death (though not all of Sedding's decorative scheme was realized, fig. 50). Sedding, who himself designed wallpaper, embroideries and church metalwork, felt strongly about the need for co-operation between architects and craftsmen, describing the architect as 'a pictorial artist on a large scale' who should use 'the best faculties of his fellow craftsmen as well as his own, much as the musical composer secures the services of the best soloists and the best chorus and orchestra to render his oratorio'.[13] Accordingly, he and Wilson employed some of the best designers and craftsmen they could find to decorate Holy Trinity Church, the majority of whom, like Sedding and Wilson, were members of the Arts and Crafts Exhibition Society and the Art Workers' Guild. Nelson Dawson (1849–1910), for example, executed the organ grille and screen to a design by Wilson; Harry Bates (1850–99) sculpted the marble altar front; Burne-Jones, Whall and William Blake Richmond (1842–1921) provided designs for stained glass (Burne-Jones's east window being the largest Morris & Co. ever produced); and the sculptor Frederick William Pomeroy (1856–1924) supplied three-dimensional figures and relief panels for the choir-stalls, including a striking design of a lion, a lioness, an elephant and a stag (figs 51–2). Pomeroy also executed the plaque commissioned by the Art Workers' Guild in memory of Sedding, their second Master, which now hangs in the north aisle. These features were designed at different stages and, apart from their installation, were executed off-site, so the craftsmen and designers would have had little, if any, interaction in the church. The Art Workers' Guild and the Exhibition Society were therefore vital networking organizations at which craftsmen and designers could meet, study each others' work, and consider ways of incorporating their respective media into a larger architectural design.

Just as we see Morris's hope for confraternity in the arts being realized, Morris himself was becoming less involved in the Arts and Crafts Movement. He had come a long way from his sheltered past – the private moat at Water

50. John Dando Sedding and Henry Wilson
Holy Trinity Church, Sloane Street, London, 1888–90

51. Frederick William Pomeroy
Choir-stalls, c.1890
Oak interspersed with bronze roundels and facing reliefs
Holy Trinity Church

House, the hushed halls of Oxford's Bodleian Library – and by 1888 was so committed to the politics of socialism that he wrote, 'I have little life now outside the [socialist] movement – which is as it should be'.[14] The man who sold part of his valuable library to fund the socialist cause, and thought nothing of speaking at socialist rallies in the driving rain, initially looked down on the societies of the 1880s as little more than child's play. An honorary member of both the St George's Art Society and The Fifteen, he attended neither, and he did not accept the mastership of the Art Workers' Guild until 1892. Even then, he only deigned to chair three out of twenty meetings. 'I do not believe', he wrote patronizingly, 'in the possibility of keeping art vigorously alive by the action, however energetic, of a few groups of specially gifted men and their small circles of admirers amidst a general public incapable of understanding and enjoying their work'.[15] Although a member of its first selection committee, Morris was equally pessimistic about the viability of the Arts and Crafts Exhibition Society:

I don't think [...] that you will find commercial exhibitors willing to pay rent for space, and the shillings at the door will not, I fear,

come to much after the first week or two: the general public don't care one damn about the arts and crafts; [...] In short, at the risk of being considered a wet blanket, a Job, or Job's comforter, and all that sort of thing, I must say I rather dread the said exhibition: this is of course my private view of the matter, and also of course I wish it success if it comes off.[16]

Morris was wrong on many counts. The catalogue for the first Arts and Crafts Exhibition lists 517 items, proving that scores of artists and craftsmen were prepared to pay to take part, and within four weeks of opening the Exhibition Society had cleared £900, which easily covered its expenses. Nor was the exhibition an inconsequential one-off: it heralded a series of annual and then triennial exhibitions, and the practice of naming designers *and* craftsmen in its catalogues, as the Century Guild had done, made progress in placing the two on an equal stage. (Morris himself changed his tune after the success of the first exhibition, and prepared a much larger display of Morris & Co. goods for the second in 1889.) The Exhibition Society also ran lectures to accompany its exhibitions, with reduced fees for artists and craftsmen. In the first series, Cobden-Sanderson spoke on bookbinding, Crane gave a talk on 'Design', and Morris

52. Frederick William Pomeroy
Relief Panel from the Choir-stalls,
Holy Trinity Church

lectured on tapestry and carpet weaving. He brought examples
to illustrate his talk, including a cherished Persian carpet
from Kelmscott House, and later gave a demonstration which
inspired one of Burne-Jones's caricatures, lovingly scribbled on
headed writing paper: Morris sits at the loom with shoulders
hunched in concentration, his buttons ready to burst and his
feet tucked under him like a small child (fig. 53). The speaker
who had the greatest impact, though, was Emery Walker, who
was new to public speaking and, according to May Morris,
suffered 'untold agonies of shyness and nervousness':[17] but he
overcame his stage fright to declaim passionately about the
beauty of good letterpress printing, illustrating his talk with
lantern-slides of enlarged letter shapes from the pages of
fifteenth-century books. His fervour captivated Morris, who had
taught himself calligraphy and illumination, and as they made
their way home after the lecture Morris asked Walker to help
him design a new typeface, and soon invited him to go into
partnership on a printing press as well. Walker declined, but
offered to advise on an informal basis. Morris was not a man
to doubt his abilities, but Walker's offer of help allayed any fears
he might have had, and in 1890 he founded his last great
artistic enterprise, the Kelmscott Press.

The Kelmscott Press shows all the signs of the
perfectionism which had characterized Morris's earlier ventures.
Ink of the right blackness was imported from Hanover, and
handmade paper was commissioned from a manufacturer in
Kent, based on a Bolognese paper of 1473. Good vellum, which
was used for a few presentation copies, was more tricky to
source, as Morris's original supplier in Italy now worked solely
for the Vatican. Morris considered contacting the Pope himself,
before settling for a more accessible supplier in Middlesex.
Morris himself designed three new typefaces, aided by Walker's
enlarged letter shapes, and in 1891 the first of a total of fifty-three
Kelmscott Press titles appeared. These included Morris's own
works such as *News from Nowhere*, his Utopian novel which was
first published in the socialist newspaper *Commonweal* in 1892.
Charles Gere's frontispiece for the Kelmscott edition, with its
tree-lined approach to the front door at Kelmscott Manor, is
one of the most famous images that the Press produced (fig. 54).
The Press also published texts by other authors including
The Poems of John Keats, a three-volume Shelley, and 'The
Nature of Gothic' from Ruskin's *The Stones of Venice*, giving
Morris occasion to call it 'one of the very few necessary and
inevitable utterances of the century'.[18]

53. Edward Burne-Jones
William Morris giving a Weaving Demonstration, 1888
Pencil on headed paper, 22.9 x 17.8 cm (9 x 7 in)
William Morris Gallery, London

54. (opposite) Charles Gere
Frontispiece to William Morris's *News from Nowhere*, 1892
Woodcut engraved by W H Hooper
Fitzwilliam Museum, Cambridge

Most ambitious of all was the enormous *Chaucer*, planned in 1891 and completed in 1896, only months before Morris's death (fig. 55). With eighty-seven illustrations by Burne-Jones and countless initial letters and borders from a now ailing Morris, the Kelmscott *Chaucer* is a *magnum opus* in every sense. 'My eyes! how good it is!'[19] cried Morris on completing its spectacular initial page. Anyone lucky enough to handle one of the thirteen vellum copies can appreciate the characteristics of the most lavish Kelmscott productions: the delicate but detailed illustrations and borders set against Morris's dense type, all carefully printed in rich black ink on vellum, with pigskin used for some of the special bindings. Such was the quality of the materials and craftsmanship of the *Chaucer* that the sale of the book did not cover the investment in it, despite the fact that it appears to have almost sold out before printing was finished. Financial concerns apart, the *Chaucer* provided the opportunity for one last, touching collaboration between Morris and Burne-Jones, a photograph of the men still twinkling in 1890 demonstrating how well the friendship had survived (fig. 56).

The Kelmscott Press, housed in a cottage which Morris rented a few doors down from Kelmscott House,

became the focus for a veritable 'Hammersmith mafia' in the Arts and Crafts. May Morris lived a matter of minutes from the Press, at 8 Hammersmith Terrace, where she managed her circle of needlewomen who produced the embroidery for Morris & Co. Walker was only five doors away, and in 1893, Cobden-Sanderson, the bookbinder and printer and a member of Morris's socialist organizations, moved to 15 Upper Mall, opposite the Kelmscott Press. The same year Cobden-Sanderson set up the Doves Bindery, named after the local pub, adding to the density of artistic talent within walking distance of Morris's London home.

Cobden-Sanderson is a colourful character in the Arts and Crafts. He had studied medicine and law and was called to the Bar in 1871, but left for Italy when his health broke down in 1881. There he met his future wife, the suffragette Anne Cobden, and when they married he supported Anne's drive for female suffrage by prefixing her surname to his. His career as a bookbinder began soon afterwards when, on 24 June 1883, the Cobden-Sandersons had dinner with the Morrises, and Thomas expressed his desire to embark on creative work. 'Why don't you learn bookbinding?' Janey suggested. 'That would add an Art to our little community, and we would work together.'[20] Thomas noted her comments in his diary, marking the addition of a new creative form to the Arts and Crafts.

One of Cobden-Sanderson's early commissions came from Morris, who asked him to rebind his French translation of *Das Kapital* which, Cobden-Sanderson wrote on the flyleaf, 'had been worn to loose sections by [Morris's] own constant study of it'[21] (fig. 57). But Morris was initially less enthusiastic about Cobden-Sanderson's new career than his wife had been. In a revealing diary entry of March 1885, Cobden-Sanderson records that he had lunched with Morris, who had 'thought my work too costly; bookbinding should be "rough"; did not want to multiply the minor arts (!); went so far as to suggest that some machinery should be invented to bind books.'[22] This comment explodes the myth that Morris was unfailingly supportive of efforts to revive lost arts, and always opposed the use of machinery: but in 1885, Morris was so involved in socialism that he saw books primarily as tools of propaganda and education, which had to be cheap and mass produced. Fortunately, by the late 1880s Morris had become more sympathetic to the bookbinder's aesthetic aims, and Cobden-Sanderson's Doves Bindery often worked with the Kelmscott Press. In private, Cobden-Sanderson thought the type in Morris's books too heavy, and criticized their narrow margins, dense layout and disjointed text, but he was happy to bind

THIS IS THE PICTURE OF THE OLD HOUSE BY THE THAMES TO WHICH THE PEOPLE OF THIS STORY WENT. HEREAFTER FOLLOWS THE BOOK IT. SELF WHICH IS CALLED NEWS FROM NOWHERE OR AN EPOCH OF REST & IS WRITTEN BY WILLIAM MORRIS.

55. William Morris and Edward Burne-Jones
First Page of the Prologue from the Kelmscott *Chaucer*, 1896
Fitzwilliam Museum, Cambridge

the special editions in resplendent morocco covers with coloured insets.

The Kelmscott Press gave life to an extraordinary Private Press Movement. In 1894 Lucien Pissarro, son of the Impressionist painter Camille, and his wife set up the Eragny Press, also in Hammersmith, and the same year C H St John Hornby, an Arts and Crafts patron 'brimful of enthusiasm for Morris',[23] set up the Ashendene Press in Hertfordshire, moving it to Chelsea in 1899. They were followed by the Vale Press which Charles Ricketts founded in Chelsea in 1896; Ashbee's Essex House Press of 1898, which took over workers and hand-presses from the Kelmscott Press when it wound up its business after Morris's death; and the Doves Press, which Walker and Cobden-Sanderson established in Hammersmith Terrace in 1900. In Ireland, Elizabeth and Lily Yeats set up the Cuala Press as part of the Dun Emer workshops, with help from Walker and their poet brother (see Chapter 4), and there were similar initiatives in Germany and America. The Kelmscott printing style itself did not last: it was unsuitable for a new era of machine-composition and photographic illustration, and even May Morris found her father's typography hard to read. But the Kelmscott Press established a commitment to high standards of printing, printing materials, typefaces and illustration, in the process legitimizing book design as an art.

Charles Robert Ashbee (1863–1942), who set up the Essex House Press, is vital to the Arts and Crafts. The son of a connoisseur of pornographic literature, whose collection of erotica formed one of the more challenging bequests to the British Museum, Ashbee was educated at Cambridge, and on graduating worked in the architectural office of Bodley and Thomas Garner in London. This was within walking distance of his parents' elegant Bloomsbury house, but Ashbee – young, earnest, opinionated, and preoccupied with the problems facing the British working class – chose instead to live in the pioneer university settlement of Toynbee Hall in Whitechapel, which aimed to provide a social interface between the young men of Oxford University and the poorer population of London's East End. As a resident of Toynbee Hall, Ashbee was expected to organize a social or educational activity, and he chose to run an evening class on the work of Ruskin. Ashbee was struck by the Ruskinian notion of the medieval guild and, like Ruskin, fervently believed that the happiness of a craftsman was the most important index of his success. Years later, when a printer claimed that he could reproduce any work of handicraft by machinery and asked

56. Frederick Hollyer
William Morris and Edward Burne-Jones, 27 July 1890

57. Thomas James Cobden-Sanderson
Cover of William Morris's Copy of *Le Capital*, 1884
Green leather binding, tooled in gold, 29 x 21.6 cm (11 ½ x 8 ½ in)
J Paul Getty Collection, Wormsley Library, Berkshire

58. Charles Robert Ashbee
'Soul of William Morris' mounted in Ashbee's Journals, 1887
Pencil on card, 12.7 x 17.8 cm (5 x 7 in)
King's College Library, Cambridge

Ashbee if it would be any less beautiful, Ashbee replied, 'Maybe not, but ultimately it is the pleasure of the producer that sets the standard.'[24] Ruskin would have approved.

At the early age of twenty-four Ashbee determined to realize his ideas on the social benefits of craft production by establishing an art school, and went to Morris for advice. Morris at the time was being curmudgeonly about the Arts and Crafts Exhibition Society, and Ashbee fared no better. Morris poured 'a great deal of cold water' on his idea, and Ashbee vented his frustration by drawing a wide-eyed, demonic Morris in his journal (fig. 58) with the comment: 'If I could draw him, it would be thus, a great soul rushing through space with a halo of glory round him, but this consuming, tormenting, and goading him on.'[25] It is refreshing to see a cheeky young newcomer refusing to be bowed by Morris's authority. Ashbee's comment also shows a side of Morris that not many appreciated at the time: a man overwhelmed by success, who on occasion struggled to reconcile his original interests with his new priorities. Undaunted, Ashbee forged ahead, fund-raising and enlisting support, and in June 1888 his School and Guild of Handicraft opened with a capital of £50 in the attic of a warehouse

almost next to Toynbee Hall. *The Times* covered the opening, noting that edifying texts had been inscribed on the beams, including Ruskin's maxim: 'Life without industry is guilt, and industry without art is brutality.'[26] Under these sombre words, Ashbee's first five Guildsmen set to work, and within months were able to exhibit seventeen items at the first Arts and Crafts Exhibition. So it was that within sight of the slums, prostitutes, and sweated industries of Whitechapel, what was to become the most visionary Arts and Crafts community of the century came to life.

The Guild of Handicraft's earliest activities were furniture, metalwork and painted decoration, in which its first craftsmen specialized. It was primarily self-governed and had a system of profit-sharing, making it the most co-operative craft workshop yet. Others in the Arts and Crafts were impressed: its early supporters and patrons included Burne-Jones and Lewis Day, and Mackmurdo wrote 'I am delighted your experiment is progressing ... This is worth all our wordy theories,'[27] his enthusiasm portraying the workshop movement not as isolated enterprises, but as a network fired by a common aim. The Guild's first three members were drawn from Ashbee's Ruskin class, and later recruits were generally local, coming from east London, or from areas rich in artisan practice in the north of the city. (Ashbee preferred to recruit unskilled workers so that he could train them in the ways of the Guild, but by the late 1890s its commercial success required him to employ skilled craftsmen as well.) The School, for its part, enrolled about eighty students in its first year and offered evening classes ranging from carving and metalwork to clay modelling and carpentry. Many of these were run by the Guildsmen, reproducing what Ashbee saw as 'one of the best features of the medieval workshops of Italy.'[28] His belief in teaching by association was to characterize Arts and Crafts pedagogical approaches as a whole, but Ashbee was more than a talented teacher. As his wife observed, he 'had unquestionably the power of seeing and knowing the human boy, through his class, of loving him, and begetting love in return.' 'It was not that he was a King among Cobblers,' she added.[29] It was that he had that rare gift of crossing class divides and uniting men.

In 1891, the Guild and School moved to Essex House, an eighteenth-century mansion on Mile End Road in east London. The School ran into financial problems and shut down in 1895, but the Guild expanded to number about thirty workmen by 1898, and branched out to include wrought-iron work, enamelling, jewellery, leatherwork and, eventually, entire decorative schemes. The Guild trod a refreshingly practical line between the usefulness of machinery and the moral and artistic superiority of handwork: while it was perfectly acceptable to cut a plank with a circular saw, it was preferable that any carving be done by hand. Moreover, Mile End was more respectable than Whitechapel, populated by native-born artisans in regular employment, and Alan Crawford, Ashbee's biographer, believes that relocating the Guild there may have been a deliberate move to attract the sort of workmen to whom Arts and Crafts ideas would have appealed. In any case, the move to Mile End was a success: there, the Guild's men and boys met for Wednesday dinners, staged plays and sang songs, planned summer river trips and games of cricket, and fashioned some of the most memorable pieces of the British Arts and Crafts. They had a special name for the products and tastes of the Movement: it was 'Jolly Art'.[30]

The Guild's most popular lines were jewellery and silverware, much of which was designed by Ashbee. Believing that 'We nowadays have lost all understanding of the colour of jewellery',[31] Ashbee introduced enamelling, inspired by the work of the leading British Arts and Crafts enamellist Alexander Fisher (1864–1936), as well as semi-precious stones of reds, blues, greens and turquoises. 'Get to love your stones,' he urged, 'handle them, finger them, play with them, dip them in the water, get to know them intimately in various lights.'[32] For jewellery, he set the stones in silver wire, contrasting the solidity of the stone or the enamelling with the delicacy of its mount. The results are often in the form of a bird, butterfly, plant or even a ship (fig. 59), anticipating the stylized figuration of Art Nouveau. Ashbee's silverware, in contrast, is notable for its restraint, with simple, sinuous handles welded carefully – but visibly, in true Arts and Crafts tradition – to an elegant, hammered body. Stones set in the finial of a decanter or in the lid of a muffin dish (fig. 60) provide quiet points of colour to complement the planes and curves of the silverware, and the duller sheen of the glass.

Ashbee created an important showcase for Guild of Handicraft work in the Magpie and Stump, the house in Chelsea which he designed for his mother in 1893. Visiting Mrs Ashbee was quite an experience. One entered the house through a large oak door, with a doorknocker in the shape of a naked boy 'with every detail shown to perfection',[33] as Ashbee's shocked secretary remarked. The door led to a hall dominated by a chimneypiece of 174 plaques of copper, some plain, some repoussé, and others enamelled in pink, mauve, crimson and gold (fig. 61). Designed by Ashbee and executed by an eighteen-year-old apprentice, probably to demonstrate experimental Guild techniques, it featured numerous emblems associated with the Guild: the sun, the Tudor rose, and a boat known as the 'Craft of the Guild'. Other Guild products were also prominently displayed, including leatherwork, furniture and Ashbee's extraordinary light fittings: that in the drawing room was a complex net of wires, from which translucent enamel balls hung like weights on a fishing line (fig. 62). These coexisted with decoration by Ashbee's friends and family, including a frieze by his sister in the dining room (fig. 63), and a mantelpiece in the drawing room painted by the artist and critic Roger Fry. The house was a great success, with the popular illustrated journal *The Studio* publishing an article on it within a year of its completion, but was demolished in 1968 to make way for a block of flats. The Guild of Handicraft, for its part, underwent a dramatic transformation as the twentieth century dawned, as we will see in Chapter 4.

In 1896 Morris died, marking the end of an era in the Arts and Crafts. For Burne-Jones, it was difficult to imagine life without him: 'What I should do, or how I should get on without him I don't in the least know. I should be like a man who has lost his back.'[34] His death offers a convenient juncture to appraise the successes and limitations of the first wave of workshops and societies, which by the early 1890s had established themselves as an integral part of the Arts and Crafts. These craft associations were predominantly urban, with the exception of the Home Arts courses: but they were in no way homogeneous. Some were clubs, some philanthropic initiatives, and some commercial enterprises. Some aimed to address social problems, while others restricted themselves to the arts alone. Some were gender-specific, and others catered for social or geographical catchment areas. And while some focused on one discipline in a single workshop, others incorporated various crafts, either under one roof or in several venues. Several of them were elitist, with membership restricted to gentlemen artists or designers, and their clannishness and high-mindedness could be intimidating. William Rothenstein wrote that Arts and Crafts artists 'made me feel that we painters were doubtful characters, with second wives hidden away somewhere, and an absinthe bottle in the studio cupboard.'[35] But their ideal of fellowship made a vital contribution to British handicraft and design.

In the first place, the communal work ethic of the 1880s and 1890s began to influence the way in which the crafts were taught, as well as the way in which they were

59. Charles Robert Ashbee
Pendant in the form of a Ship, c.1903
Enamelled gold set with a large opal and hung
with three tourmaline beads, 3.5 x 2.5 cm (1 ¹/₂ x 1 in)
Victoria and Albert Museum, London

60. Charles Robert Ashbee
Muffin Dish, c.1900
Silver and gemstones, 20 cm (8 in) diam.
Victoria and Albert Museum, London

61. (opposite) Charles Robert Ashbee
Chimneypiece, executed by Arthur Cameron,
for the Magpie and Stump, 37 Cheyne Walk, London, 1893
Plain, repoussé and enamelled copper tiles, 215 x 201.5 cm (84 x 78 ¹/₂ in)
Victoria and Albert Museum, London

made. Until the 1880s, education had been an incidental process in the Arts and Crafts: Morris might teach others a skill which he had mastered before moving on to the next, but there was no systematic way to impart the principles of good craft design. This failing was tackled by the lectures and demonstrations of the Art Workers' Guild and the Arts and Crafts Exhibition Society, and by informal day and evening classes – for example, those of Ashbee's School and the Home Arts – all of which began to impact upon the established educational institutes. Birmingham was one of the first places to respond, with the Birmingham Municipal School of Art introducing design alongside the existing elementary courses in 1885, repoussé metalwork and experiments with craft materials in 1887–8, and craft workshops in a new wing in 1893. In the 1890s, schools offering tuition in the applied arts and design also appeared in Scotland (see Chapter 4), while Crane occupied key posts in art schools in Manchester and Reading, and was eventually appointed principal of the Royal College of Art.

In London, the most important teaching initiatives were those of Lethaby, who for many years was involved in drawing up plans for art education which would provide practical teaching in different crafts. He was able to implement these ideas in 1896 when appointed co-principal of the new Central School of Arts and Crafts, later known as the Central School of Art and Design. Pupils here had to have prior experience of their chosen craft, and were taught in workshops by practising designers, many of whom were recruited from the ranks of the Art Workers' Guild: Wilson taught metalwork, and Whall taught stained glass; May Morris, who also taught at the Royal School of Art Needlework and the Birmingham School of Art, gave lessons in embroidery; and Douglas Cockerell (1870–1945), a pupil of Cobden-Sanderson, taught book design and bookbinding. When Edward Johnston (1872–1944), the calligrapher, applied to Lethaby to attend a class in lettering, he found himself running a calligraphy course instead. Evening classes were offered for those who had to work during the day, and from 1901 until the First World War the school's staff published books on their specialist areas, many of which are still definitive texts today. The Central School remains a major player in the teaching of craft and design, based in Holborn, where it moved in 1908. Lethaby, for his part, went on to be the first Professor of Design at the Royal College of Art.

62. Charles Robert Ashbee
Light Fitting for the Drawing Room, Magpie and Stump, 1895
Iron, enamelled copper, pewter and lead, 91 cm (36 in) diam.
Victoria and Albert Museum, London

63. Charles Robert Ashbee
'Dining room, Magpie and Stump', from *The Studio*, 1895

64. William Arthur Smith Benson
Lamp, c.1895
Brass and copper, 68.5 (with glass chimney) x 40 x 17.9 cm (27 x 15 3/4 x 7 in)
Victoria and Albert Museum, London

Education apart, the workshops and societies of the 1880s and 1890s made the Arts and Crafts Movement self-aware. Crane defined the Movement's aim in 1888 as being to turn 'our artists into craftsmen and our craftsmen into artists',[36] and by the early 1890s this had been achieved in a myriad of ways. Artists, architects and craftsmen now collaborated as never before, often on an equal footing; there was greater appreciation of a craft object as a work of art; there had been explorations of the social dimension of the Arts and Crafts; and, with the Arts and Crafts Exhibition Society, the Movement had acquired a public face. The Movement as a whole was celebrated from 1893 in the pages of *The Studio*, which gave extensive coverage to the designs, plans and drawings of Voysey, Shaw, Ashbee and their colleagues, as well as publishing interviews with designers themselves.

But the workshop movement reminds us of the ongoing need to weigh practice against theory. In the first place, the ticklish question of 'integrated labour' raises its head: while some designers, notably Christopher Whall, made their own products, other craftsmen had to implement the ideas of those who ran the workshops. Some Home Arts classes, for example, issued part-worked designs by artists such as Voysey and Sumner, which class members would then complete. The established designers in turn worked for commercial manufacturers, again divorcing the making of an object from the originator of its design. As well as Webb and Burne-Jones's glass for Powell & Sons of Whitefriars, Voysey, Day and Crane designed wallpapers for Jeffrey & Co. and ceramics for Wedgwood, Minton and Maw & Co., to mention just a few retail outlets. Morris, who battled most doggedly with the spectre of dehumanized production methods, collaborated with outside manufacturers for much of his working life.

In the 1880s and 1890s we also encounter complex attitudes towards 'the machine'. In some cases, the workshops employed mechanized processes without question. Benson, for example, designed objects in his furniture and metalwork workshop which exploited the capabilities of lathes and stamping-presses to the full, on occasion producing metalwork which even resembles part of a machine (fig. 64). An early designer of electrical lightfittings, Benson saw artificial lighting as a 'fine art' and in 1896 his work was described by the *Magazine of Art* as 'palpitatingly modern', all

of which makes him stand out in the Arts and Crafts. But it is important to distinguish between different sorts of machine: an industrial production line has nothing in common with a lathe, whose products still have to be fashioned by hand in some way. Other members of the workshop movement gradually revised their anti-mechanical views. Mackmurdo confessed that when he started designing for the Century Guild 'my soul wrestled with this demon of mechanics', but 'After closer acquaintance with machine printing and weaving I was able more accurately to balance the possible gains and the inevitable losses. [...] Great and unimaginable things may in the future result from a more true marriage between art and industry'.[37] Even Morris eventually acknowledged the role of machinery, provided that the men using it remained in control: 'it is the allowing machines to be our masters and not our servants that so injures the beauty of life nowadays'.[38] Ashbee went further, writing in 1911: 'Modern civilization rests on machinery, and no system for the endowment, or the encouragement, or the teaching of art can be sound that does not recognize this'.[39]

Nevertheless, Arts and Crafts designers in the late-nineteenth century never fully reconciled themselves to the fact that industrialization had irreversibly transformed British society, and some of the most exciting opportunities for designers lay in industrial design. Some bodies more than others did encourage the union between art and industry, most notably the National Association for the Advancement of Art and its Application to Industry, which was established in Liverpool in 1888. The Association was supported by many Arts and Crafts designers: Art Workers' Guild members participated at its first congress in Liverpool, and the second congress in Edinburgh in 1889 attracted several hundred delegates, among them Morris, Lethaby, Voysey, Crane, Whall and Day. Yet the Association only survived until 1890, the victim of a general reluctance among British designers to work wholeheartedly with industry. Instead, the co-operatives of the 1880s and early 1890s remained a movement in which a succession of well-educated men and women battled for social relevance and high-quality workmanship in the arts. Their ambivalent view of industrial techniques undoubtedly limited their practice, but at the same time it constitutes an endearing and unavoidable characteristic of the British Arts and Crafts.

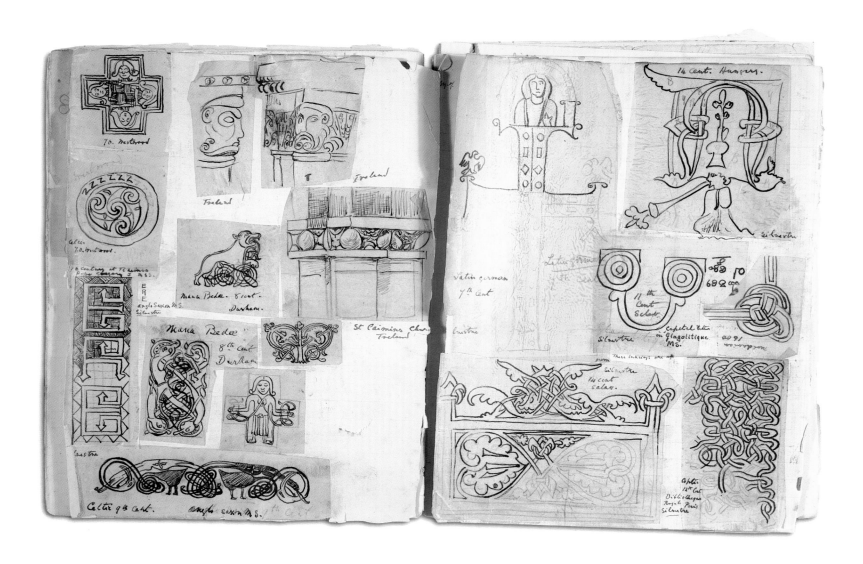

Mary Seton Watts
Designs from a Sketchbook (fig. 67)

EXPANSION ACROSS THE BRITISH ISLES

THE RICH ARTS AND CRAFTS MOVEMENT WHICH HAD DEVELOPED IN LONDON BY THE END OF THE 1880s CONTINUED WELL INTO THE NEXT CENTURY. FROM THE MID-1880s, ARTS AND CRAFTS INITIATIVES BEGAN TO APPEAR IN SCOTLAND AND IRELAND TOO, AND FROM THE 1890s THE MOVEMENT EXPANDED OUTSIDE LONDON IN A VARIETY OF WAYS.

The Home Arts classes continued to thrive, and were joined by other craft workshops and co-operatives in the provinces. Several designers and architects decided to move to the country, escaping what they saw as the spiritual impoverishment of city life. Both London-based and provincial architects won a wealth of commissions for Arts and Crafts houses in the countryside and the suburbs; and strongholds of Arts and Crafts production appeared in cities like Birmingham, Manchester and Sheffield. These processes of rural and urban dispersal resulted in the rapid expansion of the Movement throughout the British Isles.

By the 1890s, craft workshops were mushrooming throughout Britain. Many stemmed from philanthropic concerns, such as the Haslemere Weaving Industry started by Maude King (1867–1927) and her husband Joseph in 1894, and the Peasant Arts Society established in the same town by Godfrey Blount (1859–1937) and his wife Ethel in 1896. The Peasant Arts Society, which included workshops in weaving, embroidery and, later, mural decoration, woodwork and bookbinding, was religious in character and aimed to provide local women with employment. Its rural location was an important part of its ethos, as the countryside was seen as a panacea to urban degeneracy, and as the place where one could get closest to God.

Other workshops were orientated towards a particular craft, rather than a charitable or religious cause. Pottery workshops proliferated, among them the Della Robbia Pottery which the painter Harold Rathbone (1858–1929) set up in Birkenhead in 1894, and the Ruskin Pottery, which was founded near Birmingham four years later. Most remarkably, Mary Seton Watts (1850–1938), the wife of the artist George Frederick, set up an evening class in clay-modelling at her home in Compton, Surrey, to provide decorative panels for a mortuary chapel which she was designing for the village's new burial ground (fig. 65). Mary, who had studied at the Slade and South Kensington Schools of Art, had already taught pottery to shoeblacks in Whitechapel, and served on the teaching staff and council of the Home Arts: but she had no experience of architectural design. 'A few people sneered', she later wrote, 'and I believe it was generally thought that the attempt would fail, and that some big firm would come in for the order.' She proved them wrong, keeping every aspect of the work in local hands. The chapel was built of local brick; its terracotta mouldings were

65. Mary Seton Watts and Others
The Mortuary Chapel, Compton, Surrey, 1896–1906

68. Interior of the Mortuary Chapel

made of local clay and fired in a kiln in the Watts' back garden; its oak doors were carved in the village; and its ironwork was forged in the local smithy. In all, seventy-one people took part, only a handful of whom had any relevant professional training. The rector and the squire helped to make the bricks; the coachman modelled a terracotta frieze of angels' heads around the doorway; and women potters from Mary's evening class decorated the interior with what Mary called a 'glorified wallpaper'[2] of painted gesso panels in low relief (fig. 66).

The chapel followed a complex decorative scheme inspired by Celtic symbols and motifs which Mary had studied in manuscripts in the British Library: a sketchbook in the Watts Gallery in Compton, with dozens of traced drawings pasted to its pages, reveals the extent of her research (fig. 67). The iconography outside includes the River of Life and the Tree of Life, and even the seats have Celtic motifs, while the gesso panels of the interior – more intimate and resplendent than any photograph can suggest – are decorated with serried ranks of seraphim and cherubim in a kaleidoscope of ruby, emerald and gold (fig. 68). The contrast between the uniform colouring of the exterior, with its red

bricks and terracotta mouldings, and the exotic polychromy in the domed belly of the chapel could not be more pronounced. This is a Celtic Revival statement of great vigour, inflected by the tendrils and twirls of Art Nouveau.

Having learnt to pot, the Compton locals were loathe to stop, and in 1899 they began commercial production as the Compton Potters' Arts Guild, housed in a thatched shed up the road from the chapel. Within a year, they were receiving so many orders that Mary was looking to employ a paid business manager. The Guild specialized in brightly painted domestic ornaments and terracotta garden ware, which it supplied to outlets as prominent as Liberty's (the famous shop in Regent Street, London, which from about 1890 sold many goods influenced by the Arts and Crafts). It regularly exhibited at the Home Arts exhibitions in the Albert Hall, and examples of its work were commissioned for Parliament House in Pretoria, South Africa, and Adelaide Cathedral in Australia. Some of the Guild's output now seems decidedly kitsch – lamps in the form of lighthouses, for example, or a biscuit barrel in the shape of the mortuary chapel – but the battered bed-head with its painted terracotta panel, or the beautiful *Peacock Casket* of 1910 (fig. 69), show extraordinary

66. Mary Seton Watts and Assistants working
on Gesso Panels for the Mortuary Chapel

69. Mary Seton Watts
Peacock Casket, 1910
Terracotta, 9.3 x 18 x 7 cm (3 ¹/₂ x 7 x 2 ³/₄ in)
Watts Gallery, Compton, Surrey

67. Mary Seton Watts
Designs from a Sketchbook
23 x 18 cm (9 x 7 in)
Watts Gallery, Compton, Surrey

inventiveness in the use of clay. Such was the success of the Guild that Mary opened a sister operation, the Aldourie Pottery (1900–14), near her family home in Scotland. The Compton Guild continued until 1956, a lasting tribute to the local skills and enthusiasm which Mary Seton Watts had harnessed over half a century before.

The Haslemere workshops and the Compton pottery had been planned from the start as country-based enterprises, but rural life began to appeal to city artists as well. Various reports, including Andrew Mearns's *The Bitter Cry of Outcast London* (1883) and Charles Booth's *Life and Labour of the People in London* (1889–1903), highlighted the fact that, despite rising standards of living in general, parts of London were wretched in their poverty and squalor. The agricultural depression from the 1870s – the result of foreign competition, not least as cheap grain from the American prairies began to flood into Britain – was a further cause for concern, and engendered attempts to revitalize agricultural employment. From Russia, the influence of the writer Leo Tolstoy also began to be felt, with his advocacy of agricultural labour and peasant morality. These developments contributed to the 'Simple Life' Movement –

the decision of various progressive intellectuals to 'get back to the land', fuelled by a socialist vision of the self-sustaining community, and by a romantic belief in the superior value of rural life.

The most significant of the Arts and Crafts artists to leave the city was Ashbee, who had undergone a change of heart since his early desire to establish a workshop which would reflect the social concerns of Londoners. His Guild of Handicraft had in fact flourished in an urban setting: in July 1898 it had been registered as a limited company; its products were exhibited in Europe and America; and it received good reviews in the artistic press. However, Ashbee now felt that a full creative life was only possible in the country, and that 'to train up little children or fine craftsmen in London is a cruelty unmentionable'. A suitable site was therefore found in the small Cotswold market town of Chipping Campden, a Guild vote was taken, and one May morning in 1902 the Guild's younger workers piled their bicycles on to a train at Paddington station, alighted at Moreton-in-Marsh, and rode the last few miles to their new home, a disused, eighteenth-century silk mill with three floors of workshop space. Within four months the Guild had brought about 150 men, women

70. The Young Men of Chipping Campden performing Exercise Number 13 ('Double knee bend with arms bending and stretching'), c.1906

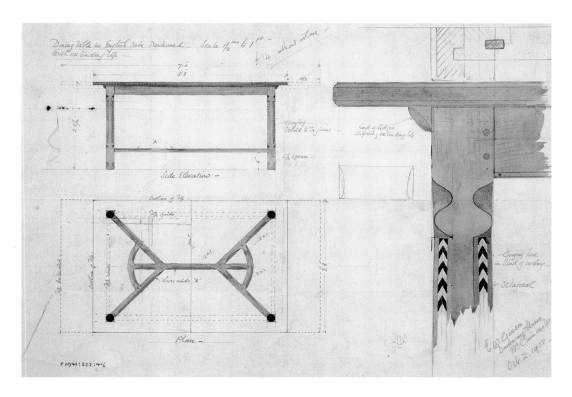

71. Ernest Gimson
Design for a Table, 16 October 1908
Pencil and wash on paper, 38 x 56.2 cm (15 x 22 in)
Cheltenham Museum and Art Gallery

and children into a town whose own population was only about 1,500. Predictably enough, there was friction with the townsfolk, not least when a local landowner evicted some of his tenants in order to enjoy a higher rent from the Londoners. The townsfolk retaliated by charging those associated with the Guild higher prices in the local shops.

Over the months, though, the rancour and distrust disappeared. Ashbee set up a Campden School of Arts and Crafts which was popular with the locals, for whom he even ran physical drill classes (fig. 70), and the townsfolk gradually accepted the Guildsmen and their curious ways: their madrigals and pageants, costumes and open-air plays. There were artistic successes as well, notably the Guild's carved decoration for the library at Madresfield Court in Worcestershire, and a stream of inquisitive visitors came to see the social experiment at work. De Morgan, whom Ashbee tried to lure permanently to Campden, paid a visit. Crane also lectured at the School and, on a cycling trip with the Guild boys in a resplendent outfit of maroon-coloured check and scarlet tie, sustained a puncture and fell off his bicycle just as a pious and unamused congregation was disgorging from the local church. Such inauspicious

encounters apart, most of the Guildsmen and their families came to feel part of Cotswolds life. As Janet Ashbee wrote in 1906: 'even the opposition, the Vicar, the pig-headed farmers, the stupid polititians [. . .] are all part of it – and seem as necessary as the mist and the rain and the rheumatism and the muddy roads.'

In one sense, Ashbee's move to the country was the ultimate Arts and Crafts statement, for here was a man prepared to take his abhorrence of urbanization to its logical conclusion. His philanthropic aspirations also found their fullest realization here, for the School provided training and employment for bored and disaffected young men. In this respect Ashbee was very much of the second generation of the Arts and Crafts, moving from the early focus on reviving lost crafts, to a wider concern for the worker's quality of life. But Ashbee's Guildsmen were almost all cockneys who had never lived in the country before, and many of their crafts – metalwork, enamelling – were urban in origin. Moving them to Chipping Campden isolated them from their roots, their patrons, and their publicity, and ultimately signalled the end of the Guild of Handicraft. It faced competition from commercial outfits such as Liberty's, whose 'Cymric' range

72–3. Philip Webb
Standen, East Grinstead, West Sussex, 1891–4, and Drawing Room (opposite)

offered cheaper, machine-made versions of the Guild's silverware, and by 1906 financial problems meant closing a London gallery which had been opened at the time of the move to display furniture, and the Essex House Press (a heart-rending operation which involved dismissing long-standing employees, and dismantling the Kelmscott presses which Essex House had acquired). The Guild itself went into liquidation the following year. It was reconstituted as a trust, under which some Guildsmen ran their own workshops with moderate success, but many left Chipping Campden and found employment as diverse as designing for Liberty's, or making moulds for the chocolate manufacturer Cadbury's. Ashbee himself never forgave Liberty's and other outlets for what he saw as plagiarism, dedicating his 1909 set of lithographs entitled *Modern English Silverwork* 'to the Trade Thief, desiring him only – if indeed he have any aesthetic honour, thieves sometimes have! – to thieve accurately'.[3]

The demise of Ashbee's Guild suggests that the romantic notion of taking craftsmanship to the country was never going to be easy. But there were other rural workshops that survived longer than Ashbee's, not least those of Ernest Gimson (1864–1919) and the Barnsley brothers Ernest

(1863–1926) and Sidney (1865–1926). These men were city-born and had met in London: Gimson and Ernest Barnsley had worked as assistants in Sedding's office, while Gimson and Sidney had collaborated with Lethaby and others in a furniture workshop called Kenton & Co. After its closure in 1892, Gimson and Sidney decided to move to the Cotswolds, persuading Ernest Barnsley to leave his comfortable architectural practice in Birmingham and join them. Initially, they settled at Pinbury Park, near Cirencester, where they worked independently as architects, craftsmen and designers, with Sidney the most industrious of the three: his wife would take in cakes for the mid-morning break and find Sidney 'hard at work at the bench, the other two standing by, often hands in pockets, whistling Gilbert and Sullivan tunes'.[4]

While Sidney Barnsley continued to work independently, making most of the furniture he designed himself, from c.1900 the two Ernests collaborated in furniture and metalwork workshops, most successfully in Sapperton, Gloucestershire, where they moved in 1903. Some of their furniture has elaborate decoration and expensive inlays, but much of it focuses on the colours and markings of local woods, and on exposed methods of construction. In a curved

74. Edward Prior
The Barn, Exmouth, Devon, 1895–7

sideboard of *c*.1910, for example, Gimson uses a segmental design to show off the grain and sheen of different planes of oak. On occasion they also echoed country woodworking techniques: the wishbone structures of rakes appear in the stretchers of tables, while the arched sides of wagons feature in cabinet and sideboard designs (fig. 71). Gimson and the Barnsleys built up their practices gradually, employing local as well as imported craftsmen. The result was an unassuming but successful business which continued to operate until the summer of 1918, suggesting that it was not being outside London which was Ashbee's problem, but his failure to adapt to his rural market and base.

While Ashbee, Gimson and the Barnsleys were running workshops in the Cotswolds, Arts and Crafts architecture was gaining currency as a mode for houses in the country. Typical of their patrons is James Samuel Beale, who came from a wealthy family of Birmingham solicitors, and in 1870 had been sent to run a new office in London. Beale also had family connections with the railways, and made a fortune by acting as the London agent of the Midland Railway. In 1891, the year he turned fifty, Beale decided to invest in a country house and settled on a site near East

Grinstead, West Sussex, to which a railway line had been extended in 1884. His aims for the house were not grand: rather than establishing a vast estate, Beale simply wanted a home where he and his family could enjoy country pursuits, and to which he would eventually retire. Webb had acquired a reputation for comfortable, sensible houses, and in spring 1891 won the commission to design Standen, Beale's new house.

At Standen, Webb showed his skill at maximizing the attractions of a site. The house enjoys spectacular views towards Ashdown Forest, but is tucked into a hillside so that it does not intrude on the landscape; natural features were accommodated from the start, with Webb noting on his plans the location of specific trees. He also acknowledged the agricultural vernacular by linking existing farm buildings to the house via an archway, keeping the new service block low and simple to match them, and using local materials and construction techniques to harmonize with the older work. The garden front alone employs local brick, tile hanging, oak weather-boarding, and sandstone quarried from the site (fig. 72), but even an array of colour and texture such as this did not satisfy Webb, who introduced variations

84

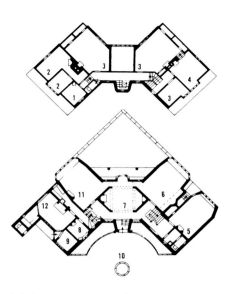

1: Bath
2: Maid's room
3: Bedroom
4: Dressing-room
5: Study
6: Drawing-room
7: Hall
8: Pantry
9: Scullery
10: Front drive
11: Dining-room
12: Kitchen

75. Edward Prior
Plan of The Barn, 1895–7

76. William Richard Lethaby
Design for Melsetter House, Hoy, Orkney, 1898
Ink on waxed linen, 42 x 45 cm (16 ½ x 17 ¾ in)
Macrae and Robertson Papers, Orkney Archives

specific to each material as well. The bricks should be '*not all of one colour, occasional grey headers and heat burred bricks to be mixed with the rest*',[5] and yellow-grey stock bricks from the local town of Horsham were used to avoid monotonous expanses of red. Webb was equally fussy about the sandstone, which was to be of the quality 'in some old walling at the back of "The Ship Inn", East Grinstead'.[6] Even the mortar was to be made of 'good clean local sand'.[7] Roughcast, a form of facing made from lime, broken stones, pebbles and tallow, was used to waterproof the brickwork of the tower, which, for an architect as interested in practicalities as Webb, was recommendation enough. But roughcast was also characteristic of humble vernacular buildings in Britain, and could be seen as suiting an unpretentious country house. As Webb confessed, 'I never begin to be satisfied until my work looks commonplace'.[8]

On entering the house, the modern visitor finds it anything but commonplace. The main rooms are decorated with Morris & Co. furnishings, De Morgan's ceramics, metalwork by Benson and John Pearson (the senior metalworker in Ashbee's Guild until 1892), and Morris-pattern hangings embroidered by members of the Beale family. To a

twenty-first-century sensibility, nurtured perhaps in the 'white cube' spaces of modern galleries, the result can seem cluttered and ornate (an effect exacerbated by the collecting activities of later inhabitants). But we have to remember the bedrock from which Arts and Crafts design was springing: the dark rooms of mahogany and chenille, every wall a collage of paintings and prints, every surface an army of knick-knacks and ornaments, and every table-leg a stylized carving. Against this, Standen's rooms, with their windowed alcoves, undecorated plasterwork, lighter decorative schemes and white panelling provided a bright, modern, liveable space (fig. 73). Webb insisted on designing every detail of his houses, down to the last bit of beading, and these fittings were only entrusted to firms with the highest standards of workmanship. Masterminding the entire project also enabled Webb to ensure that his houses actually worked: at Standen, internal doors were hung so that draughts would not blow smoke from fireplaces into the room, and even the beds were to be of 'sizes as for a tallish family', highlighting the pains the architect took to meet the needs of his client.[9]

Webb never had pupils in the direct sense and was not a prolific architect; yet his ideas were disseminated

77. William Richard Lethaby
All Saints Church, Brockhampton, Herefordshire, 1901–2

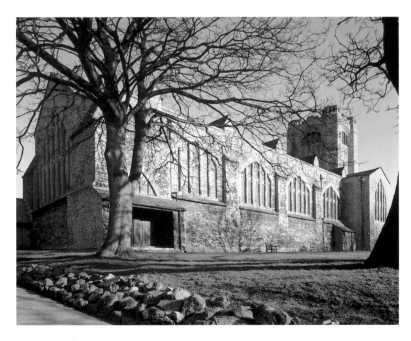

78. Edward Prior
St Andrew's Church, Roker, Sunderland, 1906

through the Society for the Protection of Ancient Buildings, whose new recruits in the 1890s included Lethaby, Macartney, Gimson, Sidney Barnsley and Detmar Blow (1867–1939). They would converse with the older architect during dinners at Gatti's restaurant, and Webb helped them to gain practical experience as clerks of works both on his own projects and on those of the SPAB (taking part in building as well as designing a project being a signal factor in the Arts and Crafts). As a result, while many of the second generation of Arts and Crafts architects trained with Sedding or Shaw, they were equally inspired by Webb. Key in this respect were William Lethaby and Edward Prior, who came from very different backgrounds: while Prior, a barrister's son, had been educated at Harrow and Cambridge, Lethaby, the son of a Devon frame-maker, had no academic education at all. They met in 1879 when Lethaby joined Prior in Shaw's office, and one might have expected some friction between the two men: Prior – athletic, assertive, well-educated and well-heeled – was soon working under a man five years his junior, who had never set foot in a university. Yet they got on well, collaborating in the St George's Art Society, the Art Workers' Guild and the Arts and Crafts Exhibition Society, and in the 1890s greatly expanded the application of Arts and Crafts ideas to architectural design.

Outstanding among the architects' domestic work are a house called The Barn which Prior built near Exmouth in Devon in 1895–7, and Melsetter House, designed by Lethaby on the island of Hoy in Orkney for a retired Birmingham businessman in 1898. The Barn (fig. 74) is remarkable on two counts: it employed unusual masonry of grey ashlar, red boulders and pebbles from the nearby coast, revealing Prior's fascination with texture; and it introduced Prior's famous butterfly plan (fig. 75) (possibly based on an earlier French form) which, with wings at a ninety-degree angle, reduced the distance between the main rooms, offered varied prospects over the sea, and created a suntrap between the two wings. Novel, convenient and adaptable to different sites, the butterfly plan often reappeared before the First World War, and comprised one of the great contributions of the Arts and Crafts Movement to domestic planning. At Melsetter, in contrast, Lethaby used Webb's room-and-passage plan, and incorporated the existing laird's house, much as Webb had accommodated farm buildings at Standen. He was concerned with fidelity to place, too, using a Scottish form of roughcast called 'harling' to waterproof the walls, and topping them with steeply pitched roofs of

79. The Nave of St Andrew's Church

80. Edward Burne-Jones with John Henry Dearle
The Adoration of the Magi, 1890–1907
Tapestry, high-warp wool, 256.5 x 370 cm (101 x 148 in) with a border of 10.2 cm (4 in)
St Andrew's Church

Caithness tiles (fig. 76). The result reminded May Morris of the 'fairy palaces of which my father wrote with great charm and dignity'. But, she added, 'for all its fineness and dignity, it was a place full of homeliness and the spirit of welcome, a very lovable place'.[10] Thus like Webb, Shaw and Prior, Lethaby combined the appeal of innovative architecture with the ease of a functioning house.

At Melsetter, Lethaby also built a small chapel, where he experimented with concrete, and installed windows by Burne-Jones, Brown and Whall. This anticipated his great design for All Saints Church, which he built in Brockhampton, Herefordshire, from 1901 to 1902. All Saints, which is based on an old English tithe barn, is of local red sandstone and thatch, offset at one end by a clapboard bell tower with shingled roof (fig. 77). Inside, pointed stone arches support a concrete vaulted nave, the plainness of which is tempered by Burne-Jones's tapestries and Whall's stained glass. The result is Arts and Crafts architecture as it might like to be remembered: an imaginative building using local techniques, rewarding materials, and fantastic combinations of colour, texture and space. Prior too turned to ecclesiastical design, with his church of St Andrew's in the seaside suburb of Roker, near Sunderland. Here, far from the crucible of Arts and Crafts ideas in London, we find an extraordinarily sustained exercise in the application of texture and craftsmanship in architectural design.

St Andrew's Church dates from the early twentieth century, when Sunderland's shipyards were booming. The suburb of Roker evolved as part of the urban expansion which followed, and in 1903 an appeal was launched to raise money for a new church. When the appeal was only partly successful John Priestman, a local shipping magnate who had risen from draughtsman to self-made millionaire, offered £6,000, but the money came with three provisos: the church tower had to be visible from the sea; a congregation of 700 had to be able to see the altar; and, as Priestman was a keen organist, the acoustics had to be good. These requirements are evident in Prior's design, as an eighty-foot castellated tower rises at the east end of the church, nearest to the sea less than a quarter of a mile away (fig. 78). The entire building is full of novelty. The walls are thicker at the bottom than at the top, so that the buttresses are subsumed into the base; the tracery of the windows is unusually straight; and thick, uneven panes of glass, made by a process called 'Early English' which Prior had developed in 1889, are placed so that their streaky lines go in different directions. The result is a mesmerizing juxtaposition

of textures and surfaces, as the rough, locally-quarried magnesian limestone of the walls and tracery gives way to the slightly convex panes of glass which, in true Ruskinian tradition, exemplify the worthy imperfection of the handmade. Inside, the nave is columnless so that the congregation can see the altar, and buttresses support high, parabolic stone arches, which make for one vast, uninterrupted space (fig. 79). The buttresses, cut away just above head height, are supported by hexagonal columns inspired by those of a Saxon church in nearby Monkwearmouth. Above them, the arches meet at a reinforced concrete ridge, and have been compared to the ribs and keel of an upturned boat – an apt simile given the local shipbuilding industry. The construction has been accused of 'dishonesty', as the arches are of stone cladding over reinforced concrete, and other parts are also reinforced with concrete and steel, but it was the use of these new materials that enabled the realization of Prior's unusual design.

If the construction of St Andrew's Church were not enough to merit its inclusion in the Arts and Crafts story, its decoration would be. There are stone tablets with the elegant lettering of Eric Gill (1882–1940), the sculptor, engraver, typographer and calligraphist who studied under Johnston at the Central School of Arts and Crafts, and in the early twentieth century frequented the Arts and Crafts Exhibition Society and the Art Workers' Guild. The pulpit, oak panelling and choir-stalls were designed by Gimson and made by Peter Waals (1870–1937), a gifted Dutch cabinet-maker who joined Gimson's workshops as foreman in 1901. Gimson also designed the candlesticks, crosses and lectern, the last of these modelled on a medieval cantor's lectern, and made of ebony inlaid with ivory, silver and mother-of-pearl. Behind it, a Morris carpet leads to the altar which, during Advent and Lent, is hung with Morris's *Bird* textile, while the reredos is adorned with a tapestry of *The Adoration of the Magi* (fig. 80), woven at Merton Abbey to Burne-Jones's design. In the church, we can get close enough to see each thread, which gives a precious opportunity to examine the craftsmanship of a Morris & Co. tapestry. The most startling discovery is that what looks like gold thread is in fact yellow, but achieves its sparkle by being thin and reflective: in contrast, the thicker, matt threads used for other colours absorb the light. This is true mastery of materials, when the density of the thread, rather than its tone, is exploited to achieve the required colour. The decoration of the sanctuary was completed with an east window by Henry Payne (1868–1940) of Birmingham,

81–2. Charles Francis Annesley Voysey
Entrance (above right) and two storey bays (above left) at Broadleys,
Lake Windermere, Cumbria, 1898

83. (below) Charles Francis Annesley Voysey
Perspective of Broadleys, Lake Windermere, Cumbria, 1898
Pencil and coloured washes on paper, 26.9 x 44.9 cm (10 ½ x 17 ½ in)
RIBA Drawings Collection, London

84. (opposite) Charles Francis Annesley Voysey
Design for *Owl* Wallpaper and Fabric, *c.*1897
Pencil and watercolour, 50.8 x 40 cm (20 x 15 3/4 in)
Victoria and Albert Museum, London

85. Mackay Hugh Baillie Scott
Inglenook in the Main Hall at Blackwell,
Lake Windermere, Cumbria, 1898–1900

who frequently worked for Prior, and by the dazzling image of *The Creation* which Eric Gill's brother, Macdonald, painted in 1927, twenty years after the church was consecrated. On the north and south walls, Adam and Eve fraternize with molluscs, fish, amphibians and a whale, while the bright blue ceiling culminates in a huge sunburst motif. Macdonald Gill worked to a design by Prior, who had envisaged painted decoration between the purlins and rafters of the nave as well, but this was never carried out: instead, we are left with the striking contrast between a jewel box of a sanctuary and the nave's stark, structural effect.

Prior eventually moved away from architectural practice and became involved in writing and education. He published acclaimed books on English Gothic architecture, and from 1912 was the Slade Professor of Fine Art at Cambridge, where he launched the University's School of Architecture. Lethaby too was as important an educator as he was an architect, and debated Arts and Crafts ideas in his elegant texts. Towards the end of his life, though, Lethaby became disillusioned: he felt that the Arts and Crafts had become as self-conscious as the styles it rejected; and he saw no way of avoiding the use of the machine. These misgivings

suggested a loss of momentum in the British Arts and Crafts Movement, and were to prove prescient of the reasons behind its demise.

Lethaby and Prior were two of many architects who combined an active involvement in Arts and Crafts organizations in London with architectural commissions in the country and the suburbs. One of their most successful peers was Charles Francis Annesley Voysey (1857–1941), a fellow member of the Art Workers' Guild, a regular exhibitor at the Arts and Crafts Exhibitions and, from 1894, Prior's neighbour in St John's Wood. Voysey, diminutive in stature but a giant in intellect, had trained with the Gothic Revival architect John Pollard Seddon and then with George Devey, and made a name for himself in media as diverse as wallpaper, fireplaces and calligraphy. He also designed over 120 houses, mainly in rural or suburban areas, which bear as little direct resemblance to Prior's buildings as Prior's do to Lethaby's, reminding us that it is a shared intellectual approach, rather than visual similarities, which underpins Arts and Crafts design.

For Voysey, one of the main tasks of an architect was to bring calm and simplicity to a house. This could be

86. Drawing Room, Blackwell

87. Stained-glass Windows, Blackwell

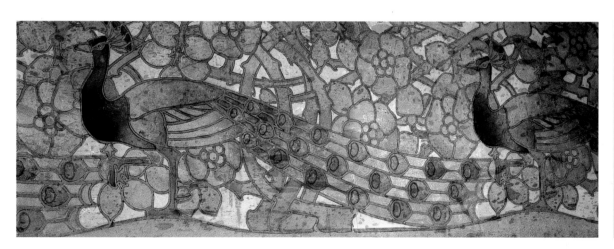

88. William Shand Kydd
Peacock Wallpaper Frieze in the Main Hall, Blackwell, 1898–9

89. Wrought-iron Window Latches, Blackwell,

achieved by emphasizing the horizontal, which he equated with natural states of rest: 'When the sun sets horizontalism prevails, when we are weary we recline [...] What, then, is obviously necessary for the effect of repose in our houses, [is] to avoid angularity and complexity in colour, form or texture, and make our dominating lines horizontal rather than vertical.'[11] Voysey added interest by introducing semicircular and polygonal bays, nestling under or breaking through low, sweeping eaves. This is beautifully achieved at Broadleys, Cumbria, which Voysey built for a wealthy Yorkshire colliery owner in 1898. The house follows Webb's L-shaped room-and-passage plan, with a long service wing emphasizing the horizontal. But in the main block the horizontality is broken: on the west front by three semicircular, two-storey bays which burst through the eaves to offer 180-degree views over Lake Windermere; and in the entrance court, by three gables over the main door (figs 81–3).

Voysey had strong views about doors, which should be 'wide in proportion to height, to suggest welcome – not stand-offishly dignified, like the coffin lid, high and narrow for the entrance of one body only.'[12] That at Broadleys is accordingly broad and low, and leads to a bright, central, two-storey hall. The dining room, drawing room and stairwell lead off this, the latter boasting newel posts rising to the ceiling and an unusual glazed balcony. Voysey also designed light fittings, furniture, and even a ventilation system with grilles to extract the stale air. The aim, as in most of his interiors, was to create a simple, clean effect (so obsessed was Voysey with cleanliness that he designed his own suits without lapels or turn-ups which might accumulate the dirt). Yet there is an irony here as, despite his advocacy of simple interiors, Voysey earned a substantial income from his naturalistic wallpaper and textile designs (fig. 84). He explained the contradiction by saying that wallpaper was redundant if one had good furniture, 'but as most modern furniture is vulgar or bad in every way, elaborate papers of many colours help to disguise its ugliness.'[13] Critics have nevertheless noted that Voysey used wallpapers in his own home where, one hopes, he liked the furniture. Was it that, like Morris, Voysey had difficulty reconciling his commercial interests with his theoretical concept of good design?

At Broadleys, we encounter another paradox in Voysey's work. The roughcast walls painted off-white and the roofs of green Westmorland slate echo local practice, in good Arts and Crafts tradition: but this was not deliberate, as Voysey used both materials irrespective of locality. (When he later wanted to use local materials, clients demanded his popular roughcast style.) Unlike many Arts and Crafts architects, Voysey was not, therefore, overly concerned with regional character. But he was exercised by the need for a *national* architecture, writing: 'Why [...] should England turn her back on her own country and pretend that she is such a born mongrel she can have no truly national architecture?'[14] His simple buildings with their geometric projections attempted to address this need for a national style.

A couple of miles from Broadleys, Mackay Hugh Baillie Scott (1865–1945), one of the few Arts and Crafts architects who was never part of the London scene, built another striking holiday house, Blackwell, for a rich Manchester brewer. Baillie Scott was the son of a Scottish landowner, and as a young man was destined to go to Australia to manage the family sheep farms there: but despite passing the relevant exams at agricultural college in 1885, he decided to become an architect instead. Four years later he visited the Isle of Man on honeymoon, and later claimed that he was so seasick on the way over that he decided to stay. Baillie Scott designed various houses on the island, not least his own home, also called the Red House (1892–3). This had an innovative plan, with the drawing room, dining room and hall separated by hinged wooden panels which, when folded back, allowed three discrete rooms to be amalgamated as one large, asymmetrical space. The study, in contrast, was wedged above the inglenook in the dining room, keeping the architect's feet warm as he laboured over his designs. These ideas reached a wide audience from 1895, when Baillie Scott published his work in *The Studio*, including designs for hypothetical houses and interiors with folding screens, inglenooks and galleries. The inglenook and gallery became a particular trademark of the architect, not least at Blackwell (1898–1900) which, after a four-year restoration project, is the only Baillie Scott house open to the public.

Blackwell, like Broadleys, is built in the Lakeland vernacular, with whitewashed roughcast walls, sandstone mullions and transoms, and a steeply-pitched roof of Westmorland slate. Like Broadleys, it also uses Webb's L-shaped room-and-passage plan, and has a double-height living hall. But if the effect of the hall at Broadleys is of a modern space well suited to the building's current function as a boat club, that at Blackwell, with its oak panelling and half-timbering, has more of a baronial air. At one end, the hall flows into a single-height billiard room, while opposite it a staircase leads to a half-timbered gallery above an inglenook (fig. 85). There is a childlike compulsion to climb that staircase, lapping up the ingenuity of a design which fits rooms together like Lego, while preserving the impressive height of the overall space. The hall opens into the dining room, with an inglenook of its own and walls covered with hessian. The drawing room, in contrast, is feminine and white, with delicate columns with basket capitals in yet another inglenook and in the west bay (fig. 86). Each room is richly decorated with naturalistic imagery inspired by the Lakeland setting: birds, rosehips, bluebells, hawthorn and acorns in the drawing-room carvings, and mountain ash in its plasterwork; tulips, bluebirds, swallows and roses in stained-glass panels; local flowers printed on the hessian in the dining room; and a frieze of rowan berries and running water carved by Arthur W Simpson's workshop in Kendal for the main hall. Particularly enchanting are the stained-glass panels of tulips which dance merrily by the front door, but stand to attention further inside (fig. 87). There are De Morgan tiles in the fireplaces, and a frieze of sapphire-breasted peacocks by William Shand Kydd (1864–1936) in the hall (fig. 88). Arts and Crafts architect that he was, Baillie Scott even designed a recently-discovered set of copper billiard lights, and each individual window latch and key (fig. 89).

Broadleys and Blackwell were both begun in the late 1890s, and it is fun to linger on the thought of the two architects working in such proximity. Travelling by train to Cumbria, did Voysey and Baillie Scott ever share a carriage? Did they swop tips – sources of material, reliable workmen, a congenial local pub? Did they perhaps even appreciate the irony that they were indebted to the abominated railway for such work? Both men went on to enjoy enormous popularity in Europe (see Chapter 5), and it is not inconceivable to picture them sharing ideas and contesting interpretations as they jolted through north-west England on a provincial railway train.

While Arts and Crafts houses and workshops were appearing from Devon to Cumbria, urban-based centres in cities other than London had begun to appear. The first of these was in Birmingham, which already had a reputation as an intellectual and cultural hub, with a rich concentration of craftsmen: in the 1840s, Pugin had relied on John Hardman of Birmingham for his metalwork and coloured glass, and the city still enjoyed a healthy output of applied art. In 1890, Ashbee's friend Arthur Dixon (1856–1929) set up the

Birmingham Guild of Handicraft, which functioned as a co-operative workshop, like Ashbee's Guild, and fostered similar social ideals. Its craftsmen produced candlesticks, jewel boxes, jugs and coffee pots inspired by Ashbee's work, and later took the motto 'By Hammer and Hand'. Another band of artist-designers, sometimes referred to as the Birmingham Group, congregated around the Municipal School of Art, first under the directorship of Edward Taylor and then, from 1903, under Robert Catterson Smith (a man immortalized by Janet Ashbee as 'so beautiful, one forgives him much, even his wife').[15] The Municipal School of Art played a crucial role in bringing Arts and Crafts sympathizers together in a way comparable to that of the Art Workers' Guild in London, and it nurtured many talents. While Arthur Gaskin (1862–1928) and his wife Georgina (1868–1934) excelled in jewellery and metalwork, Joseph Southall (1861–1944) revived the art of tempera, Mary Newill (1860–1947) invigorated the art of embroidery, and Henry Payne acquired a national reputation for his stained glass. There were links between these artists and those of the Cotswolds: the Gaskins later lived in Chipping Campden, Payne moved to a Cotswolds house altered by Sidney Barnsley, and Sidney's daughter Grace trained as a potter at the Birmingham School of Art. These movements suggest a dialogue between the new Arts and Crafts centres, echoing the web of friendships and personalities that characterized the Movement in London.

Across the Irish Sea, Dublin was also enjoying a surge of interest in the crafts, which in its case was closely connected to questions of nationalism and cultural identity. Ireland suffered from profound agricultural poverty, which had led to the almost complete disappearance of cottage craft industries. With the rural economy in tatters, many had drifted to Dublin, leading to overcrowding, unemployment, and poor health and hygiene in the disease-ridden slums. At the same time, opposition to the political Union of Ireland with Britain, which dated from 1801, was on the rise. These social and political anxieties fed into a revival of craft industries, which could provide much-needed employment for both sexes and, in promoting Irish traditions and Celtic imagery, contribute to the increasingly politicized cultural trends of the time.

Foremost among the patrons of the Irish Arts and Crafts was Lady Aberdeen, who arrived in Dublin with her husband, the new Lord Lieutenant of Ireland, in February 1886. They had not been twenty-four hours in the city before Lady Aberdeen was asked to preside over a committee

90. Wilhelmina Geddes
Joseph's Dream, c.1927
Stained-glass panel, 27.5 x 27.5 cm (10 ¾ x 10 ¾ in)
Stained Glass Museum, Ely (Gift of Elizabeth Kerr)

91. Dun Emer Guild
Hand-Knotted Rug, c.1904
Wool on a jute warp, 121.9 x 91.4 cm (48 x 36 in)
National Museum of Ireland, Dublin

92. Dun Emer Guild
Brat, c.1928
Hand-sewn Irish poplin, 163 x 105.5 cm (63 ½ x 41 in)
National Museum of Ireland, Dublin

preparing a display of Irish Home Industries work for the Edinburgh International Exhibition. This received a diploma of honour and inspired Lady Aberdeen to set up the Irish Industries Association, a local equivalent of the Home Arts: thus began her long involvement in artistic and social causes which included promoting home industries, improving housing and hygiene, setting up schemes to combat tuberculosis, and supporting Irish and Scottish crafts. Often lampooned – Lady Aberdeen's focus on tuberculosis was thought bad for tourism, while her preference for social work over hosting parties gained her a reputation for meanness – she nevertheless succeeded in galvanizing and marketing Irish handicrafts, not least in the 'Irish village' which she mounted at the Columbian Exhibition in Chicago in 1893.

Lady Aberdeen's example inspired other aristocratic patrons to support the decorative arts in Ireland. Lady Mayo revived the Royal Irish School of Art Needlework, and in 1894 her husband, the Earl of Mayo, founded the Arts and Crafts Society of Ireland. The Society's first two exhibitions were dominated by loans from England, but the third exhibition, in 1904, showed predominantly Irish work. By this stage numerous craft workshops had appeared in Ireland. Alfred Child (1875–1939), from Whall's glass workshop in London, and Oswald Reeves (1870–1967), who had trained in Fisher's enamelling studio and at the Birmingham School of Art, set up classes in stained glass and enamelling at the Dublin Metropolitan School of Art in 1901 and 1903. Evelyn Gleeson and Elizabeth and Lily Yeats, both of whom had worked in May Morris's embroidery workshops, set up the Dun Emer workshops in 1902 in Dundrum, outside Dublin (joined, in 1908, by the Yeats sisters' separate Cuala workshops). Alice Hart (1848–1931) founded the Donegal Industrial Fund to revive home industries in the west coast town of Donegal. And the painter Sarah Purser (1848–1943) established a co-operative stained-glass workshop, An Túr Gloine (the Tower of Glass), whose designers, notably Wilhelmina Geddes (1887–1955), mastered the integration of the lead cames (which hold the pieces of glass together) as part of their striking designs (fig. 90). These and other workshops raised standards of craftsmanship and engendered a sense of pride and identity among Irish craftsmen and women, and by the 1904 exhibition their work was attracting a favourable press.

Many Dublin workshops drew their inspiration from Ireland's heroic mythology and from early Celtic objects and

93. Phoebe Anna Traquair
Three Divine Powers, 1885–9
Detail of the south wall of the Mortuary Chapel in the
Royal Hospital for Sick Children, Edinburgh

94. Phoebe Anna Traquair
Psyche Chalice, 1906
Paua shell mounted on a silver stand by J M Talbot to a design by Ramsay Traquair,
decorated with enamelled plaques and suspended enamelled drops, 34.1 cm (13 ½ in) height
National Museums of Scotland, Edinburgh

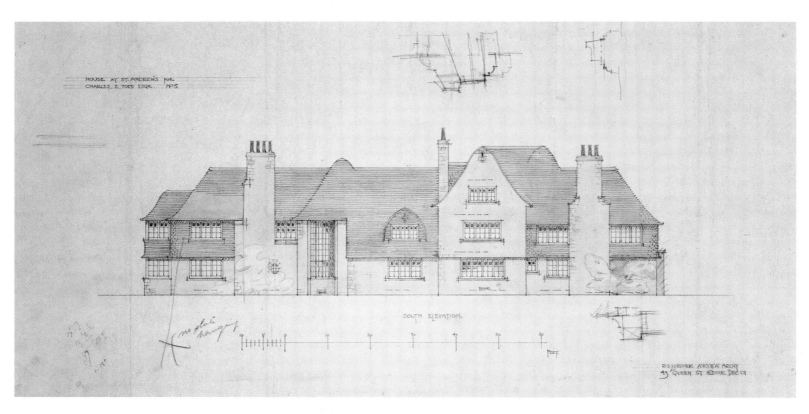

95. Robert Lorimer
Elevation of Wayside, Hepburn Gardens, St Andrews, 1901
Pencil with colour wash on tracing paper, 11.4 x 38.7 cm (4 ½ x 15 ¼ in)
Royal Commission on the Ancient and Historical Monuments of Scotland

96. A Montage of Designs for a Masque at the Glasgow School of Art, c.1904

motifs, reflecting the revival of Gaelic culture by figures such as Douglas Hyde, who in 1893 had set up the Gaelic League to revive the Irish language, and W B Yeats, who believed it incumbent on artists to convey the nobility of their indigenous culture and natural surroundings: 'I would have our writers and craftsmen of many kinds master Ireland's history and legends, and fix upon their memory the appearance of mountains and rivers and make it all visible again in their arts.'[16] Thus the mythical beast on a hand-knotted rug by the Dun Emer Guild (fig. 91) was inspired by one of Ireland's early Christian illuminated manuscripts. A brat – a cloak-like garment which assumed the role of an invented national costume – was embroidered with the natural imagery so close to Yeats's heart (fig. 92). Celtic references also abound in Honan Chapel in University College, Cork (1915–17), whose wealth of decoration included a Dun Emer cope, enamelling and repoussé silverwork by Reeves, and windows of Irish saints by Harry Clarke (1889–1931).

Scotland shared the confluence of Arts and Crafts practice and Celtic nationalism which appeared in Ireland, though not to the same extent. In Edinburgh, the Arts and Crafts Movement was galvanized by the Edinburgh Social Union which was founded in 1885 by the environmentalist Patrick Geddes and others to improve the local environment and quality of life. The Social Union ran courses ranging from window-box gardening to classes for the construction workers of the Forth Bridge; it provided local schools, halls and hospitals with original paintings by local artists, and reproductions of works by artists including Burne-Jones; and it commissioned mural decorations for public buildings, most famously those by Phoebe Anna Traquair (1852–1936).

Traquair had been born and educated in Dublin, where she attended courses in art and design, but fell in love with a Scottish palaeontologist for whom she had been illustrating fossil fish. They married in 1873 and the following year settled in Edinburgh, where Traquair's husband had been appointed Keeper of Natural History at the Museum of Science and Art. In Edinburgh, Traquair worked first in embroidery, but in 1885 was invited to decorate a mortuary chapel which the Royal Hospital for Sick Children had set aside for parents to bid farewell to their deceased children. Inspired by medieval manuscripts and the Symbolist art of Rossetti, Traquair responded with a complex and colourful interdenominational iconography which revolved around the redemption of mankind, but also featured portraits of writers and artists she admired, including Ruskin and Carlyle (fig. 93). In later murals (a medium characteristic of the Edinburgh Arts and Crafts), Traquair continued to portray real people and places. Her full-length, life-size portraits in the Song School of St Mary's Cathedral (*c.*1889–90), for example, included Carlyle, Rossetti and Morris, while her decoration for the chapel at Avon Tyrrell, a house designed by Lethaby in the New Forest, featured religious, literary and scientific figures, soldiers and workmen, and Avon Tyrrell itself. Mural painting apart, Traquair taught design at the Social Union and worked in bookbinding, calligraphy and illumination, furniture decorating and enamelling, examples of which she exhibited at the Arts and Crafts Exhibitions in London. Particularly inventive were objects which she made from silver, shells and painted enamel, such as the *Psyche Chalice* of 1906 (fig. 94). Such were Traquair's achievements that in 1920 she became the first woman to be elected an honorary member of the Royal Scottish Academy.

In 1889, Edinburgh hosted the second congress of the National Association for the Advancement of Art and its Application to Industry. Local delegates responded enthusiastically to lectures and demonstrations by Morris, Crane, Cobden-Sanderson, Walker and Whall, and the 1890s saw new energy in Edinburgh's craft activities. The Social Union established craft studios in a disused church, and by 1894 ran courses in modelling, carving, joinery, gesso, repoussé metalwork, bookbinding and leatherwork. Influential new schools promoted the applied arts, and exhibition societies such as the Society of Scottish Artists (1891) and the Edinburgh Arts and Crafts Club (1897) gave craftworkers opportunities to display their work. By 1902, even the Royal Scottish Academy grudgingly agreed to include applied art. The result was an Arts and Crafts scene of great vitality, in which scores of talented architects and designers took part. Foremost among them was Robert Lorimer (1864–1929), a local lad who had served an apprenticeship with Bodley in London before returning to his native city of Edinburgh in 1893. In Scotland, Lorimer developed a reputation for vernacular forms and, like Bodley, high-quality craftsmanship, not least in Wayside, a magnificent villa which the architect designed on the edge of St Andrews in 1901 (fig. 95). With metal fittings, fireplaces, panelling and plasterwork by Lorimer, superlative joinery containing a curved, double-height window in the central hall, and an undulating roof of Easdale, Craiglea and

97. Margaret Macdonald Mackintosh
O Ye That Walk in Willow Wood, 1903–4
Painted gesso with twine and coloured glass beads,
164.5 x 58.4 cm (64 ¾ x 23 in)
Kelvingrove Art Gallery and Museum, Glasgow

98. Charles Rennie Mackintosh
The Main Entrance to the Glasgow School of Art, 1897–9

100. (opposite) The Library at the Glasgow School of Art, 1907–9

99. Charles Rennie Mackintosh
Linen Press, 1895
Stained cypress, coloured woods and metal, 195 x 158 x 45.6 cm (76 3/4 x 62 1/4 x 18 in)
Glasgow School of Art

recover aspects of their cultural heritage in search of a national style – which elsewhere in Europe became a salient characteristic of the Arts and Crafts (see Chapter 8).

Edinburgh was far from the only Arts and Crafts centre in Scotland. There were Arts and Crafts Clubs in Dundee and Aberdeen, but it was Glasgow that hosted the most idiosyncratic developments. This began in the early 1890s when Francis Newbery (1855–1946), director of the Glasgow School of Art since 1885, set up the Technical Art Studios to offer tuition in the crafts, including an embroidery class run by his wife Jessie (1864–1948). These and other initiatives proved so popular that by the end of the century the city had a craft community large enough to sustain an Arts and Crafts Club, the Scottish Guild of Handicraft, and the Scottish Society of Art Workers. At the same time, four graduates of the Glasgow School of Art – Charles Rennie Mackintosh (1868–1928), his wife Margaret Macdonald (1864–1933), Margaret's sister Frances (1873–1921), and Frances's husband Herbert MacNair (1868–1955) – began to attract attention for the innovation of their designs. Known as the Glasgow Four, they cemented Glasgow's reputation as a hot-spot of *fin-de-siècle* art and design.

The Glasgow Four worked both independently and collaboratively, combining mystic symbolism with Celtic and Japanese influences to create highly original work in several media. Margaret was particularly skilled at gesso, her haunting, ethereal figures in delicate colours often decorating the architectural projects of her more famous husband (fig. 97). The Macdonalds and MacNair have tended to be marginalized in an attempt to contrast their work with the modernity of Mackintosh's, and their position in the Arts and Crafts Movement is subject to debate: neither major players nor staunch supporters of the Movement, they were dismissed by Voysey as 'the spook school'[17] (a sentiment which many of his colleagues shared), and their sinuous fluidity and stylized naturalism is often more characteristic of Art Nouveau. But recent research has debunked the myth that the work of the Glasgow Four was ridiculed and rejected by the Arts and Crafts Exhibition Society and vilified in the press, demonstrating instead that it appeared at several Arts and Crafts Exhibitions where it may have been seen as eccentric, but was also often admired.[18]

If the identities of MacNair and the Macdonalds have been subordinated within the Glasgow Four, Mackintosh has been lionized. There are Mackintosh tourist routes in Glasgow which include Queen's Cross Church, the part-

Ballachulish slates, the house exemplifies the architect's assimilation of vernacular ideas, and the high value which he ascribed to the crafts.

Others developed the crafts in guilds and workshops, such as the Dovecot Studio, which the 4th Marquess of Bute set up in Corstorphine, a village west of Edinburgh, to provide tapestries for his seat on the Isle of Bute. The Dovecot's panoramic Scottish narratives are bound up with ideas of Celtic identity which appeared elsewhere in Scotland. Both Edinburgh and Glasgow, for example, hosted pageants and masques with a distinct Scottish emphasis: one at the Glasgow School of Art included personifications of Glasgow University, Glasgow Cathedral, and the royalty of Strathclyde (fig. 96), while the most elaborate, in 1908, featured over 600 architects, artists, craftsmen and their families dressed up as Romans, Jacobites, and Scottish and Celtic kings. Despite references to Scotland's history prior to English political domination in 1707, however, such explorations of Scottish identity did not become overtly politicized until after the birth of the National Party of Scotland in 1928. Rather, they were a product of National Romanticism – the nostalgic quest of artists and designers to survival of the Willow Tea Rooms, the reconstruction of Mackintosh's house in the Hunterian Art Gallery, and the recent realization of his 'House for an Art Lover', which was designed but never built in 1901 (see Chapter 5). Most important of all, standing as weighty and enigmatic as the day Mackintosh built it, is the Glasgow School of Art.

The art school was built in stages, beginning with the east range and the centrepiece in Renfrew Street (1897–9), whose asymmetrical entrance introduces the dynamic between sinuous line and solid form which is so characteristic of Mackintosh's style (fig. 98). The sense of solidity continues inside in the huge timber trusses of the exhibition hall which, with their protruding wooden pegs, emphasize methods of construction. In contrast, the posts at the corners of the stairwell, with their mortar-board caps in the manner of Mackmurdo and Voysey, have no structural purpose, serving only to punctuate the large, open space. To the east of the hall, a skylit corridor to some of the studios has niches in its walls, intended to hold vases of fresh flowers which were to be changed daily by the janitor. This exemplifies the thrill of Mackintosh's work, with the imposing forms of the architecture given levity and interest by something as natural as a vase of flowers. The corridor leads to the boardroom, which now houses an array of Mackintosh furniture, including a linen press of 1895 (fig. 99). With its repoussé panels and oversize hinges as function and decoration combined, the linen press illustrates the Arts and Crafts element in many of Mackintosh's early designs.

In 1907 Mackintosh added the east stairwell, which is a clever amalgam of vernacular sources and affordable new materials. It takes its inspiration from the baronial architecture of Scottish castles, which fascinated Mackintosh: but it was built in concrete, polished to give a high sheen. Mackintosh also developed the west range and the west wing, the latter towering over Scott Street, with its three soaring bays. The shape of the bay windows is repeated inwards, creating great columns of space which slice through the famous double-height library (fig. 100). Here, there is again a hint of the baronial in the panelling and the balcony, but this is leavened by the painted insets of the balusters (fig. 101), and the modernity of the ceiling lights (fig. 102). On a bright day the windows, a full eight metres high, throw shafts of light through the geometry of the interior with all the intrigue and simplicity of a Mondrian painting.

The School of Art is one of the most famous buildings associated with the Arts and Crafts. But, in being

101–2. Details of Library Balusters and Hanging Lights, Glasgow School of Art

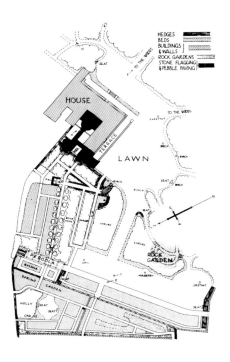

103. Edwin Lutyens
Design for the Gardener's Cottage at Munstead, Surrey, c.1892–3
Pencil, pen and watercolour, 125 x 180 cm (49 ¼ x 70 ⅞ in)
RIBA Drawings Collection, London

104. Gertrude Jekyll
Garden Plan for Munstead Wood, 1896
from G Jekyll and L. Weaver, *Home and Garden*, London, 1900

an urban school, it is also one of the most atypical, as Arts and Crafts architecture, with a few notable exceptions, continued to be primarily an idiom for country or suburban houses. As these flourished, attention turned to their gardens, drawing on Morris's dictum that a garden 'should by no means imitate either the wilfulness or the wildness of Nature [...] It should, in fact, look like part of the house'.[19] There was to be nothing natural in the manner of the eighteenth-century English landscape garden: rather, while Arts and Crafts architects took pains to fit their buildings into a landscape, they wanted their gardens to look man-made. As Sedding wrote in *Garden Craft Old and New* (1891), 'Man's imitation of Nature is bound to be unlike Nature', so 'it were wise to be frankly inventive in gardening on Art lines'.[20] Terraces, walls, and paved and pebbled walkways were used to create 'rooms' as a conceptual extension of the architecture: but as the distance from the house increased these gave way to more informal features, facilitating the transition to the surrounding landscape.

This practice of harmonizing the garden with both the house and its setting was developed most fully by Edwin Lutyens (1869–1944) and the feisty garden designer Gertrude

Jekyll (1843–1932). Their famous partnership began in the early 1890s, when Lutyens designed a gardener's cottage and small house called The Hut, both of them in the Surrey vernacular, on a plot of land which Jekyll owned in Munstead, Surrey (fig. 103). Jekyll then asked the young architect to design her a larger house, Munstead Wood (1896–7), in which Lutyens again employed the local vernacular, with a steeply pitched, tiled roof sweeping brazenly through the first floor. In the garden, Jekyll used judicious planting, an expert eye for colour, and a web of paths, pergolas and walkways to create 'rooms' to the north of the house, but to the south, she took pains to preserve the views into the surrounding woods (fig. 104). The result was widely admired and led to other Arts and Crafts gardens which, with their kitchen gardens, orchards, herbaceous borders and topiary, were expensive to maintain (at one time Jekyll employed no fewer than eleven gardeners at Munstead Wood). But this did not deter clients, and Lutyens and Jekyll collaborated on more than a hundred projects, with Lutyens planning the layout and providing seats, paths and architectural features such as terraces, while Jekyll took care of the planting. Lutyens's career continued on an upward trajectory well into the 1930s, and the vogue for his country houses spread from Devon to Northumberland, where during 1902–3 he converted Lindisfarne Castle into a private house for Edward Hudson, founder of *Country Life* magazine. Here, Lutyens demonstrated great sensitivity to the sixteenth-century castle on its rocky crag, and created interiors of which any Arts and Crafts architect would have been proud: the dining room, with its vaulted stone ceiling and blue wall, has a particularly cheeky panache.

Arts and Crafts ideas continued to resonate in Britain well into the twentieth century. One of their most important legacies lay in the Garden City Movement, which began with the foundation of the Garden City Association in 1899. Spearheaded by the social theorist and planner Ebenezer Howard (1850–1928), who in 1898 had published an ideal diagram for garden cities in his book *Tomorrow: A Peaceful Path to Real Reform*, the Garden City Movement aimed to create new cities and suburbs which combined the benefits of city and country life. There were precedents for this in the enlightened factory villages established by such philanthropically-minded individuals as Lord Lever and the chocolate kings Joseph Rowntree and the Cadbury family. Such was the influence of these villages that Rowntree's architects, Barry Parker (1867–1947) and Raymond Unwin (1863–1940), were chosen to design the first garden city in Letchworth, Hertfordshire, in 1903. Second cousins, teetotallers and socialists, Parker and Unwin complemented each other well: as Mrs Parker recalled, 'Unwin had all the zeal of a social reformer', while 'Parker was primarily an artist. [...] He wanted the home to be a setting for a life of aesthetic worth'.[21] Together, they planned a central cluster of municipal and public buildings, from which radiated broad, tree-lined avenues of semi-detached or terraced housing designed by architects such as Lethaby, Baillie Scott and Shaw. The idealism of the project attracted sandal-wearing, socialist types who became the butt of ridicule in the press, but the modest, user-friendly houses in Letchworth and other garden cities and suburbs became a lasting prototype for suburban design (fig. 105).

Despite all this energy and commitment, by the first decades of the twentieth century there were signs of crisis in the British Arts and Crafts, brought about not least by the conflicts between theory and practice which have surfaced throughout this account. Public perception fixed increasingly on the Movement's rich clientele, as opposed to its aim of offering high-quality craftsmanship as a corrective to a

105. Barry Parker and Raymond Unwin
House in Letchworth, Hertfordshire, 1907–11

dehumanized machine culture. As Ashbee wrote despairingly in 1908: 'What I seek to show is that this Arts and Crafts movement [...] is not what the public has thought it to be, or is seeking to make it: a nursery for luxuries, a hothouse for the production of mere trivialities and useless things for the rich. It is a movement for the stamping out of such things by sound production on the one hand, and the inevitable regulation of machine production and cheap labour on the other.'[22] Many British designers also continued to see the machine as a pernicious entity which could never benefit the arts. There was an attempt to correct this with the establishment in 1915 of the Design and Industries Association (DIA), whose founder members included Lethaby, Benson and Image: but this was too late for the British Arts and Crafts. As the proposal for the DIA admitted, the Arts and Crafts Movement 'has been much studied and imitated abroad, while it has been allowed to struggle helplessly at home. [...] The difficulty has been that the designer and the manufacturer have so largely remained in separate compartments'.[23] It was left to other countries to bring the designer and the manufacturer together, creating in the process a new vanguard in modern design.

Josef Emil Schneckendorf
Vase, *c*.1908 (fig. 123)

'A CRY OF DELIGHT': AUSTRIA, GERMANY AND THE LOW COUNTRIES

THE LATE NINETEENTH CENTURY WAS A RICH PERIOD FOR ARCHITECTURE AND THE DECORATIVE ARTS IN CONTINENTAL EUROPE. WHILE MANY COUNTRIES – NOTABLY FRANCE, SPAIN AND ITALY – WERE SWEPT UP IN THE EFFLORESCENCE OF ART NOUVEAU, OTHERS SAW EXCITING AND DIVERSE DEVELOPMENTS IN THE ARTS AND CRAFTS.

In the Low Countries, Germany and Austria, the Movement was largely the work of city-based artists, architects and designers, and was less concerned with the well-being of craftsmen and the guild ideal than with acknowledging regional traditions, improving the everyday environment and setting standards in modern design. To the east, in Poland, Hungary and beyond, the Movement acquired a different temper, as the Arts and Crafts became involved with vernacular revivals and issues of nationhood. The investigation here will follow an anti-clockwise route, starting in Western and Central Europe (though the narrative requires us to travel back and forth between the Low Countries, Austria and Germany). Later chapters will focus on the further reaches of the Austro-Hungarian Empire, Russia and, finally, the Nordic countries.

The first of Britain's near neighbours to develop Arts and Crafts interests was Belgium. Subject for centuries to Spanish, Habsburg, French or Dutch rule, the country had finally wriggled free of foreign control in 1830 and soon established healthy trade relations with its larger neighbours, aided by the personal contacts of Leopold I of Saxe-Coburg, Belgium's newly imported king. There were internal frictions between the largely rural, Dutch- or Flemish-speaking territories to the north, and the industrialized, Francophone region of Wallonia in the south, not least when the country was hit by agricultural and economic depression in the last quarter of the century. Nevertheless, in 1880 Belgium could look back on its first fifty years of independence with pride, and embarked on a year-long *Cinquantenaire* to mark the event. Central to the celebrations was a vast exhibition in which crafts such as embroidery, lace-making and tapestry featured alongside the glories of Belgian commerce and industry. Coming at a time when cottage industries were under threat as an impoverished rural workforce looked for city employment, these displays focused attention on the need to preserve the applied arts, and invested them with national bearing. As the progressive journal *L'Art Moderne* declared in 1883, 'In costume, furnishing, metalwork, jewellery and ceramics the soul of the people is reflected as in a clear mirror.' In the wake of the exhibition, official initiatives were launched to encourage the crafts, with considerable success – census figures for 1890–1910 reveal that the number of people engaged in artisanal production was on the rise, after a steady decline in preceding years.

106. Henry van de Velde
Bloemenwerf, Uccle, Belgium,
from *Dekorative Kunst*, 1899

In the meantime, combatants for the decorative arts were emerging from the avant-garde artists involved in the Brussels exhibition society, Les Vingt, founded in 1883 as a counterpoint to the official Société Nationale des Beaux-Arts, and its successor La Libre Esthétique (1893). Both societies contested the privileged position of painting and sculpture, and in the 1890s played a major role in the cultural repositioning of the 'minor' arts by exhibiting a range of decorative and applied art. The exhibitors included figures as renowned as Paul Gauguin, who showed ceramics and carved panels in 1891, and the rising stars of Art Nouveau. But the La Libre Esthétique exhibitions also featured architectural designs by Voysey, metalwork by Ashbee and his Guild, books from the Kelmscott Press and from Cobden-Sanderson's Doves Bindery, and designs by Image, Sumner, Whall and Crane. *The Studio*, which was available in Brussels and other European cities, also alerted a wide readership to Arts and Crafts ideas, fuelling enthusiasm for modern British design. As *L'Art Moderne* noted in 1894, 'While in France, Belgium, and Germany, furniture and decoration, given up to industrialists who possess concern only for profits, have fallen into the worst decadence, English artisans have already reignited the

flame that formerly illuminated domestic life. The love of home explains this phenomenon.'[2] The reviewer clearly subscribed to the demonization of industry, to which he attributed the excesses of continental designers. In contrast, the 'domestic' focus of British designers was seen to engender admirable qualities of simplicity, convenience, and morality.

As interest in the decorative arts spread, local artists began to work in new media. Thus the Anglo-Belgian painter Alfred William Finch (1854–1930), a founder member of Les Vingt, went in 1890 to work at the Kéramis ceramics factory in the southern Belgian town of La Louvière. Finch initially produced largely decorative pieces, combining his interest in colour effects with his desire to work in clay, but soon his fascination with colour led him to experiment with new glazes on utilitarian objects such as jugs and plates. Well-versed in the ideas of Ruskin, Morris and others thanks to his English roots, Finch alerted his colleagues to their example and, during a feast to celebrate the Les Vingt exhibition in 1892, struck up a conversation with the painter Henry van de Velde (1863–1957) on the merits of British design. Van de Velde, who happened to be showing his first experiment in applied art at the exhibition, was gripped, and within months had

107. Henry van de Velde
Chair, c.1895
Padouk wood and rush, 94 x 44.1 x 41.7 cm (37 x 17 ½ x 16 in)
Virginia Museum of Fine Arts, Richmond

turned his back on easel painting, devoting himself instead to the design of interiors, furniture, silver, ceramics, textiles, books and typography. By 1893, he was teaching a course in decorative art at the Antwerp Academy, often illustrating his argument with examples from the British Arts and Crafts (his future wife had collected Morris & Co. textiles and wallpapers during a trip to England the same year). Van de Velde also devoted eleven of the nineteen classes to local art industries, anxious that his students should appreciate their native crafts tradition. In later years, he would figure as *primus inter pares* among Art Nouveau designers, and his voice would resonate in heated debates on the role of the artist in industrial design. But at this early stage, it was the Arts and Crafts belief in the social relevance of craftsmanship which the young artist fervently espoused.

Van de Velde's earliest decorative work was in embroidery, which he was taught by an obliging aunt. He also turned to graphic design at the behest of August Vermeylen, who in 1893 set up a Flemish journal *Van Nu en Straks* (From Now On), modelled on *The Century Guild Hobby Horse*. Such was Van de Velde's commitment to his role as an artist-craftsman that it soon required a new setting, and in 1894 he began to design his own house, Bloemenwerf, in the village of Uccle (now part of Brussels). The house (fig. 106), with its hipped gables, whitewashed walls and asymmetric bay was indebted to Voysey and Baillie Scott, whose designs Van de Velde avidly perused in his copies of *The Studio* and in the La Libre Esthétique exhibitions. There is an echo of the Dutch gables which Van de Velde encountered on honeymoon in Holland, while the half-timbering – decorative rather than structural – echoes rural building traditions across Europe. The result is a sort of generic vernacular, devoid of any clear regional specificity but carrying a talismanic message of rural integration. Inside, a double-storey, skylit space, in the manner of Baillie Scott's halls, led to a series of rooms decorated and furnished to Van de Velde's designs. Naturalistic imagery pulsated in exhilarating repeats across wallpapers and textiles in a manner reminiscent of Mackmurdo and Voysey. The simple furniture in unpainted oak, for its part, was derived from the rustic prototypes favoured by Arts and Crafts designers, but Van de Velde gave these a fashionable new cast. Thus in the dining room he revitalized an old favourite, the rush-seated chair, by adding a jaunty new curve to the staves (fig. 107). Work by contemporary designers also featured, with armchairs upholstered in Morris & Co. fabric in the dining room, and special display cases to exhibit pots by Finch and

108. Gustave Serrurier-Bovy
Study, 1894, from *The Studio*, 1896

other ceramicists in the hall. So keen was Van de Velde to create a synergy between art and life that he even fashioned dresses in Morris prints for his wife, herself the designer of the *Dahlia* wallpaper upstairs. With its reinvention of traditional examples to meet modern needs and sensibilities and, in the display of ceramics, its self-conscious projection of the crafts as art, Bloemenwerf reified Van de Velde's insistence on the social and aesthetic merits of the decorative arts. It also served as a professional springboard, not least after Van de Velde exhibited the dining-room furniture with La Libre Esthétique in 1896, and was commended in *The Studio* for the elegant simplicity of its design. Such praise in Europe's most influential arts journal doubtless played a part in the artist's decision to start designing domestic furnishings on a commercial basis, working initially from Bloemenwerf, and later from a studio in Ixelles and from headquarters in Berlin. Thus like Morris, to whom he compared himself at times, Van de Velde drew on the experience of furnishing his own house to launch a successful commercial career.

Van de Velde was far from alone in Belgium in designing domestic interiors. At the first exhibition of La Libre Esthétique in 1894, Gustave Serrurier-Bovy (1858–1910)

installed a fully furnished study, in which the bare beams, stencilled wall decoration and unadorned oak furniture (fig. 108) recall projects such as the work of Ashbee and his circle for the dining room of the Magpie and Stump (see pp. 71, 74). Anxious to stress his originality, Serrurier-Bovy dismissed suggestions that he had been influenced by British work. But the artist arguably knew as much about modern British design as anyone in Belgium (he had been importing decorative and applied arts from Liberty's and other London outlets to sell since 1884, and probably visited the Arts and Crafts Exhibition in 1893), and contemporary critics noted the compelling parallels between his work and English interiors. *Le Soir* went further, linking Serrurier-Bovy's study with 'those who follow the "simple life". We too immediately want to live that life!'[3] The reviewer here clearly accepted the connection between a style of life and a style of art, but in Belgium few artists seriously entertained the possibility of cultural renewal by living the 'simple life'. The rustic simplicity and 'wholesomeness' of vernacular examples were greatly admired, but they were qualities to be explored in the comfort of one's studio, or debated over a glass of wine in a modish new café.

In the second half of the 1890s, the production, promotion and display of the decorative arts gathered pace. Serrurier-Bovy built on the success of his study of 1894 by exhibiting an 'artisan's room' with La Libre Esthétique in 1895, and the same year mounted a major exhibition devoted primarily to the decorative arts in his home town of Liège. Among the 600 or so British, Belgian, Dutch and French exhibits were many from the La Libre Esthétique exhibition, but Serrurier-Bovy complemented these with additional pieces, including more than a hundred shipped specially from the Glasgow School of Art. At the same time, European journals such as *Art et Décoration*, *Kunst und Kunsthandwerk*, and the Munich-based *Dekorative Kunst* (published in French as *L'Art Décoratif*) gave increasing coverage to the Arts and Crafts. Their interest aroused, European artists and retailers visited the Arts and Crafts Exhibitions and other collections and buildings in Britain, looking for imaginative new directions in craftwork and design. They included the designer Samuel Bing, who in December 1895 opened a shop in Paris called La Maison de l'Art Nouveau. Bing commissioned three interiors for his new shop from Van de Velde and his fellow Les Vingt artist Georges Lemmem which, with their lithe forms and writhing plasticity, conform with Art Nouveau trends rather than with those of the Arts and Crafts. Nevertheless, Bing's shop entrance was flanked by lamps by Benson, and Arts and Crafts work was on show inside, including chairs upholstered by Morris & Co. Indeed, so entranced was Bing by what was happening across the Channel that he declared: 'when English creations began to appear a cry of delight sounded throughout Europe. Its echo can still be heard in every country.'[4] While Bing's avocation of British design was to elicit relatively little support in France, in the second half of the 1890s artists in Germany and Austria began to explore Arts and Crafts practices and ideas. Theirs was no bland imitation of British or, for that matter, Belgian developments: rather, Central European designers questioned the uses, the production and the cultural meanings of the Arts and Crafts, and in the process created a new understanding of their relationship to industrial design.

The first of the German cities to merit attention is Munich, which had risen to prominence in the art world when a group of young artists had staged a Secession against the artistic establishment in 1892. Ever since, the city had been a hothouse of artistic debate and a centre for the development of *Jugendstil*, the German variant of Art Nouveau. *Jugendstil* (a term derived from the name of the magazine

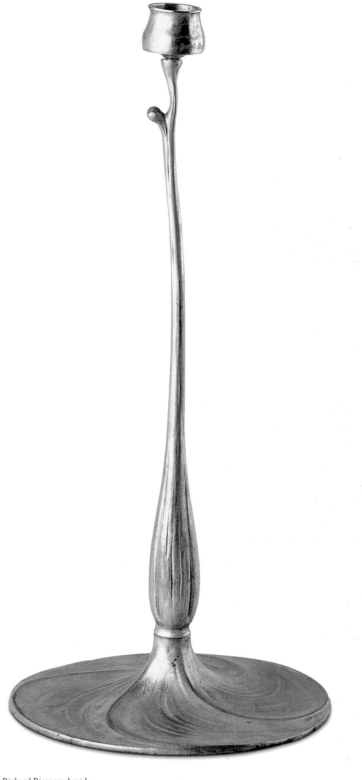

109. Richard Riemerschmid
Candlestick, 1897
Chased and gilded brass, 37 cm (14 ½ in) height
Musée d'Orsay, Paris

110. Richard Riemerschmid
Chair, 1898–9
Oak and leather, 80.6 x 47.5 x 45 cm (31 ½ x 18 ½ x 17 ¾ in)
Victoria and Albert Museum, London

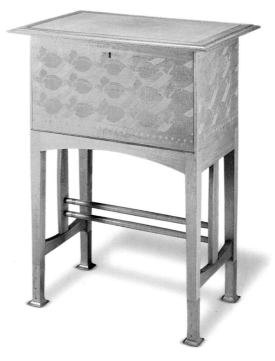

112. Leopold Bauer
Cabinet for a Postcard Collector, c.1900
Sycamore, maple and various other woods in marquetry, brass and felt
90.1 x 67.2 x 45.6 cm (35 ½ x 26 ½ x 18 in)
Virginia Museum of Fine Arts, Richmond

Jugend, meaning 'youth') tapped into the self-confidence of post-unification Germany, and the energetic modernity of its naturalistic forms met with an enthusiastic response. As the decade progressed, however, various designers, notably Richard Riemerschmid (1868–1957), Peter Behrens (1868–1940) and Bruno Paul (1874–1968), felt that many *Jugendstil* artists emphasized the aesthetic at the expense of the practical, and in 1897 decided to counteract this by forming the Vereinigte Werkstätten für Kunst im Handwerk (United Workshops for Art in Handcraft). A year later Riemerschmid's brother-in-law Karl Schmidt (1873–1948), a trained carpenter who had just spent a year in England, set up a similar organization in Dresden (Dresdner Werkstätten für Handwerkskunst) as a friendly rival to the Munich-based enterprise.

The Werkstätten designers, who over the years included many of Germany's best applied artists as well as some foreign designers, aimed to produce simple but beautiful objects for everyday use. A prime example is the candlestick which Riemerschmid modelled for the Vereinigte Werkstätten in 1897 (fig. 109). Here, we barely register the object's sensibly large footprint, so hypnotic is the visual ascent through the swirl of the base and the tapering stem to

the candle holder itself in the form of an opening bud. Similarly, the oak and leather chair from a set which Riemerschmid designed for a music salon in 1898–9 is elegant but gratifyingly solid, with the thrust of the diagonal supports gliding into a gentle curve moulded to the contours of a human back (fig. 110). Riemerschmid later wrote that 'Life, not art, creates style. It is not made, it grows', revealing a concern with functionality shared with the British Arts and Crafts. In contrast to British ideals, however, the Werkstätten artists often happily handed their designs over to skilled operators working on modern machines. Indeed, in 1897 a review in the journal *Dekorative Kunst* claimed that the metalwork of Benson had the pared-down elegance of 'a good American bicycle', clearly recognizing the potential for beauty in machine-made goods. This interest in industrial design was to become increasingly pronounced on the Continent, marking a critical point of difference with the British Arts and Crafts.

In the meantime, Vienna was developing into a heady new centre for the fine and the applied arts. As early as 1864 the Österreichisches Museum für Kunst und Industrie had opened there to promote industrial design, and four years

111. Central Hall at the Eighth Exhibition of the Vienna Secession, from *The Studio*, 1901

later it was joined by the Kunstgewerbeschule, or School of Arts and Crafts, echoing the relationship between London's South Kensington Museum and the School of Design. It was not until the 1890s, however, that Vienna witnessed its most urgent efforts to galvanize the decorative arts, inspired in part by the concept of the *Gesamtkunstwerk*, introduced by Richard Wagner in the middle of the century and elaborated in the book *Moderne Architektur* which the prominent Viennese architect Otto Wagner (no relation) had written in 1895. Wagner's book came during a period of heightened discontent with the official artistic body in Vienna, the Künstlerhaus or Society of Artists, which the city's avant-garde felt was mired in moribund practices and debates. Matters came to a head in 1897, when a group of young artists followed the example of their Munich peers and themselves staged a Secession, in their case to promote modern art and design, and to effect a democratic rapprochement between high and popular culture. 'We recognize no distinction between "high art" and "minor art", between art for the rich and art for the poor. Art is public property,'[5] they trumpeted, demonstrating both the Arts and Crafts concern to unify the arts, and its later socialist aims. Wagner's student Joseph Maria

Olbrich (1867–1908) was charged with designing a new exhibition hall, and in 1898 the first Secession exhibition opened there, organized by the painter Koloman Moser (1868–1918) and the architect-designer Josef Hoffmann (1870–1956), another of Wagner's protégés.

The Secession building, a stark white geometric confection topped with a gloriously showy cupola of gilt-bronze foliage (soon christened 'The Golden Cabbage'), has become a landmark of Art Nouveau. Its controversial exhibitions, however, included Arts and Crafts pieces in their displays of modern design. Burne-Jones, Ashbee and Crane were all made honorary members of the Secession, and the Eighth Exhibition in 1900 featured exhibits by De Morgan, the Glasgow Four, and Ashbee's Guild of Handicraft (the exhibition's second largest exhibitor), to name just a few. Mackintosh and Margaret Macdonald visited the show, meeting Hoffmann and his colleagues, and Ashbee's imposing writing cabinet of *c*.1898 was given a conspicuous position in the middle of the hall (fig. 111). The strength of its impact there is best conveyed by the critic Ludwig Hevesi, for whom Ashbee's furniture seemed like a bite of black bread after a Lucullan feast.[6] While critics were not necessarily united in their support of the British work, various Austrian designers began to respond to the ideals and to certain visual stylistics of the Arts and Crafts. The cabinet which Otto Wagner's student Leopold Bauer (1872–1938) designed in *c*.1900 (fig. 112), for example, neatly accommodates the postcard collection for which it was made, while its flawless marquetry in sycamore, maple and other woods recalls the patterns of British wallpapers and textiles, perhaps most persuasively Mackmurdo's *Cromer Bird* design (see p. 55). Bauer's work points to an increasing awareness in Austria of the nature of materials, the quality of craftsmanship, and the function of the product, and Vienna gradually became a breeding ground for artists who would devote their careers to the exploration, teaching and application of good design. By the end of the century Hoffmann and Moser had teaching posts at the Kunstgewerbeschule, and they and Olbrich were involved in other initiatives which expanded – and in some cases changed beyond recognition – the repertoire and the semantics of the Arts and Crafts.

Some of the most exciting of these initiatives were launched in Darmstadt by Ernst Ludwig, Grand Duke of Hesse (1868–1937). One of Queen Victoria's grandchildren who danced and dined in almost every royal house of Europe as the nineteenth century drew to a close, the Grand Duke had been educated under the beady eye of his grandmother after his mother died young, emerging as a renowned sophisticate with 'the urbanity of a German officer of rank and the artistic culture of an English gentleman.' During his frequent trips to England the Grand Duke had come to admire the Arts and Crafts, and in 1897 he asked Baillie Scott to remodel the interiors of a drawing room and breakfast room of his palace at Darmstadt, while Ashbee and his Guild were commissioned to produce the fittings and furnishings of the drawing room to Baillie Scott's designs. Baillie Scott was unaccustomed to the lavishness of royal hospitality and arrived at Darmstadt station with just one bag, which must have flummoxed the liveried lackeys who had been sent to help with his luggage. Ashbee, in contrast, took it all in his stride, and was quietly delighted at being hurried to complete the commission in time for the Russian Tsar's visit later that year. Both interiors were destroyed in the Second World War, but contemporary photographs and the publication of Baillie Scott's drawings in *Building News* in 1897 record the exposed beams, inglenooks, built-in furniture and different registers of wall decoration which were characteristic of his work. In the drawing room (fig. 113), white panelling and a bright orange frieze were topped by a border of tubby little birds darting around the room, while the slender colonettes with basket capitals presaged those which Baillie Scott used at Blackwell in the Lake District the following year. The furniture was predominantly blue-green, with flashes of colour inside cupboard doors, and confirmed Baillie Scott's flair for an eye-catching piece. The desk to the right of the fireplace made a virtue out of necessity by using its broad metal hinges for decorative effect, while the semicircular barrel chair (one of the few pieces to survive) was inspired by one of the Holy Grail tapestry designs which Burne-Jones had published in *The Studio* in 1894 (see p. 50).

The finished interiors deviated from the original designs and were more cluttered than Baillie Scott had intended, which was a recurrent problem for the architect. As he had lamented in 1896: 'It is a painful thing for an architect to design a mantelpiece for which he dares not hope to choose the ornaments, and which may become a resting place for he knows not what atrocities in china and glass.' Nevertheless, the rooms were widely publicized and admired, and Baillie Scott went on to win commissions

113. Mackay Hugh Baillie Scott
Design for the Drawing Room, Grand Ducal Palace, Darmstadt, from *Building News*, 23 July 1897

across Europe. The Grand Duke, for his part, expanded his activities as a patron, and in 1899 decided to finance an artists' colony in a royal park on the Mathildenhöhe, a hill to the north-east of Darmstadt. A select group of artists and designers were to work alongside local craftsmen and manufacturers, with the express aim of motivating the region's industry by providing local firms with innovative designs. The Grand Duke invited figures as prominent as Olbrich from Vienna and Behrens from Munich, creating a point of contact between two of the most vibrant artistic centres in Europe. He also offered generous terms, namely an annual salary assessed according to age, reputation and personal circumstance, in return for which the artists had to work in Hesse for a minimum of three years. Intrigued by the novelty of the idea (and by the prospect of a steady income), seven intrepid young artists from a range of professional backgrounds moved to Darmstadt, and began to build the colony from scratch. The lion's share of the architectural work fell to Olbrich, who designed a central studio block called the Ernst Ludwig House (now a museum) and six of seven houses (fig. 114). Behrens, enthused by the colony's spirit of adventure to turn his hand to architecture for the first time, elected to design his own house. This he adorned with dormer windows, brick trim, chimneys, quoins and pilasters, creating in the process four entirely different façades (fig. 115).

It is impossible to homogenize the heterogeneous voices at work at Darmstadt. The Ernst Ludwig House, conceived as a temple to art, has manifold Symbolist references, while the clean, geometric masses of Olbrich's houses and the distended ogee curves of Behrens's design are *Jugendstil* in style. At the same time, there is a firm nod to Arts and Crafts planning in those houses, Olbrich's included, which centred around a large, two-storey living space. Features such as the frieze of blue and white tiles on Olbrich's house, his Germanic, hipped roof, and Behrens's prominent gables suggested local building traditions – those of north German farmhouses, for example – while the half-timbering and red-tiled roofs drew on a more pan-European vernacular. The houses also developed the concept of the *Gesamtkunstwerk*, co-ordinating everything from the dinner services to the wrought-iron railings. Thus visitors to Behrens's house might have passed through the aluminium and gilded bronze doors of the music room (fig. 116) to relax in one of Behrens's chairs (fig. 117), perhaps enjoying an aperitif in a wine glass which the artist had also designed.

DAS·HAUS·OLBRICH·

Kunstanstalt Lautz & Jsenbeck, Darmstadt.

114. Joseph Maria Olbrich
Design for House at Darmstadt, 1901
Colour lithograph on paper, printed by Kunstanstalt, Lautz and Jsenbeck, Darmstadt
14 x 9 cm (8 x 5 ½ in)
Museum Künstlerkolonie, Darmstadt

115. Peter Behrens
Design for House at Darmstadt, 1901
Reproduced in Alexander Koch (ed.), *Die Ausstellung der Darmstädter Künstlerkolonie*, 1901
20 x 14 cm (7 ¾ x 5 ½ in)
Museum Künstlerkolonie, Darmstadt

This elision of art and life was driven home in 1901, when the colony staged an exhibition entitled *Ein Dokument Deutscher Kunst* (A Document of German Art), in which the Ernst Ludwig House and the artists' houses were opened to the public, with many of the objects in them offered for sale. Complete buildings had been exhibited before, not least at international exhibitions: but the difference at Darmstadt was that functioning and inhabited private houses were displayed as works of art. The exhibition included both exquisite one-off pieces and designs for mass production, such as Olbrich's and Behrens's cutlery, and brooches and buckles of silver and semi-precious stones by Patriz Huber (1878–1902) (fig. 118). Particularly remarkable is the dialogue between the geometric and the organic in the pewter wine service which Olbrich displayed in his own house (fig. 119). With the flask's beaky, hooked lid and the droll legs and feet of the beakers, there is something strangely bird-like about the service. At the same time, the neck and belly of the flask have been reduced to unembellished planes, looking forward to the minimalist intent of Modernism.

The 1901 exhibition in Darmstadt was followed by others, in 1904, 1908 and 1914, for which further temporary and permanent buildings were constructed, ranging from furnished apartments to model workers' houses sponsored by local firms. While some of these continued in the *Jugendstil* style, others drew on regional building techniques, a trend reflected in new building in the town itself. The hipped roof, shingled panelling and shuttered windows of Leonhard Schäfer's Rosignol House of 1909 (fig. 120), for example, are typical of local construction types. The colony also expanded to include the Hesse Ceramic Workshop, the Hesse Glass Workshop, the Hesse Workshops of Applied Art, and the Ernst Ludwig Press, all of which worked to the designs of resident artists (new recruits replacing those artists who chose to leave when their contracts expired). While the ceramic and glassware is largely *Jugendstil* in style, Friedrich Wilhelm Kleukens (1878–1956), who ran the Ernst Ludwig Press, opposed the *Jugendstil*'s 'restless and glittering tangle of frills'[7] and instead emulated the typography of Morris and his peers (fig. 121). The colony also honoured the Grand Duke's aim of boosting the local economy by providing Hessian firms with new designs. Thus the furniture manufacturer Julius Glückert was entrusted with pieces as ambitious as Olbrich's intarsia cupboard (1899–1900; fig. 122); the venerable earthenware factory Wächtersbacher Steingutfabrik (founded in 1832) produced designs by Darmstadt artists and was so

116. Peter Behrens
Door Plates from the Music Room of the Behrens House, Darmstadt, 1901
Aluminium and gilded bronze, 217 x 85.5 cm (85 ½ x 33 ½ in)
Museum Künstlerkolonie, Darmstadt

117. Peter Behrens
Music Room Chair, 1900/1
Black stained pear wood, intarsia work, leather upholstery
91 x 62 x 56 cm (35 ¾ x 24 ½ x 22 in)
Museum Künstlerkolonie, Darmstadt

117

118. Patriz Huber
Brooches and Buckles, 1900–1
Silver, semi-precious stones, various sizes
Museum Künstlerkolonie, Darmstadt

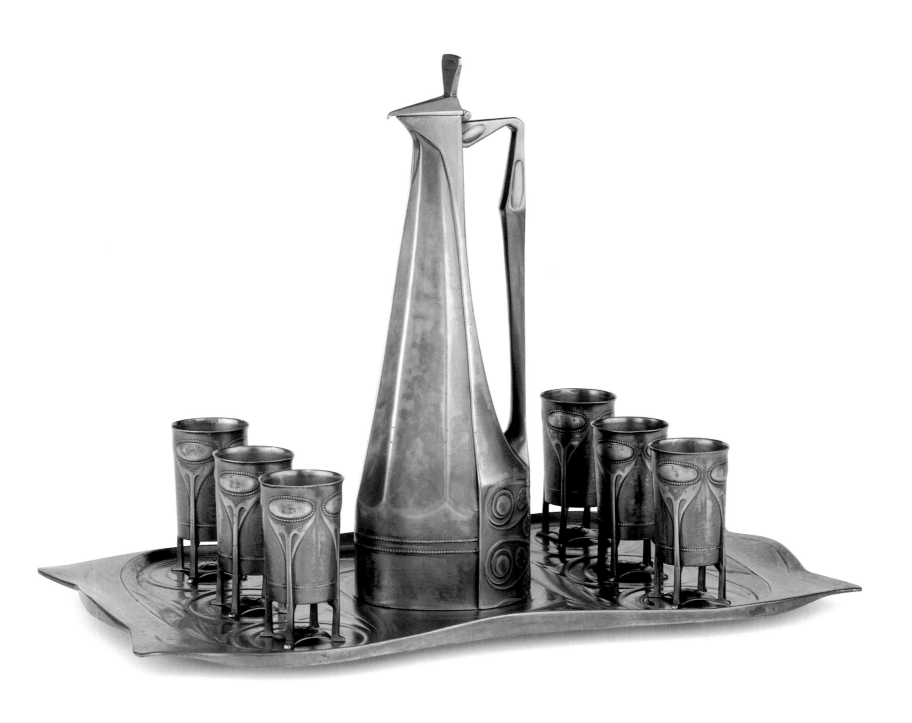

119. Joseph Maria Olbrich
Wine Service, c1901
Pewter, jug 34 (h), beaker 9.5 (h), tray 46 x 26.4 cm
(13 ½, 3 ¾, 18 ⅛, 10 ½ in)
Museum Künstlerkolonie, Darmstadt

120. Leonhard Schäfer
Rosignol House, Darmstadt, 1909

impressed with the results that it opened its own artists' atelier on factory premises in 1903; and in 1904 Paul Haustein (1880–1944), a newcomer who had worked for the Vereinigte Werkstätten in Munich, was sponsored by the local government to work with the potters of Upper Hesse in the hope of reviving the local pottery trade. These and other collaborative ventures were promoted at the exhibition of 1908, in which local artists, manufacturers and educational institutes were invited to participate for the first time. The colony also exhibited at the international exhibitions in Paris in 1900, Turin in 1902 and St Louis in 1904.

The Grand Duke's aim of popularizing good design was nevertheless thwarted, not least because of the mismatch between artistic ideals and commercial realities. In the Glass Workshop, for example, Josef Emil Schneckendorf's insistent use of expensive metal oxides to develop a shiny, metallic surface (fig. 123) made the products fragile and pricey. (Of the 615 pieces which the Glass Workshop produced between 1907 and 1909, 74 were broken or blemished and only 119 were sold, hinting at catastrophic business practices.) Likewise, when in 1904 the Grand Duke commissioned Olbrich to build three 'homes for the not over-wealthy citizen'[8] and offered two of

these for sale, their projected inhabitants could not afford them. Instead, the houses were bought by the wife of the Councillor of Commerce, and by a count in the Duke's employ. As was often the case with comparable ventures in Britain, the Darmstadt enterprise remained dependent on well-heeled patrons from the middle and upper classes.

Darmstadt was not the only colony in Austria or Germany to explore correlations between modern architecture and vernacular design. In 1900, Hoffmann included half-timbering and variations of vernacular techniques in houses he designed for an artists' colony which Moser and colleagues planned on the Hohe Warte outside Vienna. Hoffmann also worked in the Arts and Crafts mould by varying the massing of the houses, and by setting great store by a user-friendly plan. The artist Heinrich Vogeler (1872–1942), in what was perhaps Germany's most wholehearted rural retreat, made a study of peasant architecture and folk art at the Worpswede Artists' Colony from the late 1890s, and turned his hand to textiles, graphic design and furniture. This included yet another version of the rush-seated chair, the back of which is carved with a doleful owl (fig. 124). The house which Vogeler built himself, Barkenhoff, incorporated an old, thatched farm

121. Peter Behrens
Commemorative Volume of *The Darmstadt Artists' Colony*, 1901
Museum Künstlerkolonie, Darmstadt

122. Joseph Maria Olbrich
Intarsia cupboard, 1899–1900
Maple wood inlaid with various exotic woods, 183 x 71 x 40 cm (72 x 28 x 15 ¾ in)
Museum Künstlerkolonie, Darmstadt

123. Josef Emil Schneckendorf
Vase, c.1908
Colourless glass, painted with reduction colours, 18.5 cm (7 ½ in) height
Museum Künstlerkolonie, Darmstadt

building made of half-timbered brick, whose roof beams were left visible in the dining room and hall. His fellow artists and writers would gather there for warmth and revelry after performing plays outside in medieval costumes which Vogeler had designed. Vogeler also set up a craft workshop at Barkenhoff, and designed a railway station and houses for the artists and workers of Worpswede which employed the thatch and tiling typical of the local vernacular. Impressed with the Utopian ideas of Ruskin and Morris, Vogeler shared the vision of the peasant as a bearer of national heritage which often motivated those who turned to traditional crafts, though his two-dimensional work, inspired by romantic stories and fairy tales, followed a more fanciful direction than one would associate with the Arts and Crafts.

While these artistic colonies were developing, the publisher Alexander Koch (1860–1939) was deploying very different means to promote good design. Koch had begun his career by publishing *Tapetenzeitung* (Wallpaper News) – a publication, one might think, of limited appeal. But Germany was on the brink of an explosion of interest in domestic design and Koch realized that there was money to be made in this new craze, launching *Innendekoration* in 1890, and the *Studio*-inspired *Deutsche Kunst und Dekoration* (1897–1932), which paid close attention to British art and design. Both publications were a huge success and enabled Koch to live very comfortably, but it would be unfair to ascribe his motivation to financial ambition alone. He was a patriotic man who recognized a marked improvement in the decorative arts of Britain and France, and determined to respond to this foreign threat by raising standards in German design. *Deutsche Kunst und Dekoration* carried an overt appeal 'To German Artists and Friends of Art!' to shake off their subservience to foreign models, for otherwise 'the idiom of a domestic, individual German art language is in danger of being lost!'[9] So strong was Koch's desire to define the essence of 'German' art that certain articles in his magazines verged on the chauvinistic in tone. On a practical level, however, he played an enormous part in promoting German artists and the members of the Darmstadt colony in particular, almost all of whom contributed to Koch's journals or received lucrative commissions from him for interior designs.

In December 1900, *Innendekoration* launched a competition for a 'House for an Art Lover', whose objective was 'to contribute energetically to the solution of important questions confronting Modern architecture'.[10] Thirty-six architects, including Baillie Scott and Mackintosh, submitted

124. Heinrich Vogeler
Armchair, 1908
Painted oak and rush, 105.4 x 60.3 x 43.5 cm (41 ½ x 23 ¾ x 17 ⅛ in)
Hessisches Landesmuseum, Darmstadt

125. Mackay Hugh Baillie Scott
Design for the Music Room for 'House for an Art Lover', c.1901
Ink on paper, 39.8 x 52.8 cm (15 2/3 x 20 3/4 in)
Hunterian Art Gallery, University of Glasgow

127. Josef Hoffmann
Flatware Cutlery, 1905
Silver-plate on nickel silver: small fork, 18.4 cm (7 ¼ in), large fork, 21.3 cm (8 ³/8 in),
butter knife, 18.4 cm (7 ¼ in), small knife, 18.4 cm (7 ¼ in), large knife, 21.6 cm (8 ½ in),
soup spoon, 21 cm (8 ¼ in), teaspoon, 14.3 cm (5 ⁵/8 in), coffee spoon, 10.2 cm (4 in),
serving fork, 26.7 cm (10 ½ in), serving spoon, 25.4 cm (10 in)
Museum of Modern Art, New York

entries which were published as impressive lithographed plates. In the event, the judges found no design worthy of the first prize, but they awarded Baillie Scott the second prize of 1,800 marks for his *Dulce Domum*, or Dream House. Baillie Scott introduced his project with a clear statement of intent: 'There should be no object in the house which is not the product of sympathetic human craftsmanship; the knives and forks, the glasses, the daily china, should all speak of the hopes and worries, the dreams and wishes of its creator.'[11] He was evidently successful in this aim, as the judges commended the 'surpassingly artistic quality of the interior arrangement.'[12] The music room (fig. 125) in particular is crackling with confidence, from the alcove with its stained-glass windows, to the unusual carved apertures of the raised arcade. Nevertheless, the judges felt that Baillie Scott's exteriors lacked evidence of 'modernity', which cost the architect the first prize. In contrast, Mackintosh's submission was strikingly modern with, in the music room, great synchrony between the verticality of Mackintosh's furniture and the curlicues of Margaret Macdonald's panels, all of

which followed a colour scheme of silver, pink and white. Mackintosh was awarded a special prize, even though he failed to submit all the requisite drawings on time, and a much larger version of his house was eventually built in Glasgow in the 1990s, almost a century after his original designs.

The success of Baillie Scott and Mackintosh's submissions confirmed many in the view that contemporary British designers still surpassed their German and Austrian peers. European artists and theorists were anxious to get to the root of this problem, and in 1902 Hoffmann and Fritz Wärndorfer (1868–1918), a Viennese banker and avid patron of the applied arts, travelled to Britain with this objective. There, they examined Guild of Handicraft products, which Hoffmann held in high regard (he designed a covered silver dish the same year, fig. 126, whose simple form, visible hammer marks and choice of materials suggest a strong debt to Ashbee's work). Hoffmann and Wärndorfer also visited Glasgow to see Mackintosh and Margaret Macdonald, whose work they already admired, Wärndorfer having

126. Josef Hoffmann
Footed Dish with Cover, 1902
Hammered silver and turquoise, 16.2 x 7 cm (6 3/8 x 2 3/4 in)
Virginia Museum of Fine Arts, Richmond

128. Josef Hoffmann
Sugar Pot, 1906
Silver, 19 x 14 cm (7 1/2 x 5 1/2 in)
Wien Museum, Vienna

129. Koloman Moser
Music Cupboard, c.1904
Oak, carved and gilded wood, silver-plated metal, white metal and glass
119.5 x 200.5 x 65.5 cm (47 x 79 x 25 3/4 in)
Musée d'Orsay, Paris

130. Antoine Pompe and Adhémar Lener
'Little Nest' from *Le Cottage*, 1904
The Getty Research Institute, Los Angeles, CA

131. Antoine Pompe and Adhémar Lener
'Hall, Little Nest' from *Le Cottage*, 1904
Bibliothèque Royale de Belgique, Brussels

commissioned the pair to design a music salon for his Viennese mansion earlier that year. Inspired by what they had seen, the two Austrians resolved 'to create an island of tranquillity in our own country, which, amid the joyful hum of arts and crafts, would be welcome to anyone who professes faith in Ruskin and Morris'.[13] The result, the Wiener Werkstätte, opened in Vienna in 1903, financed by Wärndorfer and directed by Hoffmann and Moser, Hoffmann's friend from Secession days.

In the Wiener Werkstätte's first Work Programme of 1903, Hoffmann launched a splenetic invective against the trumpery of modern design: 'The boundless evil caused by shoddy mass-produced goods and by the uncritical imitation of earlier styles, is like a tidal wave sweeping across the world. [...] The machine has largely replaced the hand and the business-man has supplanted the craftsman'.[14] To counteract this, the Werkstätte aimed to provide craftsmen with a forum in which to practise and publicize their skills, hoping in the process to re-establish the role of the craftsman in contemporary production, and to improve the standards and availability of good design. As Hoffmann explained, 'We wish to create an inner relationship linking public, designer and

worker and we want to produce good and simple articles of everyday use. Our guiding principle is function, utility our first condition, and our strength must lie in good proportions and the proper treatment of material'.[15] True to his word, Hoffmann designed cutlery (fig. 127) which is proud, strong and devoid of fuss, with a minimum of joints and details which might be weakened or damaged by the wear and tear of everyday use. His silver sugar pot with a simple fruit motif (fig. 128), on the other hand, is a seductive exercise in truth to materials, its tactile curves exploiting the silver's polished sheen. Moser too flaunted good materials and skilled craftsmanship in pieces such as his music cupboard (fig. 129), which was treated with white lead to enhance the natural grain of the oak. The stylized female figures on its chased silver plaques point to aesthetic considerations shared with the Glasgow Four, whose work was much admired in Vienna at the time.

The Wiener Werkstätte laid great emphasis on the well-being of its workers, even if this meant charging high prices. The inevitable result was that the Werkstätte found itself working for the moneyed elite and gradually moved into the luxury of Art Nouveau. In the Palais Stoclet (1905–11)

132. The Chevalier de Wouters de Bouchout
'Seaside Interior' from *Le Cottage*, 1904
Bibliothèque Royale de Belgique, Brussels

133. Richard Riemerschmid
Maschinenmöbel from *Dresdener Hausgerät: Preisbuch*, 1906

in Brussels, for example, the bottomless pockets of the industrialist Adolphe Stoclet enabled Werkstätte craftsmen to work in materials as opulent as marble, leather, onyx and malachite. (So complete was Stoclet's embrace of the Wiener Werkstätte aesthetic that when he died he was buried with a silk handkerchief designed by Hoffmann in the pocket of his suit.) Here, the extravagance of Art Nouveau replaced the sobriety of the Arts and Crafts which had characterized some of the workshops' earlier work.

While the Wiener Werkstätte traded in increasingly exotic items through outlets in cities such as Zurich and New York (a practice which was to bankrupt its later backers), many architects were still committed to the simplicity and integrity of the Arts and Crafts. In Holland, a group of architects known as the Amsterdam School turned to their country's brick techniques to counteract classicism's grandiose stone architecture. From projects as high-profile as the Amsterdam Stock Exchange (1898–1908) by Hendrik Petrus Berlage (1856–1934) to the Amsterdam shipping office by Johan van der Mey (1878–1949), the art of building in brick was lovingly revived. At the same time, the domestic architecture of the British Movement appealed as a paradigm

for modern living. Eduard Cuypers (1859–1927) – a man who emulated Arts and Crafts workshop practices in the organization of his studio – designed country residences which bear the stamp of some of Shaw's houses. Like Shaw, Cuypers nurtured a new generation of architects who, in their later projects for social housing, took up the challenge of designing buildings which were modern, and yet acknowledged traditional Dutch techniques.

Elsewhere, it was the homely, rustic aspect of the cottage ideal which found admirers. In Belgium, Paul Hankar (1859–1901) designed the Cottage Buysse (c.1899) for a painter and industrialist in the suburbs of Ghent, in which the half-timbering, steeply pitched roofs, bay windows and, inside, an inglenook, decorative friezes and built-in furniture are unquestionably Arts and Crafts (though the application of the word 'cottage' to a building of this size shows the precarious intellectual engineering required at times to support the rustic ideal). By 1903, such was the enthusiasm for 'cottage' design in Belgium that a new association called Le Cottage launched an eponymous illustrated journal, which promoted wholesome living in a modest but comfortable exurban house. Typical of the style which *Le Cottage* advocated are the designs for 'Little

Nest' which Antoine Pompe and Adhémar Lener published in 1904 (fig. 130). The outside resembles a Voysey design which has been stretched upwards, while the interiors (fig. 131) are as clean as those in the paintings of Vermeer, with windows propped open to admit fresh air, and floors polished until they gleam. *Le Cottage* also reported on the English Garden City Movement and on workers' villages in Port Sunlight and elsewhere, and in 1904 covered the foundation of Belgium's own Association des Cités-jardins. The Association only lasted a year and the journal was only published for two, but the ideas they promoted had taken root. There was a section of model workers' housing at the 1905 exhibition in Liège to celebrate the seventy-fifth anniversary of Belgian independence, while at the Exposition Universelle et Internationale in Brussels in 1910 both Port Sunlight cottages and low-cost housing were exhibited on a green-field site. Further afield, Arts and Crafts architecture and the Garden City ideal played a part in the development of Belgian seaside resorts. In the seaside interior which The Chevalier de Wouters de Bouchout published in *Le Cottage* in 1904 (fig. 132), for example, the furniture emulates rustic models, and stylized lollipop trees provide visual continuity from the finial on the newel post to the cushion under the stairs. Realized resorts such as Westende (1895–1906), for their part, included half-timbering and tiled roofing, and used local materials to harmonize with the surroundings and to keep costs down.

In Germany, the Garden City Movement prompted the foundation of the Deutsche Gartenstadtgesellschaft in 1902, and designers such as Karl Schmidt spread word about the innovations of British architectural design. One man, however, towers above others in the promotion of Arts and Crafts architecture in Central Europe. He was Hermann Muthesius (1861–1927) who had studied his father's trade of masonry, and who in 1893 joined the Prussian civil service as a government architect in the Ministry of Public Works. In 1896 Muthesius was appointed architectural attaché to the German Embassy in London where he stayed until 1903, immersing himself in British culture with unquenchable enthusiasm and devoting himself to a searching study of British design. Indefatigable in his quest to understand contemporary British architecture, Muthesius wore his shoes to tatters as he toured the country studying buildings, workshops and art schools, and befriending leading figures of the Arts and Crafts. His labours resulted in a masterful account of British domestic architecture, *Das englische Haus*, which was published in three volumes during 1904–5. With

134. Hermann Muthesius
Am Dorffrieden Housing Group, Hellerau, *c.*1910
Sächsische Landesbibliothek – Staats- und Universitätsbibliothek Dresden, Dezernat Deutsche Fotothek

animated discussion of architects and designers from Morris and Webb to Lorimer and Mackintosh, and illustrations and plans of buildings as novel as Broadleys and Blackwell, this survey played an inestimable role in transmitting Arts and Crafts ideas. Rarely has a civil service posting had such a profound artistic impact.

After his return to Germany Muthesius began to put Arts and Crafts ideas into practice; for example, in the Freudenberg House which he built in Nikolassee, Berlin, from 1907 to 1908. Here, he adopted the butterfly plan which Prior had popularized (and which, closer to home, Baillie Scott had used in his Dream House); the exterior recalled Shaw's Old English style, and Lutyens's precipitous roof and peeping windows at Munstead Wood; and the dining room boasted panelling, a prominent fireplace, and a floral frieze. But Muthesius did not advocate the blind imitation of British Arts and Crafts practices, exhorting readers of *Das englische Haus* to 'adhere to our own artistic tradition as faithfully, to embody our customs and habits in the German house as lovingly'[16] as the British architects did in theirs. Accordingly, in the Freudenberg House, the timbering and the roofs had antecedents in north Germany, and the internal division of the plan was new, with a jigsaw of spaces replacing Prior's room-and-passage arrangement, and a large, oval hall connecting the two wings. Architects such as Paul Schultze-Naumburg (1869–1949) and Heinrich Tessenow (1876–1950) also echoed the north German vernacular in their work, and some made efforts to counteract the detrimental effects of industrialization as well. Schultze-Naumburg, for example, helped to set up the Bund für Heimatschutz (the Homeland Care and Protection Association) in 1904, which had the dual aim of safeguarding traditional building practices and supporting local economies by promoting local materials and techniques. Such initiatives fed off the discourses of *Kulturkritik*, a strand of intellectual inquiry which arose in the 1890s and which at times demonstrated an anti-modernist drive by elevating the pure morality of the common peasantry or *Volk*. At the same time, texts such as the sociologist Georg Simmel's *Die Grosstädte und das Geistesleben* (The Metropolis and Mental Life; 1903) explored the social dislocation and spiritual impoverishment of modern urban life. Such antipathy towards urbanization, coupled with efforts to preserve traditions which were threatened by a centralized, city culture, parallel the anti-industrial rhetoric of the British Arts and Crafts.

In Germany, however, there was far from a consensus of opinion concerning the merits of a pre-industrial past.

Whereas in 1880 Britain had been the world's leading manufacturing nation, by 1900 the United States had overtaken Britain, and Germany was fast catching up. There had been a dramatic shift between rural and urban populations as a result: in 1871, twice as many Germans had lived in the country as in the city, but by 1910 the ratio had been reversed. Many German designers responded positively to these changes, rejecting the sentimental view of traditional handwork which tempered responses to Modernism in Britain. By the twentieth century they were considering how progressive practices in industry and trade could help, rather than hinder, attempts to raise standards in design. In the Werkstätten in Munich and Dresden, for example, Riemerschmid, Schmidt and their colleagues welcomed advances in science and technology, and began to experiment with standardization in design. An early venture in this direction was the *Maschinenmöbel* furniture which Riemerschmid designed for the Dresden Werkstätten in 1905, in which the parts were made by machine but assembled by hand (fig. 133). Here, the balance of power within the Arts and Crafts was clearly shifting, with the emphasis on handmade production yielding to the urge to provide good design at a reasonable price. In 1908 Bruno Paul launched a comparable range, the *Typenmöbel*, which offered standardized units that could be accumulated in modular fashion, thus suiting any purse. In both cases, business interests took precedence, and machine production was welcomed as an essential means of keeping costs down. The German Werkstätten as a result achieved two aims which had often defeated the British Arts and Crafts: their products were available to a broad demographic range; and they were a commercial success. In 1907 the workshops decided to amalgamate and, under the aegis of Schmidt, moved to Germany's first Garden City at Hellerau, outside Dresden. Hellerau, which was largely planned by Riemerschmid, included not only the Werkstätten and houses for their workers, but also shops, a school, a theatre and even laundry facilities. Both the housing designed by architects such as Muthesius (fig. 134) and Riemerschmid's factory buildings (fig. 135) (the latter inspired by farm barns) drew on the vernacular associations and communitarian ideals of the Arts and Crafts.

The period 1906–7, when Hellerau was conceived, marked a turning point in German design. Many leaders of the design reform movement (the *Kunstgewerbebewegung*) now occupied key teaching posts, often thanks to Muthesius's influence. Behrens had been appointed director of the

135. Richard Riemerschmid
Factory Buildings of the Deutsche Werkstätten, Hellerau, c.1910
Sächsische Landesbibliothek – Staats- und Universitätsbibliothek Dresden, Dezernat Deutsche Fotothek

Düsseldorf Kunstgewerbeschule in 1903; Van de Velde had run the Weimar Kunstgewerbeschule since 1904; and in 1907 Paul became director of education at the Kunstgewerbemuseum in Berlin. They and others were increasingly convinced that the benefits of modernity could – and should – be harnessed to serve design. This was not to deny the importance of the independent creative spirit, and in 1906 Schmidt, Muthesius and others organized a major arts and crafts exhibition in Dresden to bolster the role of the artist in the applied arts. Individual exhibits were largely identified by artist, rather than by manufacturer, and only artist-designed objects were admitted, to the frustration of firms which did not commission artists' designs. The indignation of manufacturers intensified in 1907, when Muthesius was appointed to the first chair of applied arts in the Berlin Business School, and used his inaugural lecture to set out his vision for design reform. Muthesius began by excoriating the second half of the nineteenth century as 'the age of the worst aberrations in preposterous finery and material simulation of all kinds',[17] and praised recent developments such as the decline in superfluous ornamentation and the new emphasis on functionality and construction. But he asserted that there was still much room for improvement in German design. Public taste needed to be educated, so that the fashion for cheap, machine-made 'luxury' items was replaced by an appreciation of simple, well-made goods. At the same time, applied arts manufacturers needed to take responsibility for the impression which their work made, for only by becoming less self-serving and instead considering the nature of man's relationship to his surroundings would their products exert a beneficial moral effect, and promote honest German expression in modern design.

Incensed at Muthesius's attack on their members' practices, Germany's leading applied arts trade organization, the Association for the Advancement of Art Industry Interests, called for his resignation, but its demands went unanswered. Instead, Muthesius's supporters joined forces to found the Deutsche Werkbund, a forum of artists, critics, businessmen and manufacturers who aimed to raise standards by encouraging constructive dialogue between those involved in the creation, production and sale of manufactured goods. By recognizing the importance of the artist's contribution *and* the commercial realities of manufacturing, the Werkbund hoped to promote design which would meet contemporary needs, and in the process develop a modern, national idiom in the applied arts. With founders including Olbrich, Behrens, Hoffmann, Riemerschmid, Paul and Van de Velde, and the

German Werkstätten and the Wiener Werkstätte among the first twelve firms to join, the Werkbund soon became one of the great powerhouses in modern design.

Much of the Werkbund's early rationale derived from the wellspring of Arts and Crafts ideas. It aimed to tackle what the architect Fritz Schumacher (1869–1947) at the inaugural meeting in Munich described as 'the estrangement of the executive from the creative spirit', and instead 'regain joy in work'.[18] Muthesius also wrote eloquently of the need to get away from the semantic overload and stylistic chaos of much nineteenth-century design. In 'Die Bedeutung des Kunstgewerbes' (The Importance of the Applied Arts) which he published in *Dekorative Kunst* just before the foundation of the Werkbund, for example, Muthesius insisted on 'No imitation of any kind, each object appears as what it is, each material comes forth in its own character'.[19] To promote these qualities, the Werkbund organized lectures and exhibitions; it published pamphlets and technical literature, including handbooks on industrial materials; and it held annual meetings, which soon became vast congresses covered by the national press. More unusually, the Werkbund ran window-dressing competitions as part of its campaign to improve the standard of shop displays, and in 1909 collaborated in the foundation of a museum of modern applied arts in Hagen, which itself organized travelling exhibitions and courses for members of the retail profession. From 1912 these and other initiatives were promoted in the Werkbund's annual yearbooks. Not once, however, was there so much as a hint of the romantic nostalgia for the handicrafts which appended to the British Arts and Crafts. Rather, the Werkbund's whole ethos revolved around the need to adapt to the machine age. In his book *Stilarchitektur und Baukunst*, Muthesius even commended steamships and other icons of modernity for their *Sachlichkeit* – a word implying the practicality and sobriety which the Werkbund so admired. Nowhere was the Werkbund's desire for co-operation between designers and manufacturers better realized than in the appointment of Behrens as artistic adviser to the vast, Berlin-based Allgemeine Elektricitäts-Gesellschaft (AEG) or General Electric Company (itself a Werkbund member). For AEG, Behrens produced one of the most complete corporate identities yet, designing everything from the radiators, lights, cookers and kettles which the company sold, to its showrooms, factories, packaging and letterheads. Rarely, if ever, had there been such symbiosis between the needs of modern industry and cutting-edge design.

Over the next few years, such was the concern among certain Werkbund members to cater for a mass consumer culture that they began to investigate the concept of *Typisierung*, a word which has been used in different contexts to suggest different things. As far as the Werkbund is concerned, Frederic Schwartz concludes in his comprehensive research that *Typisierung* did not mean the standardization of parts, as has been argued, but rather the production of a limited number of standardized *products* which would enable manufacturers to control the consumer market.[20] The advantages of *Typisierung* were first mooted in Werkbund discussions by Muthesius in 1911, and the expediency of standardized output garnered considerable support. Not all Werkbund members were in agreement, though, and matters came to a head in 1914 when Muthesius circulated a set of guidelines for the future of the organization which revolved around the governing principle of *Typisierung*. A group of artists led by Van de Velde were incensed at the proposition, and the night before Muthesius was due to present his proposal they drew up a series of counter-arguments, which Van de Velde read out immediately after Muthesius's speech the next day. To an audience silenced by the tensions of the debate, the Belgian fiercely defended 'the gifts of invention, of brilliant personal inspiration' which directed an artist. 'By his innermost essence the artist is a burning idealist, a free spontaneous creator' who 'will never subordinate himself to a discipline that imposes upon him a type, a canon'.[21] After much caballing and confusion, both sides eventually beat a retreat, but the confrontation offers a revealing moment in the history of design in continental Europe. This was no polarization between the progressive forces of industrialization and a moribund craft ideal but a tense intersection between culture and economy which the Werkbund, despite its progressive thinking, had yet to resolve.

The outbreak of the First World War temporarily put paid to any grand design ambitions on the Continent. After the war, however, there was still a refracted awareness of Arts and Crafts ideology in Central Europe, filtered through the practices of the Werkbund and other initiatives which had embraced the industrialized world. Many of the Werkbund's leaders exerted a profound influence in the art schools: as well as the activities of Behrens, Paul and Van de Velde, Riemerschmid served as director of the Kunstgewerbeschule in Munich from 1913 to 1924. Behrens trained architects and designers as commanding as Walter Gropius and Ludwig Mies van der Rohe, while Le Corbusier visited Hellerau and Hoffmann's workshops in Vienna, and for a time worked with Behrens at AEG. The Bauhaus (1919–33), Germany's famous school of design which is often viewed as a cradle of functionalism, also emulated Arts and Crafts practices in its workshop-based system and promotion of the applied arts and integrated design. As its inaugural manifesto declared, 'The complete building is the final aim of the visual arts', adding that this could be realized 'only through the conscious, co-operative effort of all craftsmen'.[22] Gropius, the school's founder and director until 1928, was adamant that all art students should be trained in the crafts, and the school included teaching in media as traditional as weaving and stained glass, as well as workshops for more modern work in metal and wood. These and other examples give pause to those historians tempted to draw a clean line between the Arts and Crafts Movement and Modernism.

Most importantly, designers on the Continent recognized that financial obstacles would always plague those who advocated a retrospective craft ideal. As Muthesius wrote in *Das englische Haus*, 'the curse which weighs upon their [British] products is one of economic impossibility'.[23] By accommodating the advances of modernity, German and Austrian designers instead succeeded in making their work widely available. Moreover, by embracing the possibilities of machine production, architects and designers emerging from the Arts and Crafts tradition on the Continent were able to investigate how their work could be applied in the urban environment and, in doing so, to confront this most taxing of problems facing modern design.

Aladár Körösfői-Kriesch
Frontispiece to *Art of the Hungarian People*, 1909 (fig. 137)

A NATIONALIST MANIFESTO: HUNGARY AND POLAND

WHILE GERMAN AND AUSTRIAN ARTISTS AND DESIGNERS WERE DEVELOPING A SOPHISTICATED, URBAN DIMENSION TO THE ARTS AND CRAFTS, A DIFFERENT PICTURE WAS EVOLVING IN HUNGARY AND POLAND.

Sandwiched between the superpowers of Russia to the east and the Habsburg Empire to the west, these two countries had long been subjected to the imperialist ambitions of their neighbours. Poland had not been independent since the late eighteenth century, when Russia, Prussia and Austria had ruthlessly divided the country between them. The former state now comprised the Polish kingdom, ruled by Russia; the southern regions of Galicia and Lodomeria, which were part of the Austro-Hungarian Empire; and the Prussian section, which was known as the Grand Duchy of Poznan. Hungary fared slightly better as part of the Dual Monarchy (1867–1918), a new incarnation of the Habsburg Empire which had been formed when the Austrian powers had ceded to Hungarian nationalist pressure with the so-called Compromise of 1867. Under the terms of the Compromise, Hungary was considered a separate state with control over internal affairs, but the Dual Monarchy was dominated by Austria, and the union of the crowns of Hungary and Austria was maintained.

In the last quarter of the nineteenth century, nationalist sentiment in both countries acquired a new impetus, fuelling the move for full independence from non-native rule in Hungary and, in Poland, the desire to regain sovereign identity. Artists, architects and designers were drawn into these debates, striving to establish distinctly national forms of art as part of the wider quest for political autonomy. A century previously, the German philosopher Johann Gottfried Herder (1744–1803) had argued that a nation's soul lay in the history, language and art of the ordinary people, and had begun a systematic study of folk songs, tales and myths which he saw as the most uncorrupted expressions of cultural heritage. His views greatly influenced later generations across Europe, who carried out ethnographic, archaeological and historical research in an attempt to discover where the essential roots of national culture lay. Interest in local building traditions and the material culture of peasant communities intensified, not least in politically oppressed states where vernacular practices served as a powerful cipher for national art and design. The Arts and Crafts Movement in Hungary and Poland was, therefore, less concerned with tackling the effects of industrialization, raising design standards, or promoting the social and redemptive role of art, as had been the case further west. Rather, it revolved around what is now termed 'vernacularism' – namely, the preservation and appropriation

136. József Rippl-Rónai
Vase, c.1900
Glazed ceramic, 15.2 x 10.7 cm (6 x 4 ¼ in)
Virginia Museum of Fine Arts, Richmond

Society of Applied Arts, set up under the aegis of the museum in 1885, and its journals, *Művészi Ipar* (Artistic Crafts, 1885–94) and *Magyar Iparművészet* (Hungarian Applied Arts, 1897–1944). There was also research into peasant culture, energized by the foundation of the Hungarian Ethnographic Society in 1889. Of particular note is that of József Huszka, who worked on folk ornamentation and on the architecture of the Székely, the Hungarian-speaking people who lived in the east of the Carpathian basin and were believed to descend directly from the son of Attila the Hun. Widely regarded as the most ethnically pure of Hungarians and as guardians of the nation's eastern borders, their material culture exerted a strong nationalist appeal. Huszka was particularly interested in the origins of Székely architecture (which included Hungary's oldest domestic buildings), and in the links between Eastern cultures and Hungarian folk motifs, disseminating the results of his inquiries in publications ranging from *The Hungarian Decorative Style* of 1885 to *Hungarian Ornamentation* of 1898.

Huszka's work on the Eastern roots of Hungarian culture, both in Székely architecture and in folk decoration, formed part of a wider interest in Hungary's connections with the Asian and Islamic worlds. While some scholars traced aspects of vernacular art and architecture back to Indian sources, others focused on Islamic elements which had infiltrated Hungarian culture during the period of Turkish rule in the sixteenth and seventeenth centuries, or on the more recent arrival of Moorish influences from Spain. The equation of the national and the decorative was, therefore, far from straightforward, as the country's cultural atavism was rooted in a matrix of Indo-Islamic as well as regional and vernacular styles. On a practical level, this was evident in the new building for the Museum of Applied Arts in Budapest which the brilliant architect Ödön Lechner (1845–1914) built from 1893 to 1896. Lechner, who had studied the Oriental collections in the South Kensington Museum in London in 1888, developed lavish ornamentation for this building which drew on the Indian, Moorish and Persian decoration believed to lie at the heart of Hungarian peasant culture, as well as on local folk art traditions. Thus the museum, which included motifs from Huszka's publications, featured an orgy of decoration, from the carved hysteria of the banisters to the vast, stylized flowers on the external walls. The result, a smouldering, Gothic-Moorish hybrid, bears little visual relation to Arts and Crafts architecture, but is relevant for Lechner's investigation of the visual and historical properties of folk art. The museum also set new standards in

of vernacular skills and traditions in order to make a statement of both national and political intent.

Hungary in the late nineteenth century presented a volatile cocktail of different ethnic groups. The most dominant of these, the Magyars, who had migrated into the Carpathian basin in the late ninth century, formed the country's cultural and political elite. Below them in the social hierarchy came the Romanians, Jewish Hungarians, Slovaks and Serbs. Despite the Magyars' political and economic superiority to these more marginalized groups, many Hungarians, whatever their ethnicity, were united in their opposition to Habsburg domination. There might not have been any clear consensus on what it meant to be Hungarian, but the need to develop notions of 'Hungarianness' began to transcend ethnic divides.

Central to this developing self-awareness was the urge to construct a distinct cultural identity for the Hungarian nation, drawing on the arts as a powerful stimulus for national regeneration. Resources were invested in national collections and training programmes, including, in Budapest, a museum and school devoted to the applied arts. The activities of both institutions were given fulsome support by the Hungarian

architectural ceramics in its glazed wall and ceiling tiles by the Zsolnay Ceramics Factory, one of Hungary's premier applied arts manufacturers which had been founded in Pécs in 1862. Vilmos Zsolnay, the son of the factory's founder, had accompanied Lechner to Britain in 1888 and, convinced that creative talent should be used to improve the everyday environment, employed many gifted artists over the years. While much of their work was Art Nouveau in tone, some, such as the vase which the painter József Rippl-Rónai (1861–1927) designed around 1900, rejoices in the no-nonsense honesty which is so central to the Arts and Crafts (fig. 136).

The year 1896, when Lechner completed his Museum of Applied Arts, marked a critical point in the fortunes of indigenous architecture and craft in Hungary. That year, the country celebrated the millennium of the settlement of the Magyars in the Carpathian basin, and authorities in Budapest chose to commemorate the event by opening new museums and staging cultural events. These included a major exhibition which not only honoured the progress made in Hungarian industry and trade, but also paid tribute to the country's rural activities. In the 'Hungarian Village', visitors could watch genuine peasants practising their crafts in re-creations of rural buildings, which were furnished and equipped with peasant artefacts. There was a village church, in which peasant couples were encouraged to get married in traditional costume to increase the visitors' encounter with 'real' village life. Even the formal functions for officials and dignitaries often revolved around a folk theme, with peasant costume and entertainment the order of the day. This was more than just a celebration of Hungary's rural populace: rather, the Government hoped that the exhibition of a shared folk heritage would pour cold water on any simmering discontent between different racial groups. Hungarian peasants and rural crafts continued to feature prominently at the international exhibitions and world's fairs in Chicago in 1893, Paris in 1900, and St Louis in 1904. In the eyes of the West, these ethnographical villages served to emphasize the hierarchy between the German-Austrian core of the empire and its peripheralized ethnic groups (something which David Crowley, the foremost Western scholar of these developments, has shown was first apparent at the Weltausstellung, or World Fair, in Vienna in 1873).[1] In Hungary, however, they carried a different message, both culturally and politically. In the first place, peasant art and architecture was a signifier of difference from any Austrian or German models, and as such was promoted as central to Hungary's accelerating cultural renaissance. At the same time, during a period of

137. Aladár Körösfői-Kriesch
Frontispiece to *Art of the Hungarian People* (Vol. II), Budapest, 1909

competing notions of national identity, abstracted peasant traditions could paper over any widening ethnic divides.

One of the practical outcomes of the growing vernacularism in *fin-de-siècle* Hungary was a flourishing peasant handicraft movement, starting with the home industry association which Etelka Gyarmathy (1843–1910) launched in the region of Kalotaszeg in 1885. (Gyarmathy's peasant embroideries found clients as far away as England, where various aristocrats decided they were all the rage.) By the end of the century, the Government had made it a matter of policy to support these industries of textiles, ceramics, basketry and lace, and sponsored courses, local exhibitions, and two national displays. Hungarian artists also began to organize expeditions to remote rural areas, gravitating primarily to the eastern province of Transylvania (now part of Romania), which had been barely touched by industrialization at the time. Inspired by the material culture which they encountered there, the artists began to collect folk artefacts, and to consider ways in which these might contribute to a national school of art and design.

The most consequential of the expeditions were those organized by the artist and designer Aladár Körösfői-Kriesch

(1863–1920) and his friend Sándor Nagy (1869–1950). Nagy and Körösfői-Kriesch had met as hot-blooded young men in their twenties, working off energy in the same fencing school while they were both studying painting in Rome. Once they had shelved their foils and masks, they discovered that they shared an interest in their country's nationalist cause (Körösfői-Kriesch having adopted the prefix of Körösfői, derived from the place name of Körösfő, to emphasize his Hungarianness). They were also sensitive to ways in which Hungarians might develop a national artistic idiom, particularly after studying with Bertalan Székely (1835–1910), a venerated artist of the older generation who drew on medieval and folk imagery in his mural painting and stained glass. Inspired by Székely's example, in 1897 Körösfői-Kriesch and Nagy organized a sketching trip to the Carpathian Mountains and began to collect folk art. Similar expeditions followed, leading to an array of sketches and artefacts so rich that they formed the basis for *Art of the Hungarian People* (fig. 137), an enormous, five-volume work which was edited by Dezső Malonyay and published from 1907 to 1922. A vast, collaborative endeavour of artists, museum workers and local art teachers, *Art of the Hungarian People* was organized by region and included drawings of costumes and textiles, furniture, churches, grave monuments, and the structural and decorative arrangement of peasant houses. There were personal ramifications too, as the artists involved in the project included Körösfői-Kriesch's sister Laura (1879–1962), an art teacher who had studied at the Royal School of Applied Arts in Budapest. The daughter of Hungary's first professor of natural history, Laura had grown up surrounded by cultural and intellectual debate, and fiercely opposed the conventions of polite society. (In 1918, when women in Hungary were required to wear hats on formal occasions, she baked her own jaunty headgear out of dough and defiantly placed this on her head.[2]) Talented, wayward, and unorthodox, Laura caught the eye of Nagy (aided, perhaps, by her preference for skirts shorter than those of her more decorous peers), and the two were married in 1902.

By the time Malonyay's *magnum opus* appeared, knowledge of the British Arts and Crafts Movement had permeated the consciousness of Hungary's nationalist and artistic intelligentsia. Most Hungarian intellectuals were bilingual and could read about Arts and Crafts developments in German-language journals such as *Deutsche Kunst und Dekoration* and *Innendekoration*. In addition, Körösfői-Kriesch, among others, contributed articles on British artists and designers to *Magyar Iparművészet*; Ruskin's *The Stones of Venice*

was translated into Hungarian from 1896 to 1898; and his Hungarian translator went on to write a long essay on the British critic in 1903. There were ground-breaking exhibitions of British decorative art at the Museum of Applied Arts in 1898 and 1902, the latter derived largely from the International Exhibition in Glasgow the previous year and including reproductions of Rossetti's works, a tapestry after a Burne-Jones cartoon, and interiors by the designer George Logan which presented an artistic composite of furniture, wall painting and stained glass. Most importantly, Ashbee and Crane acquired Hungarian patrons, and travelled to Hungary to promote and develop their work. Ashbee's first contact came in 1899: 'An interesting Hungarian has turned up – see how catholic is the modern Arts and Crafts movement.'[3] His Hungarian visitor – an economist named Gyula Mandello – commissioned furniture which was exhibited en route to Hungary at the Eighth Secession Exhibition in Vienna, where it formed nearly half of Ashbee's display. Another of Ashbee's Hungarian admirers was inspired by his visits to the Guild of Handicraft to establish a reform school on his Hungarian estate, complete with workshops in embroidery and carving, evening lectures, and bonding excursions in the countryside. Ashbee's Hungarian associations culminated in 1905 when he accepted an invitation to design a house in Budapest for the politician Zsombor Szász, though there is no evidence that the house was actually built. Walter Crane, for his part, not only had works in the exhibition of 1898, but was also honoured with solo shows at the Museum of Applied Arts in 1895 and 1900. When, on the latter occasion, the artist travelled to Hungary, a veritable Crane mania set in. There was a catalogue and a special issue of *Magyar Iparművészet*, for which Crane designed title pages; he gave a lecture, which was published; and he lavished Hungarian acquaintances with examples of his work, including a drawing for a designer at the Zsolnay Ceramics Factory which Crane visited, and which later produced a vase with a Crane design. The Museum of Applied Arts purchased pieces from the exhibition for its collection, and its director-general even had the hall of his apartment in the museum decorated with the *Peacock Garden* wallpaper and frieze for which Crane had won a gold medal at the Paris Exposition Universelle in 1889.

Crane's work, and his illustrations in particular, made a lasting impact on Hungarian design. Moreover, both he and Ashbee were fascinated by local handicrafts while they were in Hungary, and their belief in the moral supremacy of the artisan and of traditional craftsmanship exerted a wide appeal.

Crane was taken on a tour through Transylvania, and filled a sketchbook with drawings of peasant embroideries and folk costumes. He thanked his guide by designing a book-plate for him which featured a traditional Székely gate (fig. 138), and even published an article on Hungarian applied art in *Magyar Iparművészet*. Ashbee in turn delighted in an evening spent with Malonyay and his collections: 'what impressed me more than all else that I saw was the wonderful living work of the Hungarian peasant', he mused, adding in admiring tones that Malonyay's studio 'was a museum of living craftsmanship'.[4] This British appreciation for the handicrafts was something to which Hungarians could relate. More specifically, the writings of Morris and Ruskin alerted Hungarian designers to the edifying power of the handicrafts, a notion fundamental to Hungary's most famous Arts and Crafts initiative: the artists' colony in the village of Gödöllő, near Budapest, which was formed after Körösfői-Kriesch bought a house there in 1901. Körösfői-Kriesch later wrote of Ruskin, 'We are all his disciples, whether we read a single line by him or not,'[5] emphasizing the importance which he at least ascribed to the British critic in this most seminal development in Hungarian design.

The Gödöllő colony is a prime example of the pluralistic reality of artistic practice which cannot necessarily be anchored to one movement or style. Many of the artists who worked there – not least Körösfői-Kriesch and the Nagys – are celebrated for their mysterious Symbolist imagery, but the colony's express purpose was to revive peasant handicrafts, giving it an irrefutable link with the Arts and Crafts. With the support of the Society of Applied Arts, workshops were set up in traditional weaving practices, such as the Kilim and Torontál techniques. (So skilled were the workshops that they later became the training centre for the Royal School of Applied Arts.) There were also experiments with vegetable dyes extracted from local plants, though these were never successfully implemented on a large scale. Approximately forty peasant girls and women were employed in the workshops at any one time, weaving tapestries and carpets to the artists' designs. For all the veneration of peasant culture, the workshops were therefore patriarchal, with the distinction between the predominantly male artist-creators and the female peasant-workers reflecting hierarchies of gender and class. What the artists were able to do, though, was to refine folk practices in a way that would appeal to modern aesthetic sensibilities – something which would have been difficult, if not impossible, for the peasants themselves. Thus Körösfői-

138. Walter Crane
Ex Libris for Kálmán Kovács, 1900
Private collection

139. Aladár Körösfői-Kriesch
Women of Kalotaszeg, 1908
Tapestry in Scherebeck technique, 164 x 145 cm (64 ½ x 57 in)
Gödöllő City Museum

140. Laura Nagy
Sándor Nagy's Embroidered Shorts, c.1904
Linen and cotton with embroidery, 52 x 46 cm (20 ¼ x 18 in)
Sándor Nagy House, Gödöllő

Kriesch drew on traditional costumes in his *Women of Kalotaszeg* tapestry, but abstracted a series of vivid geometric patterns – from the highlights in the women's boots, for example – to give the design a punchy, contemporary feel (fig. 139). This adaptation of folk traditions to suit a modern consumer market was successful, and the workshops' products were marketed not only in Gödöllő, but also in venues as exclusive as the National Salon in Budapest. Even the Hungarian Ministry of Religion and Public Education (which covered cultural matters) donated second-hand looms, recognizing an opportunity to demonstrate the Government's commitment to peasant art. The Ministry was clearly happy to turn a blind eye to the artists' more unusual advocacy of vegetarianism and nudity (the latter thankfully practised only after the mystified peasant workers had gone home).

Over the years, the Gödöllő artists turned their hand to many crafts, and their designs were regularly published in pattern books which were distributed to craftsmen in other workshops and factories. Laura Nagy made it her mission to master folk embroidery techniques, putting these to good use in the peasant costumes which she sewed to clothe her family. Even Sándor's shorts – much loved, much worn – were treated to a delicate pattern in pale gold and olive green (fig. 140). Other artists endeavoured to revive ancient practices, such as the use of egg tempera in painting, or lead in stained glass. Their iconography focused on stylized images of peasant women, or historical and mythological subjects such as the legend of the Magic Deer, which told of the origins of the Magyar race. The Gödöllő project also attracted architects such as István Medgyaszay (1877–1959), a gifted young man who designed studio houses there from 1904 to 1906. Medgyaszay had studied with Otto Wagner, from whom he learnt the importance of integrated design. He was also a friend of Huszka and Lechner, who waxed lyrical about Hungary's cultural debts to the East. For Medgyaszay, however, the true stimulus for a national architectural style lay in rural architecture (he contributed drawings of peasant building types to *Art of the Hungarian People*), and his houses at Gödöllő drew on the ornamentation of peasant houses, and on their structural features such as wide, sheltering eaves. The resulting buildings, which were celebrated for their comfortable and healthy interiors, set new standards for the appropriation of vernacular motifs in modern domestic design.

The Gödöllő colony was visited and admired by foreigners including Crane and Akseli Gallen-Kallela, an important figure in the Finnish Arts and Crafts (see Chapter 8). *The Studio*, with its vast, international readership, ran articles on it, illustrating pieces which emphasized the renewal of peasant crafts and motifs (fig. 141). And in 1906 the Hungarian Government, recognizing an apposite vehicle to promote its vision of cultural autonomy, invited the Gödöllő artists to exhibit a furnished interior entitled 'The Home of an Artist' at the International Exhibition in Milan. Largely the work of Nagy and Medgyaszay, the exhibit was decorated with murals, textiles and rustic furniture in a *tour de force* of Arts and Crafts design. In later commissions, though, we see a slippage between the Arts and Crafts and Art Nouveau, most famously in the murals, mosaics, sculpture and stained glass which the Gödöllő artists designed for the Palace of Culture in the Transylvanian town of Marosvásárhely (now Târgu Mureş, Romania) from 1912 to 1913. In his stained-glass windows based on Transylvanian folk ballads, for example, Nagy alternated between a chivalric language of medieval and folk derivation and the sinuous torsion of enigmatic damsels and tendrilled tresses which is so characteristic of Art Nouveau (figs 142–5).

As the Gödöllő artists moved beyond their early focus on the handicrafts, it was left to architects to extend the orbit of the Hungarian Arts and Crafts by combining their knowledge of British developments with the patrimony of vernacular art. Béla Lajta (1873–1920), for example, admired the comfort and simplicity of British Arts and Crafts houses (he knew Baillie Scott, and had worked in Shaw's office during a trip to England in 1898–9), and searched for similarly progressive models of form, function and structure in peasant buildings. For Lajta, certain architectural forms were emblematic of national character – the cupola, for example, which had appeared in everything from sacred tombs to beehives – and should have a role in modern Hungarian design. The group of architects known as Fiatalok (The Young) also trawled the vernacular traditions of Transylvania in search of models for modern houses. The hall and dining room for an artist's home which the group's leader, Károly Kós (1883–1977), published in *Magyar Iparművészet* in 1908 exemplifies the way in which functional features of vernacular architecture could combine with medievalizing decoration to create a strikingly original living space (fig. 146). Kós never lost his belief that vernacular practices provided a portal to a modern, national style. Even in projects as progressive as the social housing modelled on English garden suburbs which appeared from the first decade of the twentieth century, Kós and his colleagues evoked a

141. Aladár Körösfői-Kriesch
Tree Planters Tapestry, c.1906, from *The Studio*, 1908

consciously rustic style in their shingled and weatherboarded houses, and included features as typically Transylvanian as steep roofs, wooden balconies, and picturesque turrets and spires in the public buildings they designed.

Most interesting of all is Ede Toroczkai-Vigand (1870–1945), a graduate of the Royal School of Applied Arts who, like Körösfői-Kriesch, demonstrated his nationalist beliefs by changing his name (in his case by adapting that of the Transylvanian town of Torockó). Toroczkai-Vigand was one of the first Hungarians to design furniture as part of a room, drawing on ethnographic work he had carried out in Transylvania to produce pieces derived from peasant designs. These were published in one of the pattern books which featured Gödöllő work (fig. 147), and played an important part in Körösfői-Kriesch and Nagy's ventures in interior design. Gradually, however, Toroczkai-Vigand became more interested in buildings, despite having had no formal training as an architect. He wrote and illustrated books on Hungary's medieval and vernacular architecture, and in 1907 published a series of designs called *Az én falum* (My Village) which drew on peasant building types. The same year, he designed a weaving school for the Gödöllő colony whose hipped roofs,

142. Sándor Nagy
Stained-Glass Window, 1912–13
Palace of Culture, Marosvásárhely

143–5. Sándor Nagy
Cartoons for Stained-Glass Windows
for the Palace of Culture, Marosvásárhely, 1912–13

146. Károly Kós
'Hall and Dining Room for an Artist's Home' from *Magyar Iparmuvészet*, 1908

gables and turret were derived from Transylvanian churches and peasant homes (fig. 148). The weaving school was never built, but Toroczkai-Vigand went on to design many church and school buildings as part of the Government's programme to develop towns and villages in Transylvania, as well as designing furnished houses and studios for artists and other patrons who favoured his rustic style. Most of Toroczkai-Vigand's buildings were wooden and few have survived, but his work bore testimony to a thriving vernacularism in both public and private architectural design.

If many Hungarians felt compelled to promote a national artistic idiom, in Poland there was even more cause to develop forms of Polish culture which would transcend the divisions imposed by foreign rule. Conditions under the three powers which had partitioned the country varied considerably. The part of Poland which fell within the Austro-Hungarian Empire benefited from the relatively liberal Habsburg regime which had agreed the Compromise of 1867. Its inhabitants conversed in Polish (which was recognized as one of the official languages), managed their own local politics and, from 1871, were represented in Vienna by a Minister for Galician Affairs. In sharp contrast, those Poles who lived under Prussian and Russian rule had many limitations on their national expression, especially after the famous but unsuccessful uprisings in the Russian partition in

145

147. Ede Toroczkai-Vigand
'Kitchen' from *Sample Pages*, New Series 1, 1900s
Museum of Applied Arts, Budapest

1830 and 1863. The Warsaw School of Fine Arts, among other institutions, was shut down in the aftermath of these insurrections, on the second occasion remaining closed until 1904. The city itself was placed under military rule, and Polish children in the Prussian and the Russian partitions had the unnerving experience of reading Polish literature as a 'foreign' language in schools.

One of the responses to these developments was a policy known as 'Organic Work' whose advocates, in contrast to the earlier insurrectionists, aimed to work with the imperialist powers to improve social and economic conditions on behalf of Poles in all three partitions. But this did little to address the fact that the culture in each area was being adulterated (in the eyes of Polish nationalists) by that of the ruling state, not least because, in the absence of suitable training institutions in the Russian and Prussian sectors, Polish artists and architects were obliged to seek an education in centres such as St Petersburg and Berlin. With forms as culturally alien as the onion-domed churches of Russia infiltrating architectural practice, members of the Polish intelligentsia turned to native artistic traditions which might act as an antidote to the enervating effect of foreign motifs. Just as Hungarians had alighted on Transylvania as the cradle of national forms (and as Finland would iconize the region of Karelia, as we will see in Chapter 8), many gravitated towards the area of Podhale as a repository of artistic traditions which could energize Polish design.

Podhale and its key town of Zakopane lie to the south of Cracow, below the Tatra Mountains which today mark part of the Polish–Slovakian border. In the second half of the nineteenth century, it was among the most unindustrialized and impoverished areas of the Habsburg Empire, its native peasants, the Górale or 'Highlanders', continuing in the traditional occupations of farmers or shepherds in the absence of any city or factory work. With its picturesque mountain scenery and inhabitants who were linguistically and culturally distinct, the region had attracted artists and writers since the 1850s. From the 1870s, however, it became more than just an artists' retreat and began to acquire resonance as a crucible of Polish identity, fuelled by the activities of Tytus Chałubiński, a remarkable surgeon who arrived in Zakopane from Warsaw in 1873 to tackle an outbreak of cholera. As passionate about the local environment as he was about saving lives, Chałubiński founded the Tatra Society which aimed to safeguard Górale traditions by improving living conditions and increasing

148. Ede Toroczkai-Vigand
Design for the Weaving School at Gödöllő, 1907, from *Ház* (The House), 1908
Gödöllő City Museum

educational and employment opportunities. The Society also undertook to broadcast Podhale's attractions as a health resort – an unusual idea considering the cholera which had brought Chałubiński there, but one that nevertheless worked. Middle- and upper-class Poles alike were soon rubbing shoulders in Zakopane's new sanatoria or, if they could afford it, in their own private villas, spending their days hiking and exercizing and filling their lungs with unpolluted mountain air.

Among the visitors who sought respite from their aches and pains was Stanisław Witkiewicz (1851–1915), a painter and critic suffering from tuberculosis who arrived in Zakopane in 1886. Witkiewicz was immediately struck by the wooden houses typical of the region, with their steep roofs, wood tiling and sheltering eaves. Both the gables, porches, and door and window frames, and the household furniture and utensils were skilfully carved with latticework, sunbursts, geometric arrangements or floral motifs. Captivated by these and other aspects of the local vernacular, Witkiewicz uprooted his family and moved permanently to Zakopane in 1890, taking up residence in a traditional wooden house. Undeterred by his lack of architectural training, he drew on the skills of both Warsaw-based architects and local craftsmen and began to build a series of villas which echoed

149. Stanisław Witkiewicz
Design for Koliba, 1892–4
Tatra Museum, Zakopane

150. (opposite) Stanisław Witkiewicz
House under the Firs, Zakopane, 1897

the structural and decorative forms of Górale houses (fig. 149). Colleagues who shared his fascination with the Górale vernacular followed suit, designing not only houses but also furniture and smaller decorative objects in what became known as the Zakopane style.

The largest and most famous of Witkiewicz's villas is the Dom pod Jedlami (House under the Firs), which he designed in 1897 for an economist and *aficionado* of folk art (fig. 150). This was the project which put the Zakopane style on the map, with skilled local craftsmen working round the clock for nine months to complete not only the building, but also interiors, furniture and textiles based on the designs of Witkiewicz, his wife and colleagues. Parallels with the Górale vernacular were immediately apparent: the construction in unclad planks and logs; the overhanging eaves; the ornamental carving around balconies and windows; and the carved sun's rays fingering their way to the edges of the gables. Even the house's curtains carried a pattern taken from trousers which the Górale wore. But these elements were combined with new features, such as the massive stone base, and they were assembled on a scale and at a level of complexity unknown in their original

context. The interlocking puzzle of roofs, eaves and dormer windows, for example, was more elaborate than the arrangement in any peasant house. In Witkiewicz's design, the local vernacular therefore underwent a process of reincarnation but retained sufficient evidence of traditional practices to signify 'Polishness' to a generation sensitive to the need for a national focus in art and design. Significantly, Witkiewicz argued that the material culture of Podhale was typical of a style which had once prevailed all over Poland, before the processes of modernization and the cultural encroachment of other countries had obliterated it. In fact, Górale architecture had features in common with wooden buildings in other parts of the Austro-Hungarian Empire such as Transylvania, but Witkiewicz's intellectual invention of the Zakopane style as specifically Polish was nevertheless a great success. The region became a cultural nirvana for Poles living in all three partitions, and the fashion-conscious of Warsaw (a city ruled by a different country from the Podhale region) developed a penchant for Podhale peasant dress. Efforts were even made to apply the style to urban architecture; for example, in an apartment house which Jarosław Wojciechowski designed in Warsaw in 1905. Here,

however, the Zakopane style reached its limits, the techniques of assembly and decoration which worked so well in wood failing to translate into brick and stone.

While considering the Górale vernacular it is worth mentioning the School of Carpentry in Zakopane, whose history highlights the different views of those involved in developing peasant crafts. The School of Carpentry had been set up by the Tatra Society in 1876 to nurture the local woodworking industry, and originally employed a local Górale carpenter to train just nine boys. A few years later, it was reorganized as a *Fachschule*, one of the state-supported craft schools which were set up in Austria-Hungary to boost local economies by offering training in specialist crafts, particularly those which could utilize local materials or existing expertise. Along with the school's new status came a new director, who paid little attention to Górale woodworking traditions. Instead, boys at the school were expected to study the classical and historical models of design favoured by the Österreichisches Museum für Kunst und Industrie in Vienna. As pupils produced increasingly elaborate pieces, at odds with the forms and patterns of Górale work, a group of local inhabitants led by Witkiewicz

began to object. He noted sardonically in 1891 that the school had become 'the Zakopane seed-bed for Tyrolean-Viennese taste, a German poison exhausting the skills of the Górale peasants. [...] Having the aim of developing applied art from handicraft found among the peasantry, which in its independence and originality adorns all of their hand-crafted goods, [...] this school adds nothing to the development of local artistic motifs.'[6] By the end of the century Witkiewicz's point had struck home and, under new directors sympathetic to Górale traditions, the school again reflected vernacular methods and motifs. As David Crowley has pointed out, the vehement reaction of Witkiewicz and his colleagues, despite the financial benefits which came with the school's reclassification as a *Fachschule*, highlights the extent to which the nationalist lobby valued peasant culture as a reservoir of Polish identity, and resisted what they saw as the meddlesome and destructive intervention of the state.[7]

By the early twentieth century, it was not only in rural areas that Polish artists and intellectuals were intensifying their promotion of the applied arts. In Cracow, the capital of the Austro-Hungarian partition, such was the urgency of debate on modern art and design that a group of artists, designers and critics joined forces to set up the Polish Applied Art Society in 1901. This included many of the Young Poland group, an avant-garde collective of artists, writers and designers who shared an interest in Symbolism and Art Nouveau: but it was also concerned with preserving native crafts, and with the need to improve the design of commonplace objects. The ideas of the British Arts and Crafts were now circulating in Poland (texts translated into Polish at the time included works by Morris and Ruskin). There was also a rediscovery of the works of the Polish poet and critic Cyprian Norwid, who from exile in Paris in the mid-nineteenth century had argued that one route to social cohesion lay in the application of artistic principles to everyday design. Norwid's poetry struck a chord with artists and designers who saw the raising of aesthetic standards as central to the development of the Polish nation. In the words of Jerzy Warchałowski, a critic and founder member of the Polish Applied Art Society, their aim was to 'substitute ugliness with real beauty, rubbish with good work, fake with genuine materials, pretentiousness with simplicity, carelessness with conscientiousness, indifference with zeal, thoughtlessness with resolution, quantity with quality [...] and, finally, everything that attracts Polish artists of foreign origin with the prevailing spirit of our nation and the ideals of our leading figures.'[8] Warchałowski's veiled reference to the tripartite division of his country in his appeal to 'Polish artists of foreign origin' stands testament to the nationalist sentiment which he and many colleagues shared. Indeed, so anxious was the Society to bridge the cultural rifts brought about by partition that its journal was run by editors in Cracow and Warsaw, and both cities hosted its first exhibition in 1902.

Over the next decade, the Polish Applied Art Society acted as a fulcrum for designers working in many media, from metal and furniture to fresco and stained glass. Theirs was not a gripe with the changes of industrialization (indeed, the Polish designers often farmed their work out to commercial workshops). Rather, the Society adopted the dual role of watchdog over threatened or neglected areas of Polish culture, and champion of traditional forms and motifs in modern design. Notable among its members was Stanisław Wyspiański (1869–1907), the writer and designer who was as at home designing a rug or a poster as he was restoring a church or writing a play. It was Wyspiański who had produced one of Cracow's great artistic ensembles in the 1890s, when he was commissioned to renovate and decorate the Gothic church of St Francis. He responded with some of the most all-encompassing interior decoration in Polish church history, in which every wall, ceiling and window was painted or glazed in giddying geometric patterns, abstracted figurative designs, or floral or folk motifs (figs 151–6). Wyspiański also struck a stark nationalist note by including the Polish monarchic symbol of crowned eagles. With a peasant wife at his side (certain Polish intellectuals engaging in very public marriages with peasant women at the time), Wyspiański continued to strive for forms which were suggestive of both the modern and the Polish. Sadly his star burned brightly but fast, and he died in 1907 at the age of just thirty-eight.

As the first decade of the twentieth century progressed, numerous ventures furthered the applied and decorative arts in Poland, including the Society of Podhale Art founded in 1909, the Kilim Association established in 1910 and, in Warsaw, the courses run by the Museum of Handicraft and Applied Art. So successful were these in whipping up interest in vernacular traditions across the Habsburg Empire that *The Studio* published a book entitled *Peasant Art in Austria and Hungary* in 1911. The Polish Applied Art Society, for its part, continued to publish its influential journal, *Records of Polish Applied Art* (1902–12), and to stage exhibitions which promoted new trends in architecture, as well as in the decorative arts. An important development was the rise of the so-called manor style, which drew on the wooden and brick country houses of the Polish gentry. These houses were relatively sparse in decoration (though from the eighteenth century they had developed statuesque columnar porches), and were seized upon by architects searching for a specifically Polish prototype for the modern, suburban home. The Society ran competitions in 1908, 1910 and 1913 to promote the manor style, the design which Józef Galezowski submitted to the first of these exhibiting its typical features of hipped roof and dormer and bay windows anchored by the prominent, classical porch (fig. 157). In 1912, the Society also played a role in disseminating the Garden City ideal when it mounted an ambitious exhibition entitled 'Architecture and Interiors in Gardens', held courtesy of the Cracow city council in a public park. The exhibition's aim of providing 'new forms of practical, healthy and aesthetic living ... [for] all sections of Polish society'[9] came from Garden City rhetoric: but this was given a sharp injection of Catholic morality in the model house for a craftsman designed by Adolf Szyszko-Bohusz (1883–1948), in which a stained-glass window of the Virgin Mary struck a monitory note over the fictional inhabitant's bed. Szyszko-Bohusz based his design on a peasant

151–6. Stanisław Wyspiański
Decoration in the Church of St Francis, Cracow, 1896–1902

157. Józef Galezowski
Design for the Manor at Opinogóra, 1908

158. Pupils of the Cracow Workshops under the Direction of Kazimierz Młodzianowski
Metalware, 1913–14
Copper, cold-hammered and silvered inside, coffee pot 18 x 10.8 cm (7 x 4 in),
milk jug 15 x 8.5 cm (6 x 3 ¼ in), sugar bowl 9 x 9 cm (3 ¼ x 3 ¼ in)
National Museum, Cracow

159. Karol Stryjeński
Wooden Bench, 1925
National Museum, Warsaw

160. Mackay Hugh Baillie Scott
An Interior Sketch for Le Nid, 1901
Colour reproduction, 39.5 x 52.7 cm (15 ½ x 20 ¾ in)
from M H Baillie Scott, *Houses and Gardens*, 1906

house from southern Poland, illustrating the continuing promotion of vernacular traditions.

By 1912, however, a new force in the Cracovian Arts and Crafts Movement was beginning to overshadow the Polish Applied Art Society: namely the craft workshops in the Museum of Industry, a vast repository of scientific exhibits, ethnographic curiosities, and fine and applied arts which had been established on the South Kensington model in 1868. The museum had first launched courses in the crafts in the 1880s, though these had been discontinued when they could not keep up with the demand which they generated. From 1909, new workshops opened in bookbinding and metalwork, where artists such as Kazimierz Młodzianowski revelled in the properties of different materials in their designs for practical household goods (fig. 158). In 1913, the workshops, along with the museum's collections, moved into a stunning new building designed by the museum's director, the architect Tadeusz Stryjeński (1849–1943). There, they were joined by facilities for woodworking, printing and photography; by the National Institute for the Promotion of Handicraft and Industry, which monitored professional standards in the craft and manufacturing industries; and by

the Cracow Workshops, a body of artists, critics and designers who promoted a more catholic range of methods and products than those employed by the Polish Applied Art Society. The Cracow Workshops' ambition was to make art widely available through the design of interiors and everyday objects, but they had little time to realize this in the tumultuous build-up to the First World War. After the war, however, they assumed a central role in Polish design, reviving the art of batik dyeing and achieving renown for the furniture of Wojciech Jastrzębowski (1884–1963) and Karol Stryjeński (1887–1932), who produced weighty and tactile creations in native woods such as oak and larch (fig. 159). The umbilical cord with peasant traditions was still intact: in Jastrzębowski's words: 'In folk creation [...] we saw real artistic life.'[10]

Indeed, the history of Polish design in the twentieth century offers a corrective to any lingering notion that the Arts and Crafts Movement came to a halt with the First World War. The search for nationalism through vernacularism which runs as a leitmotif through the Movement in Eastern Europe reappeared in the interwar period in the debates of the Cracow School, a loosely aligned

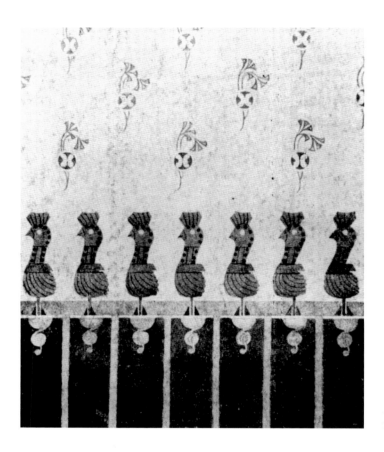

161. Apcar Baltazar
Decoration for a Dining Room, from 'Towards a Romanian Style', 1908

group of designers living in the newly reunified Poland which included members of both the Cracow Workshops and the resurrected Warsaw Academy of Fine Arts. The Warsaw Academy itself negotiated the difficult balance between disseminating the ideas of foreigners such as Ruskin, Morris and members of the Deutsche Werkbund, and launching a spirited defence of nationalist design. Most extraordinary of all was the occasion of the Exposition Internationale des Arts Décoratifs in Paris in 1925, when the Cracow Workshops mounted an acclaimed display which again appealed to the twin constructs of good craftsmanship and vernacular design. The Exposition is best known for its array of Art Deco objects (the exhibition gave the style its name), and there is a world of difference between Art Deco's embrace of modernity and the humble peasant and applied art traditions which lay behind the Cracow Workshops. Yet among the sybaritic excitements of Art Deco, the Polish section won more prizes than any other foreign display. Even in an age when bob-haired beauties caroused in flapper dresses and gleaming Cadillacs, there was still a role for the nationalist vernacularism of the Polish Arts and Crafts.

For all their success at the Exposition Internationale, the Cracow Workshops derived little financial benefit and went bankrupt in 1926. Yet the death-knell was still to sound for the Polish Arts and Crafts. The same year saw the foundation of a new organization called LAD or 'Harmony', which brought together artists and designers from the Warsaw Academy who at times still referred to vernacular practices. In the 1930s, some of them even moved out of the cities and set up weaving and embroidery workshops in rural areas to manufacture their designs. The textile initiatives apart, the LAD co-operative was often derided by designers from a different ideological standpoint as a moribund and backward-looking organization unable to compete with the sleek seduction of Modernism. But the very existence of the Cracow Workshops and the LAD community as late as the 1920s – twenty years after the foundation of the Gödöllő colony (which continued to produce textiles until 1943), and thirty years after the inception of the Zakopane style – attests to the resilience of the Movement to recover vernacular and craft practices. This was no longer a form of vernacularism designed to challenge imperial rule, as had been the case in both Poland

and Hungary. Rather, it was a defiant last gesture on the part of those who, despite the growing contempt of Modernists, continued to find in peasant conceptions a viable model for modern, national design.

As a postscript, it is worth briefly considering developments in Romania, whose difference from those in Hungary and Poland sheds light on the interrelationship between vernacularism and attitudes towards a national style. Romania was not devoid of Arts and Crafts work. Indeed, the country boasted one of the most playful Arts and Crafts projects in the form of a tree house called Le Nid which Baillie Scott designed for Crown Princess Marie in a forest above the royal summer palace in Sinaia. The sister of the Grand Duchess of Hesse, Marie commissioned Baillie Scott after admiring his work at Darmstadt, and her tree house echoes aspects of his Darmstadt designs. The decorative scheme in each of its three interiors was based on a different flower: sunflowers in the main salon, lilies in the oratory alcove, and poppies in the bedroom (fig. 160). These were complemented with inscriptions and richly decorated furniture to create a bejewelled, airborne retreat so enchanting that even Marie's uncle-in-law, the dour King Carol, took guests there, negotiating the ascent up an access tower (based loosely on Romanian belfries) and across a drawbridge which would then be raised to accentuate the frisson of escapist delight. The tree house, suspended eight metres above the ground in a group of five pine trees, blew down – perhaps unsurprisingly – in a storm after the First World War, but Marie continued to patronize the applied and decorative arts. She commissioned a series of ornate interiors, both for her main palace of Cotroceni and for her country residences and garden follies; she supported a new school of decorative art in Bucharest; and she herself designed furniture, which was manufactured by local craftsmen.

There was also a renewal of interest in Romanian vernacular culture. In 1907, the country's first Museum of National Art opened with displays of peasant handicrafts, and the architect George Sterian began a decorative arts department at the Bucharest School of Fine Art which educated students in vernacular forms and techniques. The following year, the young artist Apcar Baltazar published an article called 'Towards a Romanian Style' which advocated the distillation of the 'artistic sense' of vernacular culture in modern decoration.[11] Practising what he preached, Baltazar illustrated his article with a wall design for a modern dining room which included a row of cockerels derived from the handles of carved wooden spoons (fig. 161). Much later, in the 1920s and 1930s, Marie (by then Queen of Romania) developed a taste for the simple forms of boyar manor houses in her fanciful country retreats and took to displaying peasant craftwork, perhaps inspired by earlier coverage of folk art in *The Studio*, to which she subscribed.

In Romania, however, there was nothing comparable to the move in Hungary and Poland to recast vernacular traditions in a new, national style. Recent research suggests that this reflected the country's different political position: Romania had secured independence from Turkish governance in 1878, and had been an autonomous kingdom under Hohenzollern-Sigmaringen rule since 1881.[12] Was it as a result of the security which came with this independence that artists and designers were not compelled to trawl the country's vernacular in their affirmation of national identity, or to romanticize groups of geographically distant peasants as guardians of the nation's artistic soul? Instead, their work in what is known as the neo-Romanian style drew inspiration from the country's Orthodox traditions, and from the monuments built under Prince Constantin Brâncoveanu at the turn of the eighteenth century. Other constructs of the Arts and Crafts Movement, such as the notion of the *Gesamtkunstwerk* and the social aspirations of Ruskin and his followers, also rarely appeared in Romania. While it is difficult to draw any certain conclusions, the relative lack of enthusiasm for Arts and Crafts ideas in Romania lends weight to those accounts which emphasize the importance of the dialogue between vernacular revivalism and notions of a national style in the development of the Movement in Eastern Europe. It was the veneration of local traditions, old buildings, craft skills and peasant life which created such fertile ground for the Arts and Crafts.

Viktor Vasnetsov
Set Design for Act II of *Snegurochka*, c.1885 (fig. 165)

ARTISANS AND ARISTOCRATS: THE RUSSIAN EQUATION

RUSSIA IN THE NINETEENTH CENTURY WAS A COUNTRY BESET WITH ANXIETIES. EVER SINCE THE RISE OF THE DISTINCT GROUP OF CRITICAL THINKERS KNOWN AS THE INTELLIGENTSIA IN THE 1830s, THE AUTHORITARIAN STRUCTURES OF POWER HAD BEEN UNDER SCRUTINY.

The nature of Russia's relationship to Western Europe was also the subject of fierce debate, and had gradually divided the intelligentsia into two camps: the Westernizers, who favoured the overt westernization of Russia which had begun during Peter the Great's reign from 1682 to 1725; and the Slavophiles, who felt that Peter's much-vaunted political and cultural orientation towards Europe denied the importance both of the native people or *narod* (a word as highly charged as the German *volk*), and of Russia's Slavic and Byzantine past. With the emancipation of the serfs in 1861, which liberated an estimated twenty-two million peasant men, women and children (a massive thirty-five per cent of the total population of the Russian Empire), and the ensuing rise of Populism, a revolutionary movement which glorified the peasantry, the notion of the *narod* as embodying both the country's identity and her future salvation become enshrined in democratic debate.

In the arts, the growing interest in peasant life and in the material culture of the pre-Petrine era (the period preceding Peter the Great) spawned the so-called Russian style, a vast and ill-defined trend which spanned much of the nineteenth century and encompassed an eclectic variety of artistic styles. From the middle of the century, however, there was a sharpening of focus, with scholarly research into medieval and vernacular culture, and a more directed interest in folk art. Familiarity with the nature of peasant traditions further increased with the extraordinary Populist initiative known as 'going to the people' in 1874, in which thousands of educated, if misguided Russians, the majority of them students, moved to rural areas to reconnect with the peasantry and garner support for their anti-autocratic beliefs. Politically, their actions were a disaster, as startled and God-fearing peasants reported their seditious activities to the authorities: but the movement did increase contact between the peasantry and urban elites, and created a more informed understanding of rural ways of life.

These developments stimulated a range of Arts and Crafts practices in Russia, from the deployment of the peasant vernacular in architecture, to commercially-oriented initiatives to sustain Russia's craft industries. As was often the case elsewhere, the result was not a style of visual coherence, but a set of common intellectual approaches freighted with a commitment to indigenous sources, craftsmanship, and the possibility of social regeneration through the arts. By 1913, the

162. Fedor Solntsev
Frontispiece to *Antiquities of the Russian State*, 1849–53

Movement had spread to encompass the development of craft industries among distinct ethnic nationalities; for example, in the Caucasus, Ukraine and Turkestan. But its core revolved around Moscow, Russia's medieval capital which Slavophiles felt had been wrongly usurped by St Petersburg, the 'window on Europe' which Peter the Great had founded in 1703. So great was the enmity felt in certain quarters towards Peter's city that the ethnographer and passionate Slavophile Ivan Aksakov wrote, 'It is impossible to consider oneself a citizen of Russia and St Petersburg at the same time', his comment highlighting the extent to which the northern capital was seen as a rarefied European construct isolated from the realities of Russian life. As far as the Arts and Crafts are concerned, St Petersburg housed members of the nobility and influential figures at court who played an important patronage role, as well as educational institutions and museum collections central to the development of art industries and the study of national cultural patrimony. But in terms of actual production St Petersburg, with its neoclassical palaces and pomaded aristocrats, contributed relatively little to a movement concerned with peasant and medieval artefacts. It was primarily in Moscow, with its ancient, onion-

domed centre, and on a handful of country estates that the key Arts and Crafts initiatives of Russia took place.

The serious study of the Russian vernacular dates from the second quarter of the nineteenth century, when various individuals began to collect peasant artefacts, produce accurate scale drawings of buildings, and investigate the rationale behind different forms of ornamentation. One such scholar was Fedor Solntsev (1801–92), the son of a serf, who had studied at the Imperial Academy of Arts in St Petersburg and was then appointed to oversee the restoration of the seventeenth-century Terem Palace in the Kremlin. In the mid-1830s, at the suggestion of the President of the Academy, Solntsev began to study pre-Petrine material culture, travelling vast distances 'for the purpose of sketching our traditional customs, vestments, weapons, ecclesiastical and royal plate, goods and chattels, harnesses, and other objects pertaining to historical, archaeological, and ethnographical knowledge'. Solntsev's detailed drawings were published in the vast, six-volume *Antiquities of the Russian State* (fig. 162) which, with illustrations of objects ranging from antique saddlery to the childhood throne of Peter the Great, offered something of an encyclopaedia of medieval and vernacular design. At the same time there was an early practical attempt at the scholarly revival of the architectural vernacular – a small pavilion based on a traditional peasant hut, or *izba*, which Nikolai Nikitin (1828–1913) built in the grounds of the Moscow residence of Mikhail Pogodin in 1856. Pogodin, a historian who specialized in ancient Russian history, met there with other dissident sympathizers to debate Populist values and democratic ideals, making the hut an unmistakable statement of both cultural and political intent.

In the 1860s and 1870s, three institutions began to offer a formal design education: the Central Imperial Stroganov School of Technical Design, founded in Moscow in 1860; and the School of the Society for the Encouragement of Artists and the Baron Stieglitz School, founded in St Petersburg in 1862 and 1876 respectively. Of these, the Stroganov School was the most influential, setting up a museum after the South Kensington precedent which included old Russian artefacts and architectural details, running workshops in skills ranging from weaving and textile printing to chromolithography, and agitating for a Russian style in manufactured goods. There was also a surge in the investigation of monuments, which were studied and measured with increasing accuracy, and a number of new publications addressed the applied arts and ornamental design. In 1869 the Moscow Archaeological

Society was established and began to issue papers and reports to disseminate the results of empirical research. The following year Viktor Butovsky, the director of the Stroganov School, published in France a set of volumes entitled *Histoire de l'ornement russe du Xe au XVIe siècle d'après les manuscrits* (1870–3), which included accurate reproductions and details. In the words of its author, true to the ethos of the Stroganov School, the book was 'aimed exclusively at the needs of technical and industrial designers. It is intended to introduce Russian craftsmen to the models and sources for an original Russian style'.[2] Two years later Vladimir Stasov (1824–1906), the giant of Russian art criticism in the nineteenth century and an indefatigable advocate of nationalism in the arts, published *Russian Folk Ornament* (1872), a lavish volume which contained real pieces of embroidery, much as Henry Cole's *Journal of Design and Manufactures* had included actual samples of textiles and wallpaper twenty years before. The run of new design publications in the 1870s culminated with *Motifs of Russian Architecture*, an annual journal which drew on Butovsky's and Stasov's albums and published designs for wooden buildings, interiors, furniture, and domestic utensils, much of it in the Russian style, thus promoting ways in which the results of the earlier surveys might inspire new work.

The first place to witness the revival of medieval and folk motifs on a large scale was Abramtsevo, the country estate of the industrialist and impresario Savva Mamontov (1841–1918). Mamontov was one of a group of extraordinary millionaire patrons in late-nineteenth-century Russia who came from peasant stock, but whose fathers or grandfathers had initiated a remarkable change in family circumstance by grasping the opportunities presented by Russia's belated industrialization. In Mamontov's case, the family fortune had been made in the railways, which saw a dramatic expansion in the years following the abolition of serfdom: in 1861, there were less than a thousand miles of permanent track in Russia, but by the end of the century all of the country's major cities were accessible by rail. Mamontov inherited his family's railway holdings in 1869, and the following year bought Abramtsevo as a country retreat. Away from the thundering factories and sulphurous chimney-stacks of Moscow – a city whose rapid industrial expansion had earned it the epithet 'the Russian Manchester' – Mamontov and his wife, Elizaveta (1847–1908), created a rural haven in which to indulge their passion for the fine and applied arts.

The Abramtsevo estate had belonged to the Aksakov family, and as such resonated with Slavophile concerns:

Sergei Aksakov (1791–1859), the paterfamilias, was a writer and theatre critic who had meticulously chronicled rural Russian life in works such as *Notes on Angling* (1847), while his son Ivan, a respected scholar of Russian folklore, edited various Slavophile journals. During their time at Abramtsevo the Aksakovs had invited many intellectual luminaries to stay, and the estate's rambling, eighteenth-century house had become a congenial centre of cultural debate. This practice, typical of much of the Russian gentry, continued in Mamontov's time. But whereas the focus under the Aksakovs had been literary – guests had included the writers Nikolai Gogol and Ivan Turgenev – Mamontov's passion was for the visual and performing arts. One of his first steps was to commission Viktor Gartman (1834–73) – the artist who inspired the composer Modest Mussorgsky's *Pictures at an Exhibition* – and Ivan Petrov (1845–1908), who used the pseudonym of Ropet, to build various pavilions on the estate. Both architects drew on the form and the intricate carving or 'wooden lace' characteristic of the *izba* in their designs. From 1873, Mamontov also began to invite many of Russia's most promising young artists to spend their summers at Abramtsevo. Once there, they were encouraged by the patron, with his infamous blend of cajolery and shameless bullying – what one of the young protégés called his 'inspirational despotism'[3] – to turn their hand to the applied and decorative arts and, in theatrical productions, to engage in communal work.

Abramtsevo's celebrated series of amateur dramatics began in 1879 and involved the resident artists in every aspect of the production, from designing the costumes to performing in the plays. Valentin Serov (1865–1911), who would become the greatest Russian portraitist of his generation, found himself cheekily defined as 'a ballerina and a decorator'[4] by his friend, the artist Viktor Vasnetsov (1848–1926). Mamontov would chivvy them along in the chaotic confusion of sawing, painting, sewing and rehearsing, before himself taking a central role on the stage. Most importantly, the artists referred to pre-Petrine and vernacular models in their designs, in the process making a key contribution to the Russian Arts and Crafts. The seminal production in this respect was that of *Snegurochka* (The Snow Maiden), Alexander Ostrovsky's folklore play which was staged in Mamontov's Moscow mansion in the winter of 1882, to be followed by a performance of Nikolai Rimsky-Korsakov's operatic version at Abramtsevo in 1885. The designer was Vasnetsov, who was so inspired by Russia's

Slavic past that he once declared: 'I have only ever lived for Rus' (Rus being the political entity dating from the late ninth century which covered large parts of what are now Russia, Belorussia and Ukraine). For the costumes for *Snegurochka*, Vasnetsov used both antique peasant garments and colourful re-creations which incorporated folk fabrics, peasant head-dresses and *lapti*, the traditional bast shoes of the peasantry (fig. 163). The set design for Act I featured an *izba*, complete with the traditional peasant features of painted window surrounds and a carved ridgepole over the raised porch (fig. 164). The polychrome interior in the palace of Tsar Berendei in Act II (fig. 165), in contrast, was inspired by the Faceted and Terem Palaces of the Kremlin in Moscow; the bulbous wooden columns, with their ornate decoration, echoed those of northern Russian churches; and the animal motifs across the ceiling derived from the decoration of domestic utensils in peasant households, from wooden distaffs and battledores to gingerbread moulds. The chair and throne echo both the reassuring solidity of peasant furniture and the lavish carving more common in the house of a boyar or old Russian nobleman, while the towers at the back evoke the *shatior* – the tent-shaped roof which had flourished in Russian ecclesiastical architecture from the early sixteenth century until Patriarch Nikon had banned the form as too secular in 1653.

The employment of fine artists in the theatre at Abramtsevo, and the integration of their designs as a fundamental element of the production, underpinned Mamontov's Russian Private Opera (1885–91 and 1896–1900) and, later, Sergei Diaghilev's Ballets Russes. These became a key determinant in the emergence of Modernism in Russia and, internationally, redefined the nature of theatre art. From an Arts and Crafts perspective, the Abramtsevo productions were critical for their deconstruction of professional hierarchies, and for the spur they gave artists to investigate fairy tales, legends, and medieval and folk art. Such investigations were profoundly eclectic: there was rarely any concern to differentiate the plethora of activity which could be classified under the headings 'medieval', 'pre-Petrine' or 'folk', nor to acknowledge distinctions between Asiatic, Byzantine or Slavic roots. Favoured sources were themselves problematic: the Kremlin 'restoration' projects in which Solntsev had been involved in the 1830s, for example, had dramatically altered the original fabric of some of the interiors. Furthermore, notions of what constituted medieval imagery were at times constructions of the modern

163. Viktor Vasnetsov
Costume Designs for *Snegurochka*, 1885–6
Gouache, watercolour and pencil on paper mounted on card
26.4 x 22.2 cm (10 1/4 x 8 3/4 in)
State Tretyakov Gallery, Moscow

165. Viktor Vasnetsov
Set Design for Act II of *Snegurochka*, c.1885
Gouache, watercolour and pencil on card, 35.5 x 48.8 cm (14 x 19 in)
State Tretyakov Gallery, Moscow

164. Viktor Vasnetsov
Set Design for Act I of *Snegurochka*, c.1885
Watercolour, gouache and pencil on card
21.2 x 28.3 cm (8 ½ x 11 ¼ in)
State Tretyakov Gallery, Moscow

imagination, much as a 'medieval' artistic vocabulary had been created in Britain. Thus Vasnetsov went on to paint vast canvases inspired by the heroes and beliefs of the ancient Slavs, the visualisation of which stemmed from a largely imagined world.

In 1880, artistic activity at Abramtsevo took a new direction, when the River Vorya flooded and prevented locals from visiting the nearest church. The artists resolved to build an alternative, and began to consider medieval Russian prototypes. Vasnetsov was already familiar with ancient architectural forms in Kiev, where he had been painting the murals of the cathedral of St Vladimir since 1878. Vasily Polenov (1844–1927), the painter son of a respected archaeologist, for his part studied vernacular church design in Novgorod and Pskov. As the vodka bottle replaced the samovar and day turned unnoticed into night, they and other colleagues, wide-eyed with fatigue and adrenaline, fiercely debated how these and other medieval buildings might provide the genesis of a new, national style. After submissions from Polenov and Vasnetsov, the community eventually settled on the latter's brilliantly simple design of a cuboid church with single dome and belfry (fig. 166), inspired by the fourteenth-century Church of the

Saviour on the Nereditsa in the Novgorod region, but also incorporating features from church architecture in Moscow, Yaroslavl, Vladimir and Suzdal. The walls were unpainted, as was common in medieval churches, but outside the artists clambered up scaffolding – 'like real stonemasons,'[6] boasted Vasnetsov – to carve ornaments into the stone. Inside, several artists painted icons for an iconostasis (fig. 167) made to Polenov's design and based on the ancient *tyablyi* type, in which the wood is deeply carved but not pierced; Vasnetsov designed and helped to lay the mosaic floor; and Elizaveta Mamontova and Polenov's sister, Elena Polenova (1850–98), embroidered gonfalons (a sort of ensign) and shrouds to Polenov's designs. The church, which was consecrated in 1888, was an unprecedented collaboration, in which distinctions between the arts were consciously elided to create an organic whole. It also signalled a new approach to the question of national revivalism, with architectural and decorative features researched and integrated more meticulously than had been the case in the work of Gartman and Ropet. Vasnetsov proudly recalled: 'It seemed that the artistic impulse which lay behind the creativity of the Middle Ages and the Renaissance was again hammering in the key.'[7]

163

While the theatrical productions and the church at Abramtsevo explored ways in which art and architecture could be invested with nationalistic meaning, Elizaveta Mamontova was approaching the revival of the vernacular from a different angle. Concerned by the way in which industrialization vitiated craft production, Elizaveta had decided to channel her energies into the promotion of the cottage handicraft activities which in Russia are known as *kustar* crafts. The *kustar* handicrafts (which included both utilitarian objects such as nails and ploughs, and more decorative crafts such as carved wooden goods and lace) were not some gentle hobby in which peasants dabbled on a rainy day: a sixteen-volume report on the state of *kustar* production, published by the Imperial Russian Geographical Society in 1874, revealed that 7.5 million peasants relied on an income from *kustar* industries, particularly in the winter, and that many of these were in serious danger of decline. The threat which the structure of industrial and capitalist working relations posed to the *kustari* (those involved in the *kustar* industries) had already attracted attention in official circles: the *kustar* question was broached at congresses throughout the 1870s; government bodies had launched commissions to monitor *kustar* production; and in 1872 the State Treasury had lent 30,000 roubles to the Pavlovo *kustar* workshops.

Mamontova – a woman whose quiet good sense stood in stark contrast to the extravagant behaviour of her husband – instead chose to tackle the problem in a small and practical way, and in 1876 established workshops to teach local peasant boys the skills of joinery and carpentry on the Abramtsevo estate. Provision for ceramics, embroidery and painted decoration followed. The workshops initially aimed simply to equip the local population with a trade which would offer an alternative to factory employment, but Mamontova soon realized that the crude and clumsy objects they produced were never going to make the workshops commercially viable. She therefore recruited Elena Polenova to supply the workshops with designs, inspired by the peasant artefacts which the Abramtsevo artists had begun to collect (and which would lead to a museum of folk art on the estate). Polenova willingly joined Mamontova's philanthropic crusade, writing after an earlier experience of social work that 'to return to my former life, that is, to deprive myself of working for society in some form or another would be like depriving myself of healthy and nourishing food'.[8] Thus began the extraordinary inversion whereby members of an educated elite taught peasants how to produce variants of folk art

166–7. (opposite) Viktor Vasnetsov
Church of the Saviour Not Made by Hands, Abramtsevo, 1881–2
(above) Iconostasis made to Vasily Polenov's Design
in the Church of the Saviour Not Made by Hands, Abramtsevo, 1881–2

168. Abramtsevo Furniture Workshop
Carved Pine Armchair, late nineteenth century
State Tretyakov Gallery, Moscow

169. Elena Polenova
Column Cupboard, c.1885–90
Painted, carved and gilded birch, 56 x 50 x 23 cm (22 x 19 ¼ x 9 in)
Victoria and Albert Museum, London

which would appeal to a new, urban audience – a distinctly paternalistic arrangement which is undoubtedly the most quirky feature of the Russian Arts and Crafts (fig. 168).

Polenova derived her inspiration from a range of peasant architecture and domestic artefacts, and felt no compunction in disregarding the original context of a design. Her famous column cupboard of 1885 (fig. 169), for example, incorporated forms or ornamentation from objects as diverse as a column, a kitchen shelf and a cart. She was not alone in this indiscriminate transfer of folk patterns and forms from one medium to another: a disgruntled critic in the 1870s had branded current architectural ornamentation as 'marble hand-woven towels and brick embroideries'.[9] Polenova, however, attracted admiration for the way in which she extrapolated a new style from her vernacular source material: many of her designs, often with the geometric, three-faceted chip-carving characteristic of much Abramtsevo work, have entered the pantheon of Russian decorative art. Elizaveta, for her part, secured commercial outlets for the workshops in the Moscow Kustar Museum, which was founded by the Moscow *zemstvo* or district assembly in 1885, and by setting up two of her own shops in

Moscow in 1886 and 1890. The male artists were less involved, though Vasnetsov designed furniture for the Abramtsevo Workshops, and the brilliant young Symbolist artist Mikhail Vrubel (1856–1910) led the ceramics studio on the estate. Working with the chemistry specialist Petr Vaulin, Vrubel reduced the proportion of metal oxide in the composition of a glaze to create iridescent colouration (something which had previously been seen as a flaw), and in work ranging from majolica figures to garden benches pushed the expressive potential of ceramics to new heights. A prime example is his bust of *Tsar Berendei* (fig. 170), modelled on the composer Rimsky-Korsakov. Vrubel also produced fireplaces and tiles for stoves – the stove, a focal point of the Russian home, offering an interesting parallel to the centrality of the inglenook fireplace in Arts and Crafts houses in the West. Sadly Vrubel, plagued by self-doubt and self-harm, suffered a breakdown after the death of his infant son in 1903 and died in a sanatorium seven years later. The Abramtsevo Ceramics Studio (later the Abramtsevo Ceramics Factory) nevertheless went from strength to strength, moving to Moscow in the late 1890s, where it expanded its output to include vast tiled and ceramic panels for architectural facades.

170. Mikhail Vrubel
Ceramic figures (*Tsar Berendei* in centre), after 1903
Majolica, polychromatic painting, restored glazing, Each figure approx. 48.5 x 34.5 x 13.5 cm (19 x 13 1/2 x 5 1/4 in)
State Tretyakov Gallery, Moscow

The success of the Mamontova–Polenova partnership was not to last. Polenova left the workshops to pursue her own creative projects in 1893, whereupon the Abramtsevo craftsmen, lacking her artistic direction and, increasingly, the victims of their own success, began to produce shoddy and repetitive work to meet the growing market for their designs. The workshops nevertheless participated to acclaim in events as prestigious as the Columbian Exhibition in Chicago in 1893 and the Exposition Universelle in Paris in 1900, and the Abramtsevo experiment effected an undeniable reversal in the sagging fortunes of the *kustari*. It inspired the revival of craft industries on other private estates; and it proved that the intervention of fine artists and upper-class patrons could create a viable interface between the demands of a modern, urban consumer and the distinctive nature of the *kustar* crafts.

An unusual characteristic of the *kustar* revival is the dedicated involvement of many noblewomen, who set up workshops in spinning, weaving, embroidery and other forms of needlework in villages and on country estates. While these satisfied a sense of *noblesse oblige*, they were equally a practical response to the devastation caused by famine and fire, or to the problems which the female workforce faced in negotiating their domestic responsibilities, the decline in agricultural employment, and the irregular nature of factory work. There were initiatives in the cities too, such as the Mariinsky Lace School which Sofia Davydova founded in St Petersburg in 1883 to promote traditional women's crafts. The school, whose students were encouraged to disseminate their new skills in their home villages, was funded by the Ministry of Finance and the Ministry of State Domains and boasted Empress Maria Fedorovna as its patron, highlighting the extent to which the Russian craft industries enjoyed state, aristocratic and even imperial support which was inconceivable elsewhere. The Russian Government had initially been slow to make a financial commitment to the *kustar* industries, but from 1888, when the Ministry of State Domains was appointed to look after them, there were many practical expressions of support as official and upper-class patrons alike recognized the *kustar* industries to be vital to the rural economy, and useful mechanisms of nostalgic identification with an identifiably Russian base. Thus the Ministry of Agriculture established the St Petersburg Kustar Museum in 1892; and Grand Duchess Elizaveta Fedorovna

171. Elena Polenova
'Two Sketches for a Dining Room for Maria F Yakunchikova's
Estate of Nara, 1897–8' from *Mir Iskusstva*, 1899

172. Princess Maria Tenisheva
Bird, c.1904
Silver, copper and champlevé enamel
Victor Arwas Collection, London

(sister of the Empress and of the Grand Duke of Hesse) opened a shop for *kustar* goods in Moscow, and acted as patron of both the Moscow Kustar Museum and the Exhibition of Industrial Art and Antiques which was held at the Stroganov School in 1901.

As far as the workshops on country estates are concerned, there was something of a *kustar* revival mafia – a world of friends and relations taking up the *kustar* mantle, and of figures leaving one workshop, only to reappear in another. Thus Mamontov's niece Maria Yakunchikova (1864–1952), who in 1885 had donned one of Vasnetsov's costumes in the title role of *Snegurochka* at Abramtsevo, opened an embroidery workshop on her estate of Solomenko in Tambov province in 1891. Yakunchikova followed Mamontova's example in employing a fine artist, Natalia Davydova (1873–1926), to oversee her embroidery enterprise. Davydova, for her part, emulated Polenova in creating a new repertoire which would appeal to middle-class purchasing power, rather than simply replicating peasant art. As a colleague admiringly recalled: 'In her hands a small fragment of an object made by some anonymous serf master became the point of departure for creating something new and beautiful in line with new demands.'[10] Yakunchikova also employed Polenova (who was a relation by marriage) on various projects, the most important in this context being the dining room of her country house, Nara, outside Moscow, in 1897. Polenova's designs (fig. 171), known from their reproduction in the journal *Mir Iskusstva* (World of Art) in 1899, resonate with stylistic features which accrue to the Arts and Crafts: the sturdy, built-in furniture, the panelled and painted walls, the stylized floral decoration, and the hinges and latches which are integral to the decorative effect. The room included furniture and tiled stoves from the Abramtsevo workshops, embroidered or painted panels from the Solomenko workshop, painted and appliqué panels by Alexander Golovin (1863–1930), and a vast embroidered panneau which Polenova had designed for the Solomenko display at the All-Russian Arts and Industries Exhibition in Nizhny Novgorod in 1896. There is no firm evidence that Polenova was familiar with Voysey and Baillie Scott: rather, the scheme's astonishing resemblance to aspects of the Englishmen's work shouts of the truly international nature of the Arts and Crafts.

The last of the great craft workshops set up by a Russian aristocrat are those which Princess Maria Tenisheva (1858–1928) ran at Talashkino, her estate outside the medieval city of Smolensk. Tenisheva's personal interest was enamelling: she wrote a dissertation on the subject at the Moscow Archaeological Institute, and in her practical work realized the stunning effect which geometric champlevé enamelling in primary colours can have on a copper base (fig. 172). Enamelling apart, Tenisheva was passionate about reviving folk art: in 1894 she founded a peasant school whose curriculum included music, embroidery and design; in 1898 she established a Museum of Russian Antiquities and Folk Art at Talashkino (this eventually numbered about 10,000 objects, and moved to a specially-built museum in Smolensk in 1905); and she set up workshops in carpentry, ceramics, enamelling and embroidery on her estate. Following the now tried-and-tested arrangement of an artist-in-residence, she employed Sergei Malyutin (1859–1937) to direct the carpentry workshop in 1900, and later engaged Ivan Barshchevsky to manage the ceramics studio and curate her folk art collection, and Anna Pogosskaya, an expert on folk embroidery, to run the textile enterprise. Pogosskaya's mother had heard William Morris speak at the first Arts and Crafts Exhibition in London in 1888, which may have inspired the natural dyeing facility that her daughter set up on the estate. The products of all three workshops were both marketed locally and sold in Moscow through Rodnik (The Source), a shop which Tenisheva opened in 1903.

Talashkino proved a honey-pot for many established artists including some, such as Vrubel, who had worked at Abramtsevo, or at other estates involved in the *kustar* revival project. However, it is Malyutin whose name is most closely associated with Talashkino. The furniture which he produced there developed a new stylization of common folk art motifs, such as the sunflower. The studio known as the Teremok which he designed in 1901, on the other hand, derived its essential form from vernacular precedents, but its painted facades, complete with a rainbow-coloured menagerie of seahorses, firebirds (the Talashkino trademark) and grinning serpents supporting the overhang, are entirely atypical of peasant buildings (fig. 173). This architectural caprice was complemented by a church designed by Malyutin and Tenisheva and decorated with a vast mosaic and fresco by the painter Nikolai Roerich (1874–1947), who joined the community at Talashkino after Malyutin left in 1903. Roerich was drawn to the symbolism of Eastern religions, and the interest in traditional craftwork and the iconography of fairy tales and folk art at Talashkino gradually disappeared. The work there thus points to a movement on the cusp, yielding

173. Sergei Malyutin
Teremok, 1901
Talashkino, near Smolensk

174. Sergei Malyutin
Polar Bear Tile on the Teremok, 1901
Talashkino, near Smolensk

175. A Burnovo
Poster for the International Exhibition of Industrial Design in Furniture,
Decorative Work, Furnishings and Fittings, St Petersburg, 1908
88.3 x 57.8 cm (34 3/4 x 22 3/4 in)
Russian National Library, Moscow

to the more avant-garde expression of Art Nouveau, or Style Moderne, as it is known in Russia. But Tenisheva remained a diehard advocate of artistic unity (even overseeing the design of a prayer-book on the estate), and certain elements – the lovely conceit of a single ceramic tile depicting a polar bear on the Teremok (fig. 174), for example – look to the highly personal marriage between different arts which is so typical of the Arts and Crafts.

In the early years of the twentieth century the *kustar* industries went from strength to strength. They in no sense conformed with every aspect of the Arts and Crafts, as is clear from the unexpected history of the *matrioshka* (Russia's famous wooden nesting dolls which fit inside each other as they decrease in size). Far from being an 'authentic' folk toy, the decoration of the *matrioshka* was in fact devised by Malyutin in 1891. Nor was a set of *matrioshka* dolls necessarily produced by just one craftsman. On the contrary, in the renowned toy workshops in Sergiev Posad, an ancient monastic centre near Abramtsevo, a craftsman might spend his every working hour simply painting geese by the dolls' feet. But the successful promotion of *kustar* work against the vacuity of factory production is one of the great triumphs of the Arts and Crafts.

At the first All-Russian Kustar Exhibition in St Petersburg in 1902 a German reviewer could barely contain his delight:

> *In the Tauride halls a genuine popular spirit blows,*
> *strong and healthy like the smell of the earth; an air*
> *that makes the chest expand and the muscles relax.*
> *Here the spontaneous creativity of the people reigns,*
> *here we catch the Russian people working, not in*
> *stuffy city factories that wash away the originality*
> *and the very personality of the worker, but at home*
> *on their own land, under conditions that do not*
> *hamper the free development of native originality*
> *and inventiveness.*[11]

Such unabashed celebration of an artisanal culture inextricably linked to rude good health and national sentiment could read as a manifesto of the Arts and Crafts. Success bred success: from 1904 the Moscow Kustar Museum began to forge trade links abroad and established a shop in Paris called Koustari Russes, and the second All-Russian Kustar Exhibition opened in 1913. There were also exhibitions of domestic design, the poster for the International Exhibition of Industrial Design in Furniture, Decorative Work, Furnishings and Fittings, held in St Petersburg in 1908 under the patronage of Empress Maria Fedorovna, detailing built-in furniture, painted decoration and metalwork on the door which has strong affinities with other Arts and Crafts design (fig. 175). As the twentieth century progressed, however, the *kustar* revival – always the construction of educated outsiders, rather than an organic development – gradually became what Wendy Salmond, the great scholar of the Movement, has termed 'a highly controlled form of souvenir industry'.[12] The visceral creativity which had characterized the approach of Polenova, Davydova and others was gradually elbowed out by repetitive, commercial practice, leading to a decline in the quality and originality of the work. In some senses, though, the *kustar* industry's position at the heart of the Soviet souvenir trade, with its export organization, Sovkustexport, bringing in vital hard currency in the 1920s, can be seen as a sign of the successful transformation of industries once thought obsolescent to meet modern consumer practices both at home and abroad.

While the revival of the *kustar* craft industries created a powerful rural component of the Russian Arts and Crafts, in Moscow the Movement underwent a marked urban phase in media as diverse as architecture and graphic design. Peculiar to

Russia was the elevation of items such as menus and decrees to the status of high art. In 1896, for example, Vasnetsov produced a series of beautifully illuminated menus to mark the interminable feasts which accompanied the coronation of Nicholas II and his wife Alexandra (fig. 176). In these, ornamental headpieces typical of ancient Russian manuscripts integrate with old Slavonic lettering detailing each gastronomic marathon, from partridge soup and steamed sterlet to pheasant in aspic and vanilla ice-cream. With visual signifiers as potent as onion domes, courtiers and peasants in traditional dress, and the double-headed eagle with orb, sceptre and three crowns (the national emblem of Russia), the menus broadcast the political and spiritual authority of the Romanov dynasty, and their embrace of both nobility and *narod*. The same year Vasnetsov produced another seminal graphic design for a plate which, with its iconography of St George killing the dragon – the principal charge on Moscow's coat of arms, highlights his nationalistic sentiment and subtle retrospectivism, imbibing as he did a range of ideas from folklore, icon painting, medieval manuscripts, and heraldic art.

Questions of national identity underpinned developments in Russian architecture as well. In 1867, the foundation of the Moscow Architectural Society had created a new platform for serious academic debate, and the following year its president, Mikhail Bykovsky, argued for 'the erection of buildings which satisfy the contemporary requirements of life, and answer to local climatic conditions with solidity, convenience, hygiene and economy'. Only by accommodating function, climate and site, Bykovsky argued, would Russia acquire a distinct and national architectural style: 'the study of architectural history shows how the original and truly national is that which serves as a complete expression of the way of life and spirit of its own time'.[13] The interest in national tradition was fuelled in 1872 by the publication of Nikolai Shokhin's book *Traditional Russian Buildings*, and by the launch the same year of *Zodchii* (The Architect), the first professional architectural journal in Russia which included a regular column on the country's architectural vernacular. Controversially, the architect and theorist Eugène-Emmanuel Viollet-le-Duc (1814–79) was then invited by Butovsky, the director of the Stroganov School, to voice his opinion on the future direction of Russian architecture. The Frenchman responded by arguing in *L'Art Russe. Ses origins, ses éléments constitutifs, son apogée, son avenir* (1877) that the rational, structural framework of earlier Russian buildings, from ecclesiastical cupolas to Moscow's

176. Viktor Vasnetsov
Menu for the Coronation Banquet of Tsar Nicholas II and Tsaritsa Alexandra Fedorovna, 14 May 1896
Colour lithograph, 93.5 x 32.5 cm (36 1/2 x 12 3/4 in)
Russian National Library, Moscow

177–8. Vladimir Shervud
The State Historical Museum, Moscow, 1875–83, and Detail of a Door (right)

seventeenth-century brick architecture, might serve as the basis of a new, national architectural vocabulary, not least as (in Viollet-le-Duc's rather curious view) these forms were suited to modern materials such as iron. Many Russians disagreed with Viollet-le-Duc's conclusions, and resented the interference of a foreigner whose reputation rested on his historical method, yet who had never set foot on Russian soil. But Viollet-le-Duc's intervention focused minds on what might constitute a national style.[14]

The most interesting building to consider in this respect is the Historical Museum, which Vladimir Shervud (1833–97) constructed from 1875 to 1883 at the north end of Red Square in Moscow (fig. 177). The committee appointed to oversee this project agreed that it should be 'Russian', but found themselves at loggerheads over what precedents such a 'national' style should follow: the twelfth-century cathedrals and palaces of Vladimir and Suzdal (a development resonating with autocratic power, linked as it was to the rise of a unified Russian state); or the distinctive red brick, often with white detailing, which had characterized public architecture in Moscow in the sixteenth and seventeenth centuries. The latter view eventually prevailed on contextual grounds, as the Historical Museum was to stand next to the imposing brick construction of the Kremlin, and opposite St Basil's Cathedral at the other end of Red Square. Shervud complemented these existing buildings by including octagonal towers with tent-shaped roofs inspired by those on the Kremlin, and the stepped, corbelled gables and arched or keel-shaped windows and door surrounds of St Basil's (fig. 178). The architect also adopted the practice typical in old Russian architecture of combining individual units or *kletki* to create a picturesque whole. The Historical Museum's qualifications as an Arts and Crafts building, however, do not rest on its site-specificity alone. The interiors presented an unusual take on truth to function: the plan incorporated two parallel sequences of rooms to reflect the two centres of medieval Rus (Vladimir and Suzdal, and Novgorod and Pskov); and the roofing in individual rooms employed structural devices characteristic of the period whose artefacts they displayed – a vaulted ceiling for the ancient Russian rooms, flat beams for those concerned with the Greek settlements around the Black Sea, and cupola-shaped domes for those which displayed early Christian art.[15]

Over the next twenty years, many new buildings in both Moscow and provincial towns reflected the cultural and ideological concerns which were coursing through the Russian Arts and Crafts. Vasnetsov turned his hand to architecture with éclat with the main entrance and facade which he designed for the gallery housing Pavel Tretyakov's unrivalled collection of Russian art (fig. 179). Tretyakov had donated this to the city of Moscow in 1892, and Vasnetsov's design of 1900, with its proud inscription and towering relief of the Moscow coat of arms, is an overt celebration of his generous act. The cross-stitch of red and white brick, the protrudent door and window surrounds and the lettering of the frieze make it more a page of glorious illumination than a simple facade. Vasnetsov's design incorporated brightly coloured ceramics from the Abramtsevo Ceramics Studio, and other important buildings in late nineteenth- and early twentieth-century Moscow were similarly bedecked with ornamental tiles and majolica panels. Across the river, the Metropol Hotel sported a vast ceramic panel by Vrubel and majolica work by Golovin, and Malyutin incorporated a cornucopia of flowers and ceramic suns on the Dom Pertsova, an apartment block which he and the architect N K Zhukov designed in 1905. In the top-floor

apartment, Malyutin created a series of elaborately carved interiors in which almost every surface dripped with folk motifs, from lions and sunflowers to the mermaids or *rusalki* so popular in peasant dwellings along the River Volga. These and other projects point to one successful resolution of the *kustar* industries' confrontation with modernity, as ceramics and carving were eagerly embraced in large-scale, urban design.

By the dawn of the twentieth century the cultural scene in Russia was shifting, yet the Arts and Crafts continued to develop, albeit in different ways. The journal *Zodchii* published the first known account in Russia of the Garden City ideal in 1904, and Ebenezer Howard's book was translated into Russian in full in 1911, though the Garden City Movement did not elicit any widespread practical response for years. More important was the publication in *Zodchii* of illustrated articles on Voysey, Baillie Scott, Newton and the buildings of the Darmstadt colony, and both *Zodchii* and other periodicals discussed the work of Morris, Ruskin, Mackintosh and the American Henry Hobson Richardson (see Chapter 9) in glowing terms. The use of the vernacular and the integration of the decorative and applied arts by Western designers was particularly admired, and was echoed in some of the

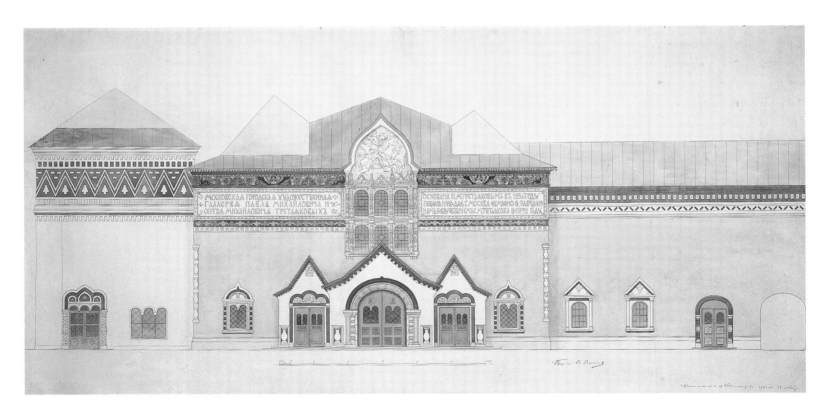

179. Viktor Vasnetsov
Design for Tretyakov Gallery Facade, 1900
Watercolour, pen and India ink on paper, 90.5 x 194 cm (35 1/4 x 75 3/4 in)
State Tretyakov Gallery, Moscow

mansions which were built in and around Moscow and St Petersburg for Russia's entrepreneurs and merchant elite. Some architects, notably V A Simon and Leonid Vesnin in the Nosikov House in the suburbs of Moscow (1909), adhered to the steep roofs, bay windows and other features of Arts and Crafts architecture in the West (fig. 180). Others, such as Roman Meltser, filtered their response through a nationalistic prism in order to invest their work with the vernacular language of Russian and Karelian architecture (Karelia being the region which straddles the Russian–Finnish border: see Chapter 8). The architects of these houses often designed fittings and furnishings too, with Meltser producing lavish work for the imperial family as well as inexpensive furniture for the middle class.

In the fine arts, the most exciting development was the Mir Iskusstva or World of Art group in St Petersburg, which disavowed the inward-looking nativism which had come to characterize Russian painting and instead, under the volcanic leadership of Diaghilev, looked to invigorate Russian art by reconnecting it with that of the West. Tenisheva and Mamontov initially co-financed the *Mir Iskusstva* journal, partly in the hope that the applied arts would feature on a par with

painting, and the first Mir Iskusstva exhibition at the Stieglitz School in 1899 duly included work by Malyutin, embroidery and ceramics from Abramtsevo, Lalique crystal and jewellery, and Tiffany glass. In its early years the *Mir Iskusstva* journal also featured the *kustar* workshops (one issue was devoted to Talashkino), and graphic work by artists such as Polenova and Ivan Bilibin (1876–1942). Polenova's flat, stylized plant forms, Bilibin's inventive use of old Russian typefaces, and the strong decorative talent, folk-tale subjects, and integration of image and text in the work of both artists hit the right associative notes for the Arts and Crafts (Polenova in particular knew and admired the work of Morris and Crane). In 1898, the year that the *Mir Iskusstva* journal was launched, the decorative arts also acquired a very different champion in the form of the periodical *Iskusstvo i khudozhestvennaya promyshlennost* (Art and Industrial Design), which included articles on architecture and folk art and ran competitions to stimulate commercial design, sponsored by applied arts manufacturers such as the Sapozhnikov and Fabergé firms. The stated aim of *Art and Industrial Design* was 'to develop the idea of 'Nationality in Art'.[16] As one editorial declared, 'We have but to cast our eyes over the folk art of the past to be convinced that it is the only sure foundation for the creation of a truly Russian tradition of industrial design.' Such overt nationalism contrasted with the pro-Western *Mir Iskusstva* circle, but both journals nevertheless shared a respect for recent developments in the applied arts, demonstrating the extent to which these were able to cut across political and cultural divides.

Indeed, so multi-layered and versatile was the appeal of the Arts and Crafts Movement in Russia that it shaped the Russian contribution to both the Paris Exposition Universelle in 1900, and the Glasgow International Exhibition in 1901. For the first of these, peasant carpenters from the *kustar* workshops at Sergiev Posad built an entire Russian village to the designs of Konstantin Korovin (1861–1939) and Golovin, both of whom were habitués of the Mamontov circle. Within the Russian village a Kustar Pavilion, organized by Yakunchikova and under the patronage of Grand Duchess Elizaveta Fedorovna, displayed Tenisheva's balalaikas alongside a range of work from Abramtsevo, Solomenko and other workshops, and won a crop of medals and awards. The following year, nearly 200 craftsmen from the Stroganov School were shipped over to Glasgow at enormous expense to construct a series of polychrome pavilions designed by Fedor Shekhtel (1859–1926). In Moscow, Shekhtel would reign as the architect supreme of Style Moderne, producing

180. V A Simon and Leonid Vesnin
Nosikov House, Moscow, 1909, from *Ezhegodnik Moskovskogo arkhitekturnogo obshchestva*, 1910–11

eloquent statements of ascendant bourgeois aspirations in projects such as the Ryabushinsky Mansion and the Derozhinskaya House, both of which pulsate with the rhythmic undulations of Art Nouveau. Shekhtel's pavilions in Glasgow, however, are purely Arts and Crafts (fig. 181). The main pavilion, drawing on both the famous twenty-two-domed wooden church in Kizhi and the columnar, hipped-roof churches of the Russian North, rang with national specificity, while the employment of trained Russian craftsmen broadcast the successful revival of their skills to an outside world.[17] As the twentieth century progressed, cultural, political and ideological tensions would propel Russian artists in new directions, from the aesthetics of mass production to the explosive innovation of the Russian avant-garde. The success of the Russian pavilions in Paris and Glasgow nevertheless testifies that the ideas and approaches first juggled by the Abramtsevo stable of artists a quarter of a century earlier had led to something which was seen as identifiably Russian, and promoted as such in the most prominent arena abroad.

181. Fedor Shekhtel
Russian Pavilions at the Glasgow International Exhibition, 1901
Phototype taken from a photograph, 20 x 30 cm (8 x 12 in)
A V Shchusev State Museum of Architecture, Moscow

Gunnar Gunnarson Wennerberg
Textile, late-nineteenth century (fig. 205)

NORDIC IDENTITIES: SCANDINAVIA AND FINLAND

IN THE LATE NINETEENTH CENTURY, THE FOUR COUNTRIES WHICH TODAY FORM SCANDINAVIA AND FINLAND DIFFERED WIDELY IN THEIR MEANS OF ADMINISTRATION, CREATING CULTURAL AND POLITICAL ATTITUDES WHICH PLAYED A SIGNIFICANT ROLE IN THE DEVELOPMENT OF THE ARTS AND CRAFTS.

Sweden, while no longer the superpower she had been in the seventeenth and eighteenth centuries, was an autonomous nation. Norway, in contrast, was wriggling uncomfortably in the Union she had formed with Sweden in 1814, which gave Sweden control over foreign policy and a veto on Norwegian constitutional legislation. Norway eventually dissolved the Union in 1905, becoming fully independent for the first time since 1384. Finland, like Norway, was also bound to a larger, more bullish neighbour, having been a Grand Duchy of Russia since 1809. While this was initially welcomed by most Finns (their autonomy as a Grand Duchy being preferable to the Swedish rule which had preceded it), as the century progressed they became irked by Russia's attempts to curtail their rights and draw Finland into the Slavic fold. Denmark, for her part, had plummeted in international prestige after the Napoleonic Wars and was now smaller than she had been for centuries, having relinquished Norway to Sweden in 1814, and Schleswig-Holstein to Germany in 1864. Political tussles between Left and Right followed, until the country elected her first truly democratic parliament in 1901.

This brief outline points to a diversity of allegiances and anxieties across the region. What the political and territorial manoeuvring had created, though, was a common concern with how both national and regional identities might be constructed and defined. In the arts, this led to a vibrant National Romantic Movement, which in Scandinavia and Finland is often referred to as Art Nouveau, or as the Jugend style. But a vast spectrum of practice is subsumed under the National Romantic rubric, within which a clear subset of ideas, objects and buildings sits most comfortably under the banner of the Arts and Crafts. Still largely agrarian (just fourteen per cent of the Finnish population was urban at the outbreak of the First World War), the Nordic countries witnessed nothing like the tension with industry which stimulated the Arts and Crafts Movement in other parts of Europe and the United States. Rather, they shared its interest in indigenous traditions; the drive for simplicity and comfort in domestic buildings; an emphasis on function and site; and concern for the role of the craftsman. Overriding it all was the desire to define a modern design aesthetic. Thus we find progressive, internationalist debates grafted on to National Romantic concerns, giving the Arts and Crafts Movement in Northern Europe a decidedly Modernist edge.

Finland, so long a pawn between Sweden and Russia, presented an unusual arena for the development of the Arts and Crafts. She had an exciting new capital city, Helsinki having replaced Turku (the capital when Finland had been under Swedish rule) in 1812. She had her own civil service and Senate, with Russian intervention limited to the appointment of a Governor General to chair the Senate, and a Finnish Secretary of State to report to the Tsar on Finnish affairs. Finland's position as an autonomous Grand Duchy also allowed for social, educational and economic improvement, including the first Finnish stamps in 1856, the first publication of doctoral theses in Finnish in 1858, and an official Finnish currency in 1860. Russia initially encouraged Finland's expressions of self-assertion, trusting these to further the region's alienation from Sweden. Thus in 1863 the Russian authorities recognized Finnish, the demotic tongue, as an official language alongside Swedish, which had long been the language of the upper classes and the administration. The literary credibility of Finnish had been greatly enhanced in 1835, when Elias Lönnrot (1802–84), who would later hold a university chair of Finnish language and literature, compiled *The Kalevala*, a series of tales based on the tradition of oral poetry in the eastern province of Karelia. While Lönnrot inevitably changed the nature of the narratives by writing them down, he provided the Fennomane (Finnish-speaking) movement with a national epic, and with a Finnish mythological imagery which would inspire artists, writers and nationalists for years.

Over the following decades, the concern with constructing Finnish traditions which had appeared in literature spread to the visual arts. In 1846, the Finnish Art Society was founded to inform public taste and to educate the nation's artists, opening Finland's first official art school in 1848; and in the 1870s a number of organizations began to promote the applied arts. These included the Central School of Applied Arts (Veistokoulu), founded in 1871; the Finnish Museum of Art and Design (Taideteollisuusmuseo, now the Designmuseo), dating from 1873; the Finnish Society of Crafts and Design (Suomen Taideteollisuusyhdistys) which appeared in 1875; and the Friends of Finnish Handicraft (Suomen Käsityön Ystävät) which the painter Fanny Churberg (1845–92) and others established in 1879 to preserve and revive Finnish craft skills, and foster good design. The Friends initially specialized in textiles but soon broadened their remit to include metalwork, furniture, and interior design. They also

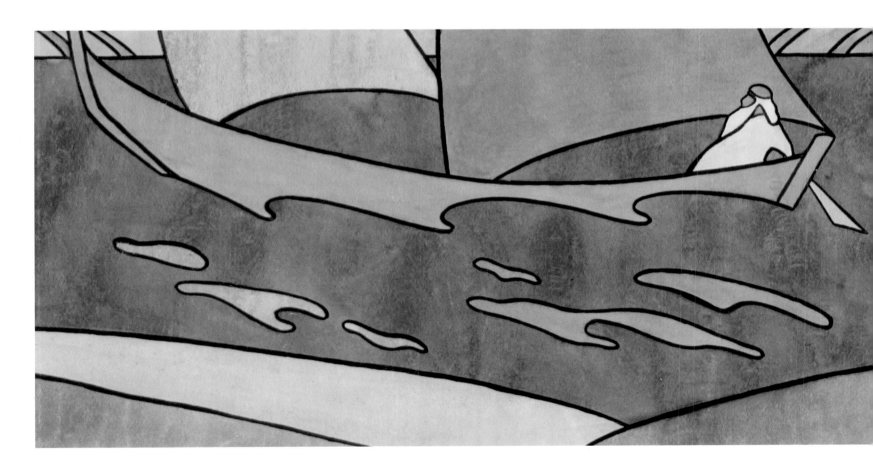

ran exhibitions and competitions which enticed the vanguard of Finland's architects and artists to contribute designs, for which the society retained exclusive rights. These included simple, homely pieces such as Aili Tallgren's linen tea-cosy of 1904–9 in which a solemn, button-nosed girl carries a steaming bowl of soup (fig. 182), and Germund Paaer's sketch for a tapestry of c.1910, which appealed to the national psyche by depicting activities as popular as boating and sledging (fig. 183). The Friends of Finnish Handicraft also spearheaded the revival of *ryijy* rugs, the hand-knotted affairs that peasants in Finland and Sweden had used as covers in beds, boats and sleighs, but which were now recast as floor and wall adornments. Particularly striking is Jarl Eklund's *Seagull ryijy* of 1905 (fig. 184), in which a halo of seagulls hovers neatly over the crest of a breaking wave.

Two key figures who designed for the Friends were Count Louis Sparre (1863–1964) and his wife, Eva Mannerheim-Sparre (1870–1957). Sparre was Swedish, and in his youth had shown little interest in the Finnish lands to the east of his homeland. However, while studying in Paris he befriended Axel Gallén (1865–1931), the great Finnish painter who later changed his Swedish name into the more Finnish-

182. Aili Tallgren
Tea-cosy, 1904–9
Embroidered linen
38.5 x 35 cm (15 x 13 ³/₄ in)
Designmuseo, Helsinki

183. Germund Paaer
Sketch for a Tapestry, c.1910
Watercolour on paper
32 x 88 cm (12 ¹/₂ x 34 ¹/₂ in)
Designmuseo, Helsinki

184. Jarl Eklund
Seagull Ryijy, designed 1905–9, made 1914
Tapestry wool, 366 x 204 cm (144 x 81 in)
Designmuseo, Helsinki

185. (opposite) Eva Mannerheim-Sparre
Album, *c.*1900
Cream leather, with metal clasps decorated with heart shapes
32.5 x 28.5 cm (14 x 11 ¼ in)
National Museum of Finland, Helsinki

sounding Akseli Gallen-Kallela. The latter invited Sparre to visit Finland in 1889, and Sparre was so enraptured that he moved there in 1891. Eva Mannerheim-Sparre, for her part, studied wood-carving and leatherwork at the Stockholm Technical School, and was then employed as a leatherwork instructor at Helsinki's Central School of Applied Arts. Her speciality of bookbinding is exemplified in an album of *c.*1900 (fig. 185), its creamy leather embossed with the flimsiest of gold stems and its pages held together by heart-shaped clasps.

Both Eva and her husband were interested in modern European design, and studied this closely during a tour of Europe in 1896. In Paris, they took part in a prominent exhibition of modern bookbinding in Bing's galleries, and met Julius Meier-Graefe who, as editor of the magazine *Pan* and a prolific writer, was a key commentator on contemporary art. In Britain, they met Charles Holme, founder of *The Studio* and owner of Morris's Red House, which he invited the Sparres to visit. The couple returned to Finland enthused with the spirit of the Arts and Crafts, and in 1897 set up the Iris Workshops in Porvoo to produce furniture, household goods and made-to-order interiors constructed to the highest standards and exhibiting the latest trends in domestic design. Alfred William Finch (see Chapter 5) was persuaded to move from Brussels to Porvoo to head a ceramics department, and while he perfected his glazes and simple, incised patterns (fig. 186), the Sparres focused on good, solid furniture, such as Louis's waxed ash armchair which Eva decorated with leather inlay (fig. 187). Cross-cultural exchange was central to their endeavours. Sparre was the Finnish agent for Liberty's, from whom he imported upholstery fabrics, and the Iris showroom in Helsinki included work from the Vereinigte Werkstätten in Munich, Tiffany lamps, and Benson's brass and copperware. At the same time, Finch reported on British art in *Ateneum* (Finland's first colour-illustrated art journal, founded in 1898), and Sparre disseminated the latest in Finnish art and design as the Finland correspondent for *The Studio* and *Pan*.

The Iris Workshops were initially a success, partly because of Sparre's judicious decision to base them in Porvoo, a cabinet-making centre which could supply the skilled labour required by the workshops. While Sparre was content to keep the enterprise small, his financial backers (a group of wealthy young industrialists) were anxious to expand, and in 1898 the workshops moved into a purpose-built three-storey factory which boasted Porvoo's first mechanical lift. Sparre fell out with his profit-hungry shareholders, resigning as creative director of the Iris Workshops in 1900, and the factory went bankrupt in

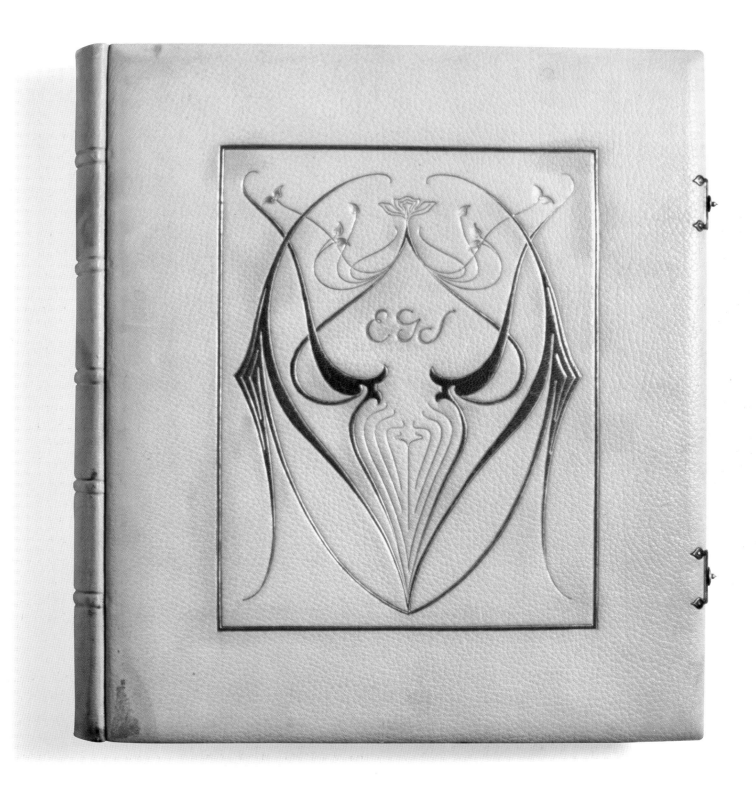

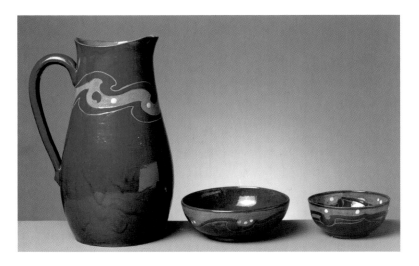

186. Alfred William Finch
Pitcher and Bowls, 1897–1902
Ceramic, pitcher 35 x 18 cm (14 x 7 in)
Designmuseo, Helsinki

187. Louis Sparre and Eva Mannerheim-Sparre
Armchair, 1903
Waxed ash, with inlaid leather decoration and new broadcloth cover
similar to original fabric woven in France
Private collection

1902. Finch went on to work as the first ceramics teacher at the Central School of Applied Arts, and the Sparres bounced back with the Eva & Louis Sparre Design Bureau, whose products are often referred to as Iris work. With enviable energy and rude good health (Louis lived to the age of 101), the couple extended their repertoire to include book illustration, embroidery, weaving and metalwork. Sparre's patinated copper ceiling light of 1905, with its stylish construction of hooks and rings and its ingenious arrangement of light bulbs inside the circular drum (figs 188–9), exemplifies their continuing desire to create a modern design aesthetic, and other craftsmen shared their approach. Valle Rosenberg's compot bowl of 1911 (fig. 190) is a case in point, its elegant form and stylized apples and pears on the handle of the spoon and at the top of the paired legs echoing the skilful understatement of Ashbee's designs.

The Friends of Finnish Handicraft and the Iris Workshops both made efforts to establish a Finnish style: the former's intention was 'to promote Finnish handicrafts and to refine them in a patriotic and artistic direction', and it and other applied art manufactures (the Nuutajärvi glass factory, for example) ran competitions for 'Finnish' designs. Towards the end of the century Gallen-Kallela and the composer Jean

Sibelius were similarly credited with initiating a national idiom in their respective arts. Architecture, however, was thought not yet to have pulled its weight in the construction of a national culture, a concern which by the 1890s recurred in both the professional and the popular press. The architect Vilho Penttilä, for example, published several articles in *Suomen Teollisuuslehti* (The Industrial Magazine of Finland) in 1893–4 which considered the potential of Finnish wooden building traditions, and lambasted the deficiencies of modern design. 'The principle that the exterior should always reflect the inner construction, and at the same time it should never try to hide the special character of the material used, too often remains unobserved,' Penttilä thundered. The question of what constituted 'Finnishness' in architecture was contentious, not least as Finland could not lay claim to any obvious historical precedent. The country boasted some splendid castles, but these had likely as not been built by Swedes, denying Finnish architects the native medieval example which had so captivated Arts and Crafts architects elsewhere.

In search of national models, a number of artists and architects began to travel to Karelia, where the roots of Finnish culture were supposed to lie. The Sparres made their

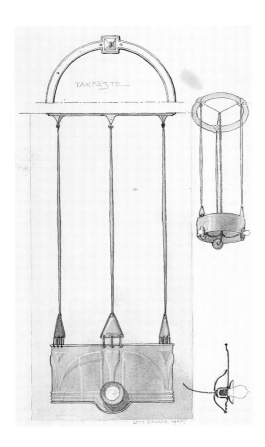

190. Valle Rosenberg
Silver Compot Bowl, 1911
24 cm (9 ¹/₂ in) height
Designmuseo, Helsinki

188–9. Louis Sparre
Sketch for a Ceiling Light and Ceiling Light, 1905
(Sketch) India ink and watercolour on paper, 34.5 x 21.5 cm (13 ¹/₂ x 8 ¹/₂ in)
(Light) Patinated copper, 127 cm (50 in) height
Porvoo Museum, Finland

191. Herman Gesellius, Armas Lindgren and Eliel Saarinen
The Finnish Pavilion at the Exposition Universelle, Paris, 1900

first trip to the region with Gallen-Kallela in 1890. Four years later, the architects Yrjö Blomstedt, Victor Sucksdorff and Lars Sonck (who later withdrew) applied for a grant from the Finnish Antiquarian Society to study Karelian architecture and published their findings as a book of photographs and drawings of buildings in 1900, followed by a volume of text in 1901. In the perceived absence of an ancient architectural heritage, Karelia, whose peasant values had been untouched by industrialization, was embraced as the last remaining depository of a wooden vernacular architecture which might stimulate a new, national style. Karelian motifs duly appeared in furniture design and in wooden architecture – Sonck's log houses, for example, or Blomstedt and Sucksdorff's villas and towers – but no serious attempt was made to develop the style in stone buildings, and Karelianism in architecture dwindled as the nineteenth century drew to a close. Instead, the year 1900 brought a new and more workable model for a national style of architecture, in the Finnish Pavilion which the brilliant young partnership of Gesellius, Lindgren and Saarinen designed for the Exposition Universelle in Paris – the same venue which provided such a showcase for the Russian Arts and Crafts.

The story of the Finnish Pavilion made headlines. The very fact that Finland had been granted permission to construct her own pavilion was unusual, as she was a territory of Russia, and not an independent state. While the pavilion was officially designated 'Section Russe, Pavillon Finlandais',[2] Finland's coat of arms took pride of place above the main door and, cheekily, visual references to Russia – the Romanov coat of arms on the tower, for example – were retouched out of many official photographs. Coming hot on the heels of the February Manifesto of 1899, when Tsar Nicholas II had left the Finns fearful for their autonomy by replacing both Finnish and Swedish with Russian as the only official language and increasing the centralization of Finnish affairs, the nationalistic message of the pavilion was unmistakable.

The three men who designed this most ideologically charged of buildings, Herman Gesellius (1874–1916), Armas Lindgren (1874–1929) and Eliel Saarinen (1873–1950), had formed their architectural partnership in 1896, a year before graduating from the Helsinki Polytechnic Institute (the alma mater of most Finnish architects at the time). They won the commission to design the pavilion in 1898, and responded with what is now considered a keystone of National Romantic architecture (fig. 191). The building was cruciform in plan and semicircular at one end, echoing the layout of a medieval cathedral. This

192. Herman Gesellius, Armas Lindgren and Eliel Saarinen
East Facade of the National Museum of Finland, Helsinki, 1904
National Museum of Finland, Helsinki

193. Herman Gesellius, Armas Lindgren and Eliel Saarinen
South Facade of the Suur-Merijoki Manor House, 1902
Watercolour on board, 64 x 104 cm (25 x 40 ¹/₂ in)
Museum of Finnish Architecture, Helsinki

impression was enforced by the tower, and by the Gothic vault which soared over the crossing and the nave. But the medieval tone was given a specifically Finnish modulation by the steep shingle roof and lantern, both features of Finland's old church architecture, and by a system of ornamentation saturated with Finnish references. Sculpted bears were in abundance, at the base of the tower and in a frieze around the door, and both the architecture and the display stands inside were decorated with foxes, squirrels, pine cones and floral motifs. Gallen-Kallela painted the crossing vault with scenes from *The Kalevala* (one of which featured a snake who, in an outrageous jibe, was depicted wearing the imperial Russian crown), and an entire room was given to a display of Iris work which included Finch's ceramics and Gallen-Kallela's *Flame* rug. While acknowledging international developments in architecture, the result was a proud advertisement for the innovation of modern Finnish design. Indeed, Saarinen had been encouraged to move away from certain European trends by Gallen-Kallela who exhorted him to 'simplify and simplify and throw those sweet arabesques and mawkish [forms] copied from *The Studio* to hell'.[3] Gallen-Kallela was far from antagonistic towards European design: he had studied in Paris and London and, like many Finnish artists,

was an avid reader of *The Studio*. Nevertheless, his advice to Saarinen reveals the strength of feeling behind the desire to create a Finnish style.

The pavilion struck a chord not only with Finnish nationalists, but also with foreign observers who viewed Russia's circumscription of Finland's political liberties with concern. It received wide coverage in the international press, and its architects went on to win many prestigious commissions. These included the National Museum (first design 1901, revised design 1904; fig. 192), a wondrous hybrid which, like the Historical Museum in Moscow, rejected the idea that a museum should look like a palace, and instead tailored its spaces to suit the different collections on display. The building's tower, its vertiginous gothic roofs, and the crowd of crenellations, turrets, and door and window openings make references to Olavinlinna Castle and other medieval buildings in Finland. There are also startlingly modern touches, such as the way in which the squared insets of coffered ceilings reappear in wall friezes and under flights of stairs in a manner reminiscent of Hoffmann and Mackintosh, and the cutaway openings which offer bird's-eye views into the domed entrance hall. (Gallen-Kallela here reluctantly repeated the frescos he

194. (opposite) Herman Gesellius, Armas Lindgren and Eliel Saarinen
Library of the Suur-Merijoki Manor House, 1903
Watercolour and ink on paper, 46 x 66.5 cm (18 x 26 1/4 in)
Museum of Finnish Architecture, Helsinki

195. Herman Gesellius, Armas Lindgren and Eliel Saarinen
Great Hall of the Suur-Merijoki Manor House, 1902
Watercolour and ink on card, 48.5 x 45.5 cm (19 x 18 in)
Museum of Finnish Architecture, Helsinki

had painted for the Paris pavilion, muttering darkly that any work of art was one of a kind.) Outside, slate and copper roofs and brick and soapstone details are anchored on a massive granite base, granite being native to Finland and increasingly popular in National Romantic architecture. Its use was inspired by some of Henry Hobson Richardson's work in the United States (see Chapter 9), and resourceful Finnish architects even studied granite-working techniques in the Scottish city of Aberdeen.[4]

The National Museum exemplifies National Romantic architecture in Finland: it is adventurous, athletic architecture, often with soaring roofs, a reassuring granite base and, in between, varied masses which carry the political valence of the vernacular by using native materials and architectural conceits. In domestic architecture, the style reached its acme in houses such as Suur-Merijoki, which Gesellius, Lindgren and Saarinen built outside Vyborg for a wealthy factory owner from 1901 to 1903. Like the National Museum, the manor house stands on a granite base, above which the white walls, steeply pitched roof and other details vividly recall Voysey's work (fig. 193). One can imagine the tiny Englishman, with his firm views on doors (see p. 93), approving of that at Suur-Merijoki, which shouts a

welcome from under its massive stone arch. The house was damaged in the Second World War and subsequently dismantled, but we know of the interiors as, inspired by Baillie Scott's paintings in *The Studio*, Gesellius, Lindgren and Saarinen produced superb watercolours documenting individual rooms in the house (figs 194–5). These featured painted inglenooks and ceiling ribs; flamboyant furniture from Sparre's workshops; decorative light fittings and banded hinges; and fabrics and furnishings which kept the Friends of Finnish Handicraft busy for months.

Most famous of all is Hvitträsk, the house which Gesellius, Lindgren and Saarinen built for themselves in the still idyllic setting of Lake Vitträsk, following the quest for communal working practices in a congenial setting which is so typical of the Arts and Crafts. Each architect designed his own living quarters (of which only Saarinen's has survived in its original form), and those of Lindgren and Saarinen were then linked by a single-storey, skylit studio (fig. 196). This main building, constructed in the local materials of granite, logs, roughcast and shingle, cleaves to the lakeside ridge much as Shaw's Cragside seems an organic part of its similarly steep, wooded site (fig. 197). Of particular effect is the way in which the irregular granite blocks gradually thin out to suggest that the building grows out of the rock. Doors with vast, spiralling wrought-iron hinges lead into mysterious storage spaces under the raised lawn, while lozenge-shaped shingles make the columns on the balconies resemble the feathered legs of a giant bird. Inside, the coloured walls and exposed beams of Saarinen's voluminous living room (a space inspired by Karelian farmhouses) offset a wealth of custom-made furnishings, including Saarinen's oak settle of 1905–6, and the splendid cartwheel chandelier which his wife Louise (Loja) designed in 1903 (fig. 198). A version of Gallen-Kallela's *Flame* rug (a gift from the artist) acts simultaneously as wall, sofa and floor covering, while opposite it a vast brick kiln curves round to the fireplace (there are no fewer than twelve fireplaces and tiled ovens in the house).

In the dining room next door the ceiling – decorated by Väinö Blomstedt, a regular designer for the Friends of Finnish Handicraft – plunges to create a more intimate space which is rich in references to life at Hvitträsk (fig. 199). Eliel and Loja Saarinen included vignettes of family activities in the rug in this room. Eliel Saarinen depicted the tower which formed part of Gesellius's pavilion in the dining room sconces

(the tower reappears in the rug and the furniture, and became the emblem of the house). Most irreverently, Olga Gummerus-Ehrström referred in her stained-glass window to the drama which unfolded when Gesellius fell in love with and married Saarinen's wife Mathilda, whereupon Saarinen married Gesellius's sister Loja instead (fig. 200). Many of the creators of this supreme *Gesamtkunstwerk* went on to share the skills and ideas which they had developed there, Lindgren as artistic director at the Central School of Applied Arts. Lindgren's responsibilities were such that he moved back to Helsinki in 1905, and Gesellius took a back seat at Hvitträsk as his health deteriorated, but Saarinen and his family kept the house as a summer residence long after he – and his son Eero – were forging impressive careers as architects in the United States.

Hvitträsk was joined by many other 'wilderness studios' in the National Romantic style. Gallen-Kallela even built two. That at Tarvaspää on the Gulf of Finland (1911–13) offers a lesson in Ruskinian 'changefulness', with a vast two-storey studio (a regular feature in these artists' houses), a single-storey arcade, and a castellated, decahedronal tower. Inside, a spiral staircase leads to an Escher puzzle of rooms and terraces on different levels, the most enviable of which is

196. Herman Gesellius, Armas Lindgren and Eliel Saarinen
Elevation Drawing of the Lateral Facade of Hvitträsk, 1901–3
Watercolour and ink on board, 56 x 133 cm (22 x 52 in)
Museum of Finnish Architecture, Helsinki

197. Herman Gesellius, Armas Lindgren and Eliel Saarinen
Hvitträsk, Lake Vitträsk, 1901–3

198. Living room at Hvitträsk, 1901–3

199. Dining Room at Hvitträsk, 1901–3

200. Olga Gummerus-Ehrström
Stained-Glass Window, Hvitträsk, 1901–3

201. (opposite) Lars Sonck
West Facade of St John Cathedral, Tampere, 1901
Watercolour, pencil, ink on paper, 137 x 109 cm (54 x 43 in)
Federation of Tampere Evangelical Lutheran Parishes

202. August Malmström
Oak 'Dragon' Chair designed for Axel Key's Villa Bråvalla, c.1870
Nordic Museum, Stockholm

the bathroom in which a cutaway wall by the bath gives views into the studio downstairs. National Romanticism also informed ecclesiastical architecture in Finland, most notably the church (later the cathedral) of St John by Lars Sonck (1870–1956) in the growing industrial city of Tampere (designed 1897, built 1902–7; fig. 201). Sonck made a virtuoso display of the different uses of granite, from the vast boulders at the base of the walls to the smaller, neater blocks above, and craftsmen complemented this with superlative carving – the whimsical birds by the main entrance, for example – in a partnership which owes much to the ethos of the Arts and Crafts. The interior of the cathedral, however, is very different in mood, with Symbolist frescos by Hugo Simberg (1873–1917) reminding us of the diversity of style which coexisted in Finland at the time. By the early twentieth century both architects and designers were moving away from Arts and Crafts practices to experiment with new ideas. This is most apparent in the project to build a new railway station in Helsinki. Saarinen, working solo, won this competition in 1904 with a design which, like the National Museum, Hvitträsk and other National Romantic buildings, placed emphasis on the use of natural stone and on stylized castle motifs. However, following criticism from others in the profession who felt that a building as functional as a station needed to be overtly 'modern', Saarinen revised his design to produce a geometric monolith. The picturesque masses, vernacular references and high-quality craftsmanship of the Arts and Crafts Movement had been firmly dismissed.

The scale and inventiveness of Arts and Crafts developments in Finland surpassed those in Scandinavia, but Denmark, Norway and Sweden nevertheless made distinctive contributions to the Movement. In Denmark, there was a move away from the bland uniformity of urban housing: instead, bays and balconies gave honest expression to interior plans so that houses or apartment blocks differed from their neighbours, their asymmetrical facades arranged along winding streets to recall the picturesque informality of medieval towns. Most importantly, Martin Nyrop (1849–1921) and others rejected the classical style in public building and instead revived the use of unadorned brick, which had been Denmark's main building material for centuries, in projects such as Copenhagen's Town Hall (1892–1905). This included such National Romantic elements as medieval battlements, pinnacled turrets and a pitched roof, while its sculptural decoration, mosaics and tiles drew on Norse mythology, Danish history, and the country's flora and fauna. It was also decorated with tapestries produced

203. Gerhard Munthe
Design for *The Suitors* tapestry, 1897

by a workshop housed in the building itself (one of three new tapestry workshops in early-twentieth-century Copenhagen which used traditional techniques to produce ambitious, patriotic designs). With such local focus, the Town Hall could be seen as a repository of national memory, drawing on the 'Lamp of Memory' which Ruskin had developed in *The Seven Lamps of Architecture* almost half a century before. Later, P V Jensen-Klint developed the Danish brick-building tradition even further in the Grundtvig Church and surrounding housing which he built in Copenhagen from 1921. While the church presented a monumental, abstracted version of the stepped gables typical of Danish village churches, the single-family housing around it, built, like the church, in yellow brick, echoed the intimacy and individualism of the Garden City ideal.

While Nyrop and Jensen-Klint's designs were local to Denmark, a popular development across Scandinavia was the Viking Revival (also known as the Norse Revival or the Dragon style), which drew on old Norwegian architecture and on the mythology and decoration of the Viking period, driven by the excitement which surrounded the recent excavation of Viking ships. The style's most dedicated patrons were the two Swedish doctors Professor Carl Curman and

Professor Axel Key, who in the early 1870s commissioned summer villas, in the coastal resort of Lysekil and in the inner Stockholm archipelago respectively, in which their passion for Viking imagery knew no bounds. The eminent doctors' furniture was carved with Viking motifs and dragons' heads, designed by August Malmström and made by the joiner Carl Johan Ekelund (fig. 202). The plates off which they ate, specially commissioned from the Gustavsberg porcelain factory, bore a dragon motif. The white damask linen had a dragon pattern woven by the Almedahl linen factory. Curman even had a Viking ship in his garden, and liked his guests to don Viking dress. The two houses became a *cause célèbre*, and the Viking Revival maintained its popularity into the 1880s in Sweden and Denmark and even later in Norway, where it was used for the Norwegian pavilions at international exhibitions, for sanatoriums and for the hotels which were built to cater for the budding tourist industry. The style's unmistakably Nordic message clearly appealed to nations whose changing situation *vis-à-vis* their neighbouring countries had prompted a new appreciation of the glorious Viking past.

The Viking Revival was just one manifestation of a growing interest in indigenous traditions and industries.

204. Gerhard Munthe
A Corner of the Dining Room from
The Artist's Home at Lysaker, after late 1890s
Watercolour over graphite on paper,
35.9 x 43.8 cm (14 x 17 ¼ in)
National Gallery, Oslo

From the 1870s museums were established across Scandinavia to display these, starting with the Nordic Museum which the linguist Artur Hazelius (1833–1901) founded in Stockholm in 1873. Hazelius's project whipped up huge popular support, with Swedes the length of the country staging fund-raising events and acting as local agents to help him assemble a representative collection of Sweden's material culture. It was followed by Skansen, the open-air architectural museum which Hazelius established just down the road from the Nordic Museum in 1891, and by open-air museums and collections of applied and folk art in Denmark and Norway, all of which aimed not only to categorize and display, but to preserve the surviving remnants of a threatened rural past.

Other initiatives were more concerned with encouraging the actual practice of the applied arts. In Denmark, the Folk High Schools inspired by Nicolai Frederik Severin Grundtvig (1783–1872), a historian, writer, and passionate advocate of lifelong learning, included tuition in the arts and crafts (the schools numbered eighty-three by 1914, and still exist today). In Norway, there were wood-carving schools and, from 1891, the Norwegian Society for Home Crafts (Den norske Husflidsforening), which aimed to

provide training in craft skills, and to project cottage industries as a qualifying force in national design. Tapestry enjoyed a particularly vigorous revival in Norway thanks to the painter Gerhard Munthe (1849–1929) and the designer Frida Hansen (1855–1931), both of whom trawled Norse mythology and folk tales to find subjects for their designs. Hansen founded a tapestry weaving studio in the 1890s and devised a method which enabled her to leave areas of the warp bare, to set off the vibrant floral designs of the woven areas. Munthe, for his part, was inspired by his collection of old Norwegian tapestries to create forceful, stylized designs which were soon hailed as the genesis of a new, national style. There is certainly something modern in the flattening and abstraction of *The Suitors* (fig. 203), with its crazed maidens and snuffling bears. Both Munthe and Hansen won gold medals at the Exposition Universelle in Paris in 1900 (which included *The Suitors*), but it was the marriage of the national and the modern in Munthe's work which Norwegian critics most admired. Munthe had by this time moved with other artists to an area around Lysaker, west of Kristiania (now Oslo), where he painted his house in colours inspired by the polychromy of farmers' homes, and decorated it with furniture, textiles and ceramics which he had gathered during his travels in the Norwegian hinterland (fig. 204). This commitment to the regeneration of folk culture, coupled with Munthe's undoubted modernity as an artist, confirmed the role of native decorative traditions in the formation of a modern Norwegian aesthetic.

In Sweden, a Society of Crafts and Design (Svenska Slöjdföreningen) had been founded as early as 1845, running a programme of courses, exhibitions, and publications on subjects as varied as basketry and welding. It was joined in its mission of encouraging good design by the Association of Friends of Textile Art (Föreningen för Handarbetets Vänner) in 1874, and the Association of Swedish Handicrafts (Föreningen för Svensk Hemslöjd) in 1899. The Friends of Textile Art invited peasant women to teach weaving to its largely middle-class members, hoping to revive these and other textile skills, and to enable their practitioners to make an independent living. The Association of Swedish Handicrafts, for its part, was set up under the patronage of Prince Eugen (the unorthodox young royal who defied court protocol to become a painter) to promote the collection and production of traditional Swedish crafts. Both organizations inspired new standards in craftsmanship; for example, in the textile which Gunnar Gunnarson Wennerberg (1863–1914) produced for the Friends of Textile Art (fig. 205). Here, he used a combination of appliqué and different embroidery stitches to capture the contrasting textures of the tendrils, berries and leaves. The work of the Friends of Textile Art clearly appealed to those concerned with the construction of a national culture, as it was exhibited at the Exposition Universelle of 1900. At the same time the group was invited to sell textiles through Samuel Bing's shop in Paris, revealing that observers of design trends abroad also held its work in high regard.

By the turn of the century, the ideals of the British Arts and Crafts Movement were familiar in Swedish artistic circles. Gustaf Steffen, a scientist and social commentator who had worked as a foreign correspondent in London, published the first detailed account in Swedish of Ruskin's aesthetic and social views in 1888, and in 1897 Ruskin's work began to be translated into Swedish. Steffen, who was acquainted with May Morris, also wrote on William Morris, describing in detail his workshops, fabrics, wallpapers, and the furnishings of Kelmscott House. In the 1890s, as Swedish craftsmen and architects travelled to London with increasing frequency, further articles on Morris, De Morgan and other British Arts and Crafts designers appeared in publications such as *Svenska Slöjdföreningens Meddelanden* (The Review of the Swedish Society

205. Gunnar Gunnarson Wennerberg
Textile, late-nineteenth century
Nordic Museum, Stockholm

206. Carl Larsson
'Brita's Little Nap', from *Ett hem*, 1899
National Art Library, Victoria and Albert Museum, London

207. Carl Larsson
Karin is Reading, 1904
Watercolour, 46 x 65 cm (18 x 25 ¹/₂ in)
Zorn Collections, Mora

of Crafts and Design), and *The Studio* attracted Swedish subscribers from its launch in 1893. Most importantly, Sweden made its own contribution to Arts and Crafts literature in the writing of Ellen Key (1849–1926), a social reformer and leading intellectual who was strongly influenced by Ruskin and Morris. Convinced of the impact of the everyday environment on social behaviour, Key published a series of articles on domestic design during 1895–7. These were gathered together as a single pamphlet called *Skönhet för alla* (Beauty for All) in 1899 which, with its clarion call for truth to purpose, is a seminal Arts and Crafts text:

> *Always, when we buy something for our homes, we should ask ourselves if it fulfils the most vital requirement – namely, that everything should answer the purpose it is intended for. A chair should be comfortable to sit on, a table comfortable to work or eat at, a bed good to sleep in. Uncomfortable chairs, rickety tables, and narrow beds are, therefore, automatically ugly. But it does not follow that comfortable chairs, steady tables and broad beds are beautiful. Things must, as everywhere in nature, fulfil their purpose in a simple and expressive manner, and without this they do not achieve beauty even if they satisfy practical requirements.[5]*

Key was adamant that good aesthetic standards should be available to everyone, and her ideas, which were reiterated in her lectures and later publications, prompted many design initiatives, such as an exhibition of furnishings for low-income households which opened in Stockholm in 1899. This featured a suite of furniture for working-class families designed by the architect and designer Carl Westman (1866–1936) which, with its sturdy construction and cheerful red paint, met Key's insistence on good, simple design (though the furniture proved to be beyond the pockets of those for whom it was intended). The Association of Swedish Handicrafts also echoed Key's ideals in promoting light, airy rooms with brightly painted furniture in place of the dark wallpapers and fusty drapes which had dominated recent interior design. Most importantly, Key developed a close professional relationship with Carl Larsson (1853–1919), the artist and designer whose work continues to inspire nothing short of a cult following in Sweden.

Larsson came from the very classes whose environment Ellen Key was so determined to improve. The son of a casual labourer and an occasional prostitute, he grew up in working-class slums in which he was often left as a child

while his parents went to work. Larsson nevertheless progressed through a series of art institutes in Stockholm, and by the late 1870s he was studying in France. There, he met Karin Bergöö (1859–1928), a doe-eyed twenty-two-year-old painter who became the love of his life. They married in 1883 and Carl's career as a painter and illustrator began to take off, with Karin providing an entrée into the comfortable middle-class circles from which she came. In 1888 Karin's father gave the young couple Lilla Hyttnäs, an old log cottage in the village of Sundborn in the central Dalarna province, which had previously been the home of Karin's aunts. Carl's first impression was of 'a small, humble, ugly and insignificant building, situated on a slag heap',[6] but over the next three decades he and Karin transformed it with numerous extensions, every inch of which they painted and furnished to suit the rumbustious demands of family life (they had eight children, of whom one died in infancy). Local craftsmen including Erik Ericsson, the village blacksmith, and Hans Arnbom, a carpenter and general handyman, were recruited to help realize their designs. (Carl later registered his appreciation for this by painting portraits of Ericsson and Arnbom in front of examples of their work.) In the 1890s, Carl also began a series of watercolours of Lilla Hyttnäs, often with members of his family eating, working or simply larking around the house, and in 1897 he exhibited twenty of these at the Stockholm Exhibition of Art and Industry. So enthusiastic was the response, with Ellen Key describing the interiors in glowing terms in *Skönhet för alla*, that Larsson published an enlarged collection of twenty-four watercolours in a book entitled *Ett hem* (A Home) in 1899. Similar albums such as *Larssons* (1902) and *Åt solsidan* (On the Sunny Side; 1910) followed, continuing the tone of domestic contentment which had characterized *Ett hem*. Before Larsson knew it he and his children had been catapulted into the limelight, and Lilla Hyttnäs had been embraced as a solution to the demands of modern family life.

The Larssons were no sticklers for flawless workmanship, and would often knock up a cupboard or paint an old door in a couple of hours. Nor did they insist on natural materials, with Karin happily using aniline dyes in her textile designs. Rather, it is their ingenious responses to the requirements of modern living, their attention to every aspect of their house, and their efforts to make it as practical and comfortable as possible which relate to the Arts and Crafts. At Lilla Hyttnäs, the family's presence is felt at every step, from the individual coat pegs ascending the side of the staircase in order

208. Carl Larsson
'It is Evening, Good Night', from *Åt Solsidan*, 1910
Carl Larsson House, Sundborn

209. Karin Larsson
Cover of a Christmas Magazine for Konstnärs Klubben (Artists' Club), 1895
Carl Larsson House, Sundborn

of seniority, to the ribboned frieze which Carl painted around Karin's bedroom to celebrate her name-day in 1894. The frieze and other home-painted decoration in Karin's room take pride of place in 'Brita's Little Nap' (fig. 206), one of several *Ett hem* watercolours in which the interior is the main subject, with the sleeping child just visible in the bottom left of the picture. In other paintings the human content is given more emphasis, but the interior is always a key component of Larsson's work. Thus *Karin is Reading* (fig. 207) documents the wealth of decoration in the dining room, from the mottoes and family portraits on the walls (a favourite Larsson device) to the home-made lampshades. On the far wall, a built-in cupboard envelops one of the house's original windows, which Carl painted with the hatted profiles of himself and his wife, while *It is Evening, Good Night* (from *Åt solsidan*: fig. 208) depicts the opposite end of the dining room, with its settle and other furniture painted in the red and green colours which had been popular in the Viking Revival style. The settle is enlivened by Karin's textiles which, after she had abandoned her career as a painter, was the main medium in which she worked. Of particular significance is a rare work in a medium other than textiles, the cover for a Christmas magazine which Karin designed for the Artists' Club

in 1895 (fig. 209). Here, the pattern of interlinking palettes and brushes was possibly inspired by the frieze in an illustration of Ashbee's dining room which had been published that same year in *The Studio*, to which Carl subscribed (see p. 74).

The Larssons were strongly influenced by local crafts (Karin even designed folk costumes for Sundborn based on those she had seen in a neighbouring parish). They also found inspiration in Viking Revival interiors and in the Gustavian style, an unpretentious form of decoration which had been in vogue during the reign of Gustav III (1771–92). But despite the attention lavished on it, Lilla Hyttnäs never became rarefied or precious, and was instead ever subjected to the rough-and-tumble of its inhabitants, and constantly evolved to meet their changing demands. As its fame spread, the house became a manifesto for modern living and Carl became almost evangelical in his quest to spread the ennobling effect of art. In a letter of 1889, in which he decried the money wasted on academic art teaching, he pleaded with artists to engage in practical designs, urging them to 'carve tankards, doors and cupboards, storm the porcelain factories [...] and teach them to love the wonderful medium, blow glass into fantastic forms, scrawl on the walls and wake up those engineers hypnotized

210. Carl Westman
Press House (Interior Elevation of Dining Room and Living Room), 1902
Watercolour on paper, 22 x 35.8 cm (8 ¹/₂ x 14 in)
National Museum, Stockholm

211. Lars Israel Wahlman
Engelbrekt Church, Stockholm, 1906–14

212. Brick work at Engelbrekt Church, 1906–14

213. (opposite) Ragnar Östberg
Chamber of Councils, City Hall, Stockholm, 1909–23

by the academy, who are called architects. Yes, build your own houses, you painters who have not already had your imaginations killed.'[7] It is this disregard for artistic hierarchies, a principle which Larsson followed faithfully in his own home, which locates him so firmly in the canon of the Arts and Crafts. His work was seen to have launched a new Swedish style as early as 1910, when the critic August Brunius published an article entitled 'Carl Larsson and a National Style of Furniture'. The legacy of his airy interiors and painted furniture is still evident in the products of IKEA, the Swedish firm whose international chain of superstores is a market leader in affordable domestic design.

By the beginning of the twentieth century, Arts and Crafts concerns were stimulating not only the applied arts and interior design in Sweden, but also architecture. In 1900, the budding young architects Carl Westman and Lars Israel Wahlman (1870–1952) travelled to England, and over the next few years both responded to developments which they encountered there. One of Westman's more remarkable projects was the Press House, a one-family home in Stockholm which was commissioned in 1901 by a journalists' association to offer as first prize in a lottery. Westman designed every aspect of the house, his cross-sections detailing a large tiled stove, a built-in settee, cupboards fitted round windows, and bookshelves slotted under the stairs (fig. 210). While the wooden walls and tiled roof paid homage to medieval architecture and to simple peasant houses in the manner of National Romanticism, the vivid colours, painted walls and white woodwork inside created a truly modern home. Wahlman also adopted Arts and Crafts ideas in his domestic architecture, notably in the villa of Tallom which he designed for himself in Stocksund from 1904 to 1906, and both architects were influential in the 'Own Home' Movement which governed Swedish urban expansion in the early twentieth century. Wahlman is best known, though, as the author of the Engelbrekt Church (fig. 211), a building conceived as the centre of a new suburb in Stockholm, and named after a national icon who in the fifteenth century had led a revolt against the oppression of Danish rule. Sited at the top of a steep hill, the Engelbrekt Church dominates its parish, thrusting its asymmetrical gables and slender tower skywards like a red-brick colossus bursting out of its granite base. Wahlman loved bricks and missed no opportunity to show off with them, teasing patterns out of every wall and window frame in both the church and its hall (fig. 212). The vast expanse of brick is leavened by a festal throng of

214. Ragnar Östberg
Chair, c.1919
Oak with woollen seat
176 x 69 x 57 cm (68 3/4 x 27 x 22 1/2 in)
Thielska Gallery, Stockholm

windows, by copper sills and gutters, and by carved sandstone mouldings, resulting in one of the most felicitous explorations of material in any Arts and Crafts design. Later, other leading architects were employed to design the surrounding buildings, echoing the church's forms and techniques in streets of housing which followed the natural contours of the land.

Even a building as prominent as the Stockholm City Hall (1909–23) by Ragnar Östberg (1866–1945) has a debt to the Arts and Crafts in its integration of architecture and the applied arts. Here, craftsmen set up workshops inside the building which they were employed to decorate and, as Östberg recalled, were sometimes given designs which stipulated only the measurements and 'the general lines of composition,'[8] leaving the craftsmen with creative control over the final details. The result is astounding, from the painted ceiling in the Chamber of Councils (fig. 213), to the dazzling Golden Hall which a hundred craftsmen apparently spent two years decorating with over nineteen million pieces of mosaic. They and their colleagues are given fulsome recognition in the carved heads of the project's builders and artisans which line the corridor leading to the Chamber of Councils. Those who view the outside of the City Hall, however, can be forgiven for questioning its Arts and Crafts credentials as, for all the talk of Swedish references and National Romantic influences, the building resembles nothing so much as the Italian Renaissance palaces and piazzas by which Östberg had also been inspired (he designed the City Hall while he was living in Italy). His most compelling contribution to the Movement lies in a very different direction – in the monumental chairs which the millionaire banker and patron Ernest Thiel commissioned for his new house (now the Thielska Gallery; fig. 214). While the house is a clear attestation of Swedish Art Nouveau, the chairs, with their rough carving and huge, spiral armrests, instead exemplify the rustic solidity and simple decoration of the Arts and Crafts.

In 1917, the Swedish Society of Crafts and Design organized a Home Exhibition in Stockholm at which a series of interiors were furnished entirely with industrially made products. The event marked a turning point in the Arts and Crafts Movement in Scandinavia, as increasing efforts were made to persuade designers to work for industry. Certain craftsmen proved to be particularly adept at maintaining high standards of craftsmanship on the one hand, and adapting their work to suit new methods of production on the other. In Sweden, Carl Malmsten (1888–1972), who had won the competition to design furniture for the Stockholm City Hall, both catered for factory production and ran a workshop which emphasized traditional crafts skills. In Denmark, the architect Kaare Klint (1888–1954) produced exquisite hand-crafted furniture at the same time as designing mass produced desks and storage units in which function was paramount. And in Finland, Alvar Aalto (1898–1976) brought a superb level of workmanship to his supremely modern, streamlined designs (see pp. 243–5). It would be wrong to suggest that these and other examples of modern Scandinavian design are necessarily Arts and Crafts in character, but the Movement's ethos is evident in the importance attached to everyday surroundings which still prevails in Finland and Scandinavia. Never was this more apparent than in 2000, when the Finnish Government announced its two main objectives in the field of design: the first of these was to nurture design as a competitive factor in industry; and the second was to use it to improve the environment in which the Finnish people live and work.[9] We come back to the conviction that lies at the very heart of the Arts and Crafts: that well-made objects make a nation happier and healthier.

Elizabeth E Copeland
Casket, 1922 (fig. 223)

ACROSS THE ATLANTIC: TRANSFORMATIONS IN THE UNITED STATES

IN THE LAST THIRD OF THE NINETEENTH CENTURY, THE UNITED STATES OF AMERICA ESTABLISHED ITSELF AS A COUNTRY OF RISING AMBITION AND DRIVE.

With the East and West Coasts linked by railways in 1869, many Americans were better able to comprehend the extent and potential of their country and, moving forward from the horrors of the Civil War, they became increasingly self-confident, prosperous, and self-aware. As fortunes were made in the railways, factories and urban development, wealth and power moved into the hands of those industrialists who best adapted to, and exploited, the Industrial Age. At the same time, the growing availability of diverse and progressive employment enabled those of more modest means to achieve new levels of domestic comfort and financial security. These changes in the social and commercial fabric of America, which provided people with the money and inclination to live in different sorts of houses surrounded by different sorts of objects, stimulated many artistic and architectural developments, not least a rich and distinct Arts and Crafts Movement.

It is a challenge to identify the narratives of the American Arts and Crafts. In the first place, one cannot approach the United States in the same way that one might approach a European country: such is its physical extent that regional centres emerged, with their own characteristics and

areas of excellence. Nor can one maintain the chronological approach which mapped out the rich tapestry of British collaborations. The regional movements need to be examined separately, and the work in certain media was so prolific and geographically dispersed that these demand their own history and chronology, as is the case with the art potteries. But an analysis by medium is not always appropriate, as the interaction and exchange so typical of the Arts and Crafts also took place. In other words, the three methodologies most frequently used to discuss the Arts and Crafts – geographical, chronological and material – do not work in a country as vast as the United States. To avoid oversimplification, this chapter therefore employs different approaches at different stages. It begins with America's awakening consciousness of questions of design in the 1870s, and the beginnings of the art needlework revival and the art pottery movement. The latter developed to a greater extent than in any other country, but its relationship to the Arts and Crafts Movement requires careful thought. The chapter then turns to localized communities and enterprises, and to the way in which some of these – Stickley's furniture empire, for example – transcended regional boundaries to exert a national appeal.

215. Associated Artists
Indian Motif Tri-Fold Screen, c.1881
Glass, copper wire and rosewood, 169.2 x 68.6 x 2.2 cm (66 ½ x 27 x 1 in)
Virginia Museum of Fine Arts, Richmond

In 1876, one of the ways in which the United States of America celebrated a century of independence was by staging the Philadelphia Centennial Exhibition, the country's first World's Fair (as international exhibitions in America became known). As had been the case with Britain's Great Exhibition of 1851, the Philadelphia Centennial not only provided a vast showcase for industry and technology, but also galvanized debates concerning the state of applied art and design. It included a wealth of foreign art, ranging from an entire court of work by London's Royal School of Art Needlework to designs by Morris and Crane: but while relishing the opportunity to view these works, many commentators felt that they highlighted a lack of distinction in the American exhibits, just as the Great Exhibition had been thought to expose weaknesses in British design. According to the American ceramics designer Isaac Broome, there was 'nothing to approach even the lower grades of European ware'. The United States, like Britain twenty-five years earlier, had to confront the growing belief that the processes of modernization had stultified areas of applied art and design.

Over the next few years, certain state governments attempted to address these problems by following the South

Kensington precedent and establishing museum collections and design schools. Private philanthropists and voluntary organizations, both of which were fundamental to the development of high culture in the United States, also launched educational or social initiatives revolving around the crafts. In 1877, for example, Candace Wheeler (1827–1923), who had admired the work of the Royal School of Art Needlework at the Philadelphia Centennial, founded the New York Society of Decorative Art to enable women to make a profit from their handiwork. Railing against 'the invisible wall of prejudice and custom' which prevented 'well-bred women from [...] money gaining enterprise',[1] Wheeler challenged both the belief that it was unseemly for women to earn a living, and the condescension which was directed towards female craft. Nor did Wheeler stop with the Society of Decorative Art. 'I had in my mind larger ambitions, [...] ambitions toward a truly great American effort in a lasting direction,'[2] she wrote, and in 1879 joined with Louis Comfort Tiffany (1848–1933) to set up Tiffany & Wheeler, which specialized in embroidery. In 1881, this was absorbed into Louis C Tiffany & Co., Associated Artists, an up-market design firm in the mould of Morris & Co. The firm's products, such as the jewelled and painted screen of *c*.1881 (fig. 215), confused the boundaries between furniture and art, and it soon won commissions as prestigious as decorating the White House for President Arthur, and carrying out work for the author Mark Twain. The founders parted company in 1883, Tiffany eventually to follow his stellar career in Art Nouveau art glass. Wheeler, who retained control of the name of the Associated Artists, continued with designs as bold as the glorious goldfish who dance across a portière of *c*.1885 (fig. 216) and, with her family, kept her textile and embroidery enterprise going until 1907.

Wheeler was not alone in responding enthusiastically to the work of the Royal School of Art Needlework. Many American needlewomen admired the display, and the late 1870s saw the beginnings of an art needlework revival in the United States. By 1879 the Museum of Fine Arts, Boston, included a School of Art Needlework, which offered lessons every weekday, and free tuition on Mondays and Thursdays. Cincinnati also boasted talented needlewomen whose work had featured in the Women's Pavilion at the Philadelphia Centennial, and in 1879 the Women's Art Museum Association in Cincinnati rented premises in which to offer upper- and middle-class women tuition in embroidery and other crafts. Nor was it just needlework which was stimulated by the Centennial displays. Many American potters visited or participated in the exhibition, and were soon practising their craft with such invention that a distinct art pottery movement emerged.

There are two issues to address in establishing the relationship of the art pottery movement to the Arts and Crafts. First, the art potteries flourished for a good decade before there was sufficient activity in other fields to speak of an Arts and Crafts Movement in the United States. But just as Morris's work was integral to the Arts and Crafts in Britain before the Movement had a clear identity, so the art potters feature here (albeit working in just one medium, compared to Morris's many) as an important early feature of the American Arts and Crafts. Second, while many potteries stemmed from clear Arts and Crafts concerns – experimenting with materials and methods distinct to the craft, reviving lost techniques, and providing training and employment to disadvantaged groups – others shared none of these interests, and to a European audience their products can seem more Art Nouveau than Arts and Crafts. Yet these potteries are viewed by American scholars as Arts and Crafts, and the American Movement needs to be assessed on its own

216. Associated Artists
Portière, *c*.1885
Cotton, discharge printed with silk embroidery, plus couching of foil over paper-wrapped silk, 264.2 x 127 cm (104 x 50 in)
Private collection

terms. The account here acknowledges the wider, American definition, but offers examples with particular kinship to the Arts and Crafts.

One of the first centres of art pottery was in Cincinnati, which witnessed such a flurry of female potting from the late 1870s that a writer for the *Crockery and Glass Journal* of 1879 wrote: 'the ladies of Cincinnati are slightly demented on the subject of art.'[3] Activity began with Mary Louise McLaughlin (1847–1939), one of the great amateur polymaths of the Arts and Crafts. The daughter of a leading Cincinnati architect, McLaughlin studied drawing, wood-carving and china painting, reaching a standard sufficient to exhibit at the Philadelphia Centennial. There, she became fascinated by French Limoges ware, and during 1877–8 developed various underglaze coloured slips in a distinctive faience known as 'Cincinnati Limoges'. In 1879, McLaughlin also founded the Cincinnati Pottery Club which she invited local women to join, but one crucial invitation, to Maria Longworth Nichols (1849–1932), herself a craftswoman of repute, went astray. Piqued by the apparent snub, Nichols set up her own Rookwood Pottery in an empty schoolhouse in 1880 (fig. 217). Initially, the two potteries enjoyed a close, if competitive, relationship: Rookwood supplied the Pottery Club with pots and fired their work after it was decorated, and both organizations experimented with glazes to create different aesthetic effects. At Rookwood, Laura Fry (1857–1943) developed an atomizer method for applying slips smoothly on to wet clay, so that a relief design could be built up in coloured slip under a high gloss or matt glaze, while Kataro Shirayamadani (1865–1948), Rookwood's first non-American employee, was sent to Japan in 1893 to study his native country's decorative motifs and glazing techniques. These had caused a sensation at the Philadelphia Centennial, and were incorporated to great success: Rookwood won a gold medal at the Paris Exposition of 1889, commissioned new premises in 1890, and continued production for over forty years. The Cincinnati Pottery Club did not fare so well, particularly after Rookwood closed its facilities to amateurs, and McLaughlin turned to other pursuits such as metal etching, for which she won a silver medal at the Paris Exposition. In the late 1890s she returned to pottery, developing a form of porcelain in a kiln in her backyard which she called Losanti, after Cincinnati's early name of L'Osantiville, but it was not a commercial success. McLaughlin 'stopped short

of putting my furniture in the kiln',[4] and turned back to metalwork instead.

The work of McLaughlin and Nichols was followed by countless potteries of varying scales: there were so many in Zanesville, Ohio, that it acquired the nickname of 'Clay City'. For some, the challenge was to perfect a particular technique. In Biloxi, Mississippi, for example, George E Ohr (1857–1918) used clay he had dug from local riverbanks to throw earthenware pots with walls as thin as porcelain, keeping his handlebar moustache away from his home-made wheel by tucking it behind his ears. The most distinctive of Ohr's pots are twisted, crumpled or compressed, sinking into overlapping folds like a chocolate vase left in the sun (fig. 218). They led Ohr to the conclusion that he was the greatest art potter on earth,[5] but in 1909 he decided to deal in Cadillacs instead. Other potters were motivated by social concerns. Thus the Newcomb Pottery at the women's affiliate of Tulane University in New Orleans was set up in 1895 to provide women with a vocational training. Under the directorship of the china painter Mary Sheerer (1865–1954), the Newcomb potters developed a distinctive style, depicting local plants such as magnolia and palm trees in subtle blues and greens

217. Women Decorators working at the Rookwood Pottery, c.1890

(fig. 219). 'The whole thing', wrote Sheerer, 'was to be a southern product, made of southern clays, by southern artists, decorated with southern subjects,'[6] revealing a commitment to locality as well as to education in the crafts. The pottery maintained traditional gender divides, as men were employed to throw pots for the women to decorate: nor could the women earn a substantial income, being paid on a piecework basis. But the Newcomb Pottery created an economic outlet for their work, and later expanded to include instruction and production in embroidery, needlework, metalwork and stained glass. Edward J Lewis, the founder of the American Women's League, also set up a pottery in Missouri as part of his drive to promote female education and employment, persuading expert potters to work for him, including the editor of the highly-regarded *Keramic Studio*, Adelaide Alsop Robineau (1865–1929). In 1911 Robineau won the Grand Prix at the International Exposition of Decorative Arts in Turin for her *Scarab Vase* (fig. 220), causing her husband to wax lyrical about 'the beetle or scarab pushing a ball of food, symbolizing the toiler [...] taking pride and pleasure in his work'. Others, however, have noted that the scarab in fact pushes pieces of dung into which it lays its eggs before burying them to gestate in the ground, suggesting a less poetic reading of Robineau's work.

The art pottery movement continued long into the twentieth century. In the last decade of the nineteenth century, however, a fuller and more varied picture of the American Arts and Crafts began to emerge. Americans by now had considerable exposure to the British Arts and Crafts. Both Morris and Ruskin's writings were widely available (Morris had a publisher in America, and in 1895 designed a book specifically for the American market), and special reading groups studied their texts. Morris also employed agents to market Morris & Co. goods in the United States, and in 1883 had ensured that his firm was well represented at the Boston Foreign Fair (see Chapter 2). So effective was this marketing that by the turn of the century the *Ladies' Home Journal* declared that 'a William Morris craze has been developing, and it is a fad that we cannot push with too much vigour'. Other British designers also made their mark. In 1891, Walter Crane gave a series of lectures in the United States to accompany an exhibition of his work which travelled to Boston, Chicago, St Louis, Philadelphia and Brooklyn. C R Ashbee, for his part, began a long association with the United States when he made the first of eight lecture tours there in 1896.

218. George E Ohr
Pitcher with Snake, c.1895–1900
18 cm (7 in) height
Private collection

219. Newcomb Pottery
Vase, c.1900–10
Pottery, incised and painted with a magnolia blossom design,
in green and white tones, glossy glaze, 30.5 cm (12 in) height
Brooklyn Museum (Dick S Ramsay Fund)

220. Adelaide Alsop Robineau
Scarab Vase, 1910–11
Porcelain, excised, perforated and glazed, 42.2 cm (16 ¹/₂ in) height
Everson Museum of Art, Syracuse, NY

As these links were developing, Arts and Crafts practices in Boston were gathering pace. The city was already the American centre of high-quality book printing, and in the early 1890s it witnessed a flowering of Arts and Crafts printing and book design. In 1892 the local architect Ralph Adams Cram (1863–1942) launched a publication called *The Knight Errant*, which was modelled on *The Century Guild Hobby Horse* and devoted attention to Morris's typography and the publications of the Kelmscott Press. Cram's partner, Bertram Grosvenor Goodhue (1869–1924), designed the first cover (fig. 221) which recalls the layout of Image's famous cover for *The Hobby Horse* (see p. 56) and, with its visored knight riding through the undergrowth, is replete with the medievalizing imagery of the Arts and Crafts. Printing offices and publishing houses also appeared, notably the Merrymount Press which Daniel Berkeley Updike (1860–1941) founded in 1893. The most renowned Merrymount production was *The Altar Book* (fig. 222), a monumental collaborative effort designed by Updike, illustrated by Robert Anning Bell (1863–1933), and with initials, borders, binding and a new typeface by Goodhue, all of which took three years to complete. It eventually appeared in 1896, the same year as the Kelmscott *Chaucer*, and is clearly inspired by work at the Kelmscott Press: Goodhue's Merrymount font was modelled on Morris's Golden font, while the wide, floral borders and elaborate initial letters recall Morris's designs. Updike gradually rejected the dense Morrisian look in favour of a more restrained style, and later refused to sign a copy of *The Altar Book*, which he saw as 'too reminiscent of a particular period'.[7] When it appeared, however, it was acclaimed as 'the most interesting piece of bookmaking yet produced in this country'.[8]

Private presses soon abounded on the eastern seaboard, delighting its bibliophiles with ornamented tomes, often in luxurious bindings. These were not just the preserve of wealthy connoisseurs. In Portland, Maine, Thomas Bird Mosher (1852–1923) – a man known as the 'Passionate Pirate' for publishing the work of English authors without their permission – produced books of great flair in elegant formats, but kept his publications reasonably priced. Will Bradley (1868–1962), who had worked for the Merrymount Press, also set up his own business, the Wayside Press, in Springfield, Massachusetts, in 1895. Wayside publications included a small monthly magazine called *Bradley, His Book* (1896–7) which owed a debt to the lettering and design of Morris, Crane, and Charles Ricketts of the Vale Press in London: but the sinuous lines, recondite symbolism and

221. Bertram Grosvenor Goodhue
Front Cover of *The Knight Errant*, 1892
Columbia University Libraries, New York

powerful use of solid masses and negative space bring to mind the work of Aubrey Beardsley and other protagonists of Art Nouveau. *Bradley, His Book* ran interior design competitions, stimulating artists and craftsmen much as *The Studio* was doing in Europe, and Bradley himself became famous both in the United States and abroad where *The Studio*, among other journals, promoted his work.

By 1897, such was the explosion of Arts and Crafts interests in the Boston area that several local architects and designers, including Cram and Goodhue, decided to launch the Boston Society of Arts and Crafts. They elected as president Charles Eliot Norton (1827–1908), Harvard's first Professor of Fine Arts who was a friend of Ruskin, and himself wrote on medieval architecture and promoted courses in manual skills and model housing for the poor. The Society organized lectures, classes, social occasions, and the first exhibitions in America dedicated solely to the decorative arts, combining the social, didactic and promotional aims of the Art Workers' Guild and the Arts and Crafts Exhibition Society in London. It also managed a craft salesroom, in which standards were upheld by a jury of

222. Daniel Berkeley Updike, Robert Anning Bell
and Bertram Grosvenor Goodhue
Pages from *The Altar Book*, 1896
Black and red ink on white paper,
37.5 x 28.3 cm (14 ¾ x 11 in)

EASTER·DAY. THE COLLECT.

ALMIGHTY God, who through thine only-begotten Son Jesus Christ hast overcome death, and opened unto us the gate of everlasting life; We humbly beseech thee that, as by thy special grace preventing us thou dost put into our minds good desires, so by thy continual help we may bring the same to good effect; through Jesus Christ our Lord, who liveth and reigneth with thee and the Holy Ghost ever, one God, world without end. Amen.

THE EPISTLE. Col. iii. 1.

IF ye then be risen with Christ, seek those things which are above, where Christ sitteth on the right hand of God. Set your affection on things above, not on things on the earth. For ye are dead, and your life is hid with Christ in God. When Christ, who is our life, shall appear, then shall ye also appear with him in glory. Mortify therefore your members which are upon the earth; fornication, uncleanness, inordinate affection, evil concupiscence, and covetousness, which is idolatry: for which things' sake the wrath of God cometh on the children of disobedience: in the which ye also walked some time, when ye lived in them.

THE GOSPEL. St. John xx. 1.

THE first day of the week cometh Mary Magdalene early, when it was yet dark, unto the sepulchre, and seeth the stone taken away from the sepulchre. Then she runneth, and cometh to Simon Peter, and to the other disciple, whom Jesus loved, and saith unto them, They have taken away the Lord out of the sepulchre, and we know not where they have laid him. Peter therefore went forth, and that other disciple, and came to the sepulchre. So they ran both together: and the other disciple did outrun Peter, and came first to the sepulchre.

223. Elizabeth E Copeland
Casket, 1922
Silver, parcel gilt, painted and cloisonné enamel,
12.7 x 17.6 x 13 cm (5 x 7 x 5 in)
Private collection

selectors, and from 1902 produced an authoritative monthly called *Handicraft* which broadcast the objectives and achievements of the Arts and Crafts. Such was the success of these enterprises that the membership (of architects, designers, craftsmen, philanthropists and connoisseurs) expanded from seventy-one to almost a thousand within twenty years. The Society took pains to promote and reward applied artists, many of whom had not had an easy path to success. In 1916, for example, it gave its Medal of Excellence, one of the highest marks of recognition in the crafts, to Elizabeth E Copeland (1866–1957), who was in her thirties before she even contemplated an artistic career. Starting by pinning assignments from her art teacher over the ironing board, she learnt how to design in enamel and silver and eventually set up her own Boston studio. Copeland did not aim for a high standard of workmanship: in her enamelled silver casket (fig. 223), the metalwork is roughly finished and the enamel is applied with incontinent imprecision, like some skewed medieval reliquary. The result is a flagrant display of irregular but honest craftsmanship, a powerful bid for anti-professional accessibility, a Ruskinian exaltation of the imperfections of the handmade.

Of all the regional Arts and Crafts centres in the United States, the Boston Movement was most like that in Britain. It produced not only scholarly book printing and design akin to that of British publications and private presses, but also a wealth of church decoration comparable to that of High Anglicanism. Here, there was a clear link in the person of Christopher Whall, the leading British stained-glass designer and an inspired teacher at London's Central School of Arts and Crafts (see Chapter 3). In the early twentieth century, Whall was commissioned by Cram to design windows for churches in the Boston area, including a series of clerestory windows for the Church of the Advent in Boston. Produced from 1909 to 1910, these windows exemplify Whall's ability to animate his characters, and his revelational use of painted and leaded glass to manipulate colour and light. Never has the gravitas of St John Chrysostom been conveyed so convincingly as by Whall's inclusion of an awestruck child hovering nervously behind the saint (fig. 224). The windows were so densely painted that the bemused glaziers installing them showed them to Charles J Connick (1875–1945), the budding leader of American Arts and Crafts stained glass. Connick, too, puzzled at their technique until they were lifted up to the light, whereupon he 'awoke again to the charm of glassiness' and 'gloried in the discovery of Christopher Whall'.[9] Within weeks Connick had travelled to England to meet Whall, and in 1912 he set up a studio in Boston which long maintained Whall's focus on the resplendent colours and glazing tradition of medieval stained glass.

While Boston attended to the scholarly worlds of book printing and church decoration, in Chicago a very different picture was emerging. Birthplace of the skyscraper and engine-room of the Midwest, Chicago was a thrusting city embracing the technology and industry of modern life. As Janet Ashbee observed on a visit in 1900:

> When a man has finished with Hell, says a proverb, he is sent to Chicago; and when you first arrive you endorse the statement. Smoke, darkness, noise; the clashing of car-bells, engine-bells, steamer-bells; the grating of endless trolleys as they dash along the streets; the shriek of the American voice trying to make itself heard above the uproar. The rattle and thunder of the elevated railway, the unearthly buzzing of electric cabs [...] and the thudding of power houses that shakes a whole street.[10]

224. Christopher Whall
St John Chrysostom Stained-Glass Window, 1909–10
Church of the Advent, Boston, MA

Within this throbbing metropolis, there had since the 1880s been signs of interest in the Arts and Crafts. In 1885, the industrial magnate John Jacob Glessner and his wife had hired the Boston architect Henry Hobson Richardson (1838–86) to design them a residence in the exclusive neighbourhood of Prairie Avenue. Richardson responded with a rusticated fortress of a house (the neighbours were none too pleased): but both he and his patrons were devotees of British design (Richardson had met Morris at Merton Abbey and Kelmscott House in 1882), and the austere exterior yields to panelled rooms in which custom-made furniture by the American cabinet-maker Isaac Scott is offset by Morris wallpaper, Morris chairs, and De Morgan ceramics and tiles.

At the other end of the social spectrum, a community of philanthropists and craftsmen had gathered around Hull House, a settlement in an impoverished area of Chicago which Jane Addams (1860–1935) and Ellen Gates Starr (1859–1940) had founded in 1889. Taking its inspiration from Toynbee Hall in London (which Addams had visited), Hull House ran classes in language, literature, manual skills and craftwork for local residents, the majority of them recent immigrants, with the aim of integrating the immigrants into the community and regenerating its creative life. With Morris wallpaper on its walls, Hull House also promoted British design: Ashbee exhibited and lectured there, there were talks on his peers, and Lethaby was held in such esteem that his brother-in-law found himself basking in reflected glory when he visited in 1905. The set-up at Hull House was unusual, with black-clad Sicilian mammas and Russian babushkas weaving in one room while design aficionados debated the British vernacular in the next. But it worked. In the evocative words of Janet Ashbee, who stayed there:

> [...] at Hull House the pot is nearly boiling; and a curious mixture it is inside. Every race, every grade of human creature, seems to pour into the great caldron of Chicago – and what will be the blend at the last who shall say? Hull House itself stirs and mixes the brew, its clubs and meetings bring the motley crowd together – Russians and Greeks are taught English – the children get singing lessons, and what is even more valuable, the capacity for enjoyment – the boys have workshops – the young people dancing rooms – the older ones lectures. The great block with its forecourt of tiles attracts all sorts and conditions; it is a Beacon in that

loveless street, 26 miles long; its fame has gone out through all the earth, and its words to the end of the world.[11]

While Hull House was addressing the needs of its multi-ethnic community, other initiatives in Chicago were also invigorating the fine and applied arts. In 1893 the city commemorated the landing of Columbus in America with the Columbian Exhibition, which included the wealth of art and architecture now characteristic of international exhibitions. One of its venues, a vast, neoclassical edifice on Michigan Avenue, became the new home for the Art Institute of Chicago's growing collections of painting, sculpture and decorative arts. From 1896 the Chicago magazine *House Beautiful*, whose motto read 'Simplicity, Economy and Appropriateness in the Home', published articles and designs by Morris, Ashbee, Voysey, Baillie Scott and Crane. Morris & Co. products became available in the department store Marshall Field & Company and in the Tobey Furniture Company, which later had a dedicated William Morris Room. And in 1897, just four months after its Boston predecessor, the Chicago Society of Arts and Crafts was founded at Hull House. These initiatives fuelled the already considerable momentum of local craft industries. Starr, frustrated by teaching, travelled to England to study with Cobden-Sanderson, and on her return established a successful bookbindery at Hull House. Soon after, in 1900, Clara Barck Welles (1868–1965) set up the Kalo Shops, a place for women to practise leatherwork, weaving, copper and brass metalwork and, later, silverware, in which the Shops came to specialize. The simple, handwrought products of the Kalo Shops, with their exaggerated hammer finish and occasional decoration with enamel or semi-precious stones, recall Guild of Handicraft designs. (Ashbee's work had featured in the first exhibition of the Chicago Society of Arts and Crafts in 1898, and his 1900 lecture tour through fourteen American states, Illinois included, again raised the profile of his work.) The Kalo workshops enjoyed lasting success: the enterprise expanded to include the Kalo Art-Craft Community in Park Ridge and a retail outlet in New York, and in 1918 moved to Chicago's Fine Arts Building, home to many craft workshops, where it continued production for over fifty years.

The Arts and Crafts Movement in Chicago involved scores of craftsmen and women as talented as Welles and Starr. However, their importance, and at times the Movement in Chicago as a whole, is overshadowed by the reputation of just one man – Frank Lloyd Wright (1867–1959), a figure whose artistic genius, self-promotion, and a private life veering from the tempestuous to the tragic made him both the most lionized and the most vilified American architect of his time. Wright is often distanced from the Arts and Crafts to emphasize his role in the development of Modernism. Yet he was a founder member of the Chicago Society of Arts and Crafts, and some of his early work unquestionably forms part of the Movement, albeit a part which needs to be kept in perspective.

Wright began his career as an apprentice in the Chicago office of Dankmar Adler (1844–1900) and Louis H Sullivan (1856–1924), with whom he worked from 1887 to 1893. Partners since 1883, Sullivan and Adler were renowned for their development of high-rise office blocks, and had established themselves as a linchpin of the vibrant architectural scene which evolved in Chicago in the decades following the great fire of 1871. Sullivan contributed volubly to the debates accompanying the city's reconstruction by insisting that contemporary designs should not copy from earlier styles, but should grow 'out of their own social circumstances', reflecting the purpose for which they were intended. To emphasize the point he coined the famous phrase 'Form follows function',[12] which Wright was to revise as 'Form and function are one'.[13] Inspired by the poetry of Walt Whitman, who celebrated the Midwest as a locus of American cultural identity, Sullivan also urged his colleagues to respond to the idiosyncratic nature of the prairie, himself juxtaposing naturalistic forms of flowers and grasses with strong, geometric shapes which referred to its simple, horizontal landscape. A manic depressive, Sullivan was too testy, and often too drunk, to endear himself to clients: but his example inspired many young architects, and he was one of the few influences whom Wright later deigned to acknowledge.

In 1889 Wright moved to the suburb of Oak Park where, thanks to a loan of $5,000 from Sullivan, he purchased a plot of land and began to build himself a house (fig. 225). Recently restored to its appearance of 1909, Wright's house was built primarily in the Shingle style, a late-nineteenth-century development in America which rejected the flamboyance of High Victorian architecture and instead advocated disciplined restraint. Characteristic features include shingle coverings (inspired by early settler architecture), pitched roofs and broad gables, all of which appear in Wright's house. But Wright also introduced new ideas. The house sits on a brick base, known as a water platform, which lifts it above the damp ground; it features

225. (above) Frank Lloyd Wright
Architect's Home, 1889–98
Oak Park, Illinois

226. Frank Lloyd Wright
Arthur Heurtley House, 1902
Oak Park, Illinois

227. Frank Lloyd Wright
The Robie House, 1908–9
Chicago, IL

228. (opposite) Living Room, The Robie House

banded 'ribbon' windows, which had been pioneered by Richardson in the 1870s and 1880s; and it was built round an existing tree to create an organic link between the building and its surroundings (though the trunks of the tree which were inside the house later died). Inside, there is an organic flow from room to room, emphasized by the absence of interior doors and by co-ordinating colour schemes; and the furnishings are designed with as much care as the building itself. These features, all of which aimed to accentuate the horizontality of the building, its bond with the topography of the prairie, and the organic nature of its development, became characteristic of what is known as the Prairie style.

The Prairie style is a misleading term for those unfamiliar with its buildings. The name itself and its much-vaunted association with the landscape suggest that its architecture is somehow evocative of the rugged outdoors, with wide vistas on to the prairie. In fact, Wright's Prairie houses are long, geometric, suburban villas which often extend to the breadth of their plots, and are frequently hemmed in by other suburban homes. Rather than being literally expressive of the prairie, they are more a conceptual response to its flat, horizontal terrain. Shallow, hipped roofs

and banded windows stress the horizontal axis, while broad, overhanging eaves were seen to extend the architecture into the landscape. Internally, there is rarely a rural simplicity to their decoration, but rather a studied artfulness – a pot plant here, a pane of art glass there. They were designed not for outdoor types, but for Chicago's middle and upper classes who in the early twentieth century were attracted to suburban life. With its response to a particular landscape, ingenious planning, and integrated design, the Prairie style became the most important architectural expression of the Midwest Arts and Crafts. Wright officially launched the style in February 1901 when he published designs for 'A Home in a Prairie Town' in the *Ladies' Home Journal*, and over the next eight years it formed the backbone of his work. The best examples in Oak Park and the neighbouring suburb of River Forest include the Arthur Heurtley House, a fabulous gingerbread house of a building with its courses of pink and terracotta brick (fig. 226): and the Isabel Roberts House (1908), in which a British elm tree grows straight through the roof of the south porch. However, it was not in the suburbs but on a site next to the campus of the University of Chicago that Wright built his most spectacular exposition of the Prairie style – the Robie House (fig. 227).

229. Dining Area, The Robie House

Frederick C Robie was a manufacturer of bicycle and automobile parts. Brash, rich and ambitious, he was, in Wright's words, one of the 'American men of business with unspoiled instincts and untainted ideals'[14] whom the architect so admired. The two met in 1908 and Wright began work on the Robie House that year, though he later dated it 1906 to stress the innovation of his design. The narrow city lot was not easy, but Wright turned it to his advantage by designing a series of planes whose every feature, from the water platform to the hipped roof, emphasizes the horizontality of the building and the length of the site. The Roman bricks with which the house is constructed are themselves long and thin, and even the pointing plays its part, with the vertical joints disguised by using red mortar to blend with the colour of the bricks, while the horizontal joints are gouged out to create dark, recessed grooves. The horizontal thrust culminates in the cantilevered overhang, supported by steel beams developed in Chicago's shipyards and employed here for one of the first times in domestic design. Ever mindful of the image of his work, Wright later accentuated this feature in photographs by airbrushing out the buildings behind.

One of Robie's stipulations was that he be able to 'look out and down the street to my neighbors without having them invade my privacy'.[15] Wright complied with low walls along the sidewalk and the balconies to obscure views into the house (a device which still frustrates inquisitive pedestrians), while continuous fenestration provided uninterrupted views out. The overhangs allowed Robie to open his windows whatever the weather, dissolving the distinction between the building and its environment. Wright also included copious urns and built-in planters, believing that if one could not live in the country or have a garden, one should bring the garden into the house. Yet these attempts to 'embrace nature' are more an abstract response than a real effort to blend a building with its surroundings. No matter how many windows of the Robie House are open, and however verdant the foliage of its urns and planters, it is still an urban building on a restricted city plot, and a far cry from the expansive landscape of the Midwest.

Inside the Robie House, the living room extends the length of the first floor, its wall of art-glass windows dappling the room with flickering, diaphanous light (fig. 228). The sitting and dining areas are separated only by the inglenook

230. William Drummond
Charles Barr House, 1912
River Forest, IL.

and staircase, emulating the interpenetrating spaces of Japanese architecture which Wright so admired (he had been impressed by the Japanese Pavilion at the Columbian Exhibition, and from 1905 travelled and worked in Japan). In the dining area Wright's famous tall-backed chairs (once likened to 'some fiendish instrument of torture')[16] create a 'room within a room'[17] in which guests could focus on the social repartee: lights on pedestals illuminated the table area alone, enhancing the sense of an intimate, inner space (fig. 229). All the fittings were to Wright's design, from the oak sconces and prow-windows to the decorative ceiling grilles backed with frosted glass. Most ingenious of all are the drawers on the second floor, which project under planters outside the house so as not to obtrude into the bedrooms. (At times the architect even designed dresses so that his patrons would match his houses, and he often rearranged the furniture of clients and friends.) Superlative egoist that he was, Wright described the Robie House as 'the cornerstone of modern architecture'. But there is substance to his claim: the house is a legendary example of the living environment as art, yet also moves towards the clutter-free interiors which still preoccupy architects today.

The Robie House's unified design, which evolved from human, as opposed to stylistic needs, shows the extent to which Wright shared the mindset of the British Arts and Crafts architects, whose work he would have known from *House Beautiful*, from his acquaintance with Ashbee (whom he first met in 1900), and from activities at Hull House. But unlike many of his British peers, Wright believed that the future of design depended on the intelligent use of the machine, which alone had the ability to democratize art. As he inveighed in his famous lecture on 'The Art and Craft of the Machine' at Hull House in 1901, the machine had a 'wonderful cutting, shaping, smoothing, and repetitive capacity' which enabled both rich and poor to enjoy 'beautiful surface treatments of clean strong forms'.[18] He later reiterated that mechanized production was 'the tool which uniquely characterizes our cultural epoch and creating a work that is fitting for this machine is an important task'.[19] Transfixed by his self-constructed role of misunderstood genius, Wright claimed to have stood alone in this argument, 'voted down and out by the enthusiastic disciples of Ruskin and Morris'.[20] Yet in Chicago, with its bustling shipyards and department stores, its elevated railway and, from 1899, an

Industrial Art League to foster links between artists and manufacturers, industry was recognized as an indispensable feature of everyday life. The Chicago Society of Arts and Crafts accepted the machine 'in so far as it relieves the workman from drudgery';[21] Hull House had a Labor Museum where immigrants practised spinning and weaving to demonstrate to younger audiences the continuities between craft and industry; and in 1911 the joint exhibition of the Society of Arts and Crafts and the Chicago Architectural Club included a working-man's rooms to show 'how inexpensively and yet how practically and artistically such a home could be furnished with things made by machinery'. Wright's accommodation of machinery, far from being that of a lone pioneer, was very much part of the Chicago Arts and Crafts.

In 1909, Wright sensationally abandoned his wife, family and professional practice to elope to Europe with a client's wife, but by then a number of Midwest architects – Robert Spencer (1864–1953), Walter Burley Griffin (1876–1937), and Wright's pupil William Drummond (1876–1948) among them – were working in the Prairie style. A fine but little-known example of their work is the Charles Barr House (fig. 230) which Drummond built in River Forest, based on the 'Fireproof House for $5,000' which Wright had published in the *Ladies' Home Journal* in 1906. With its hipped roof, green-stained board and batten, and protective cantilevered overhangs, the Charles Barr House is decidedly horizontal: the house specification book reveals that Drummond even wanted the upright edges of the bricks to be flush against each other to disguise the vertical joins, though this request was not carried out. Inside, the Roman-brick fireplace opens on three sides to heat the hall, living room and dining room, Drummond's triangular light fittings and art glass cast a warm, autumnal glow, and even the boot cupboard nestles up to a hot pipe. Designed for a librarian, the house exemplifies how the Prairie style could be deployed on a relatively modest scale to create a warm and inviting family house. Wright himself moved away from the Prairie style on his return to America in 1910, but aspects of his later work reveal the legacy of the Arts and Crafts. Memories of Chipping Campden, which Wright visited that year, may have inspired his rural home at Taliesin, Wisconsin, and the residential community of architects that he established there (though the Taliesin Fellowship was less a community than a cult which one had to pay to join). His so-called 'Usonian' houses (inexpensive homes for middle-income families) and Fallingwater, a luxury Pennsylvania holiday home for a

Pittsburgh millionaire, have the innovative planning and site specificity characteristic of the Prairie style. Wright's concept of 'organic architecture', which would evolve continuously in response to local topography and to changing human situations and needs, was also in many senses a child of the Arts and Crafts. America's most notorious architect reinvented himself repeatedly throughout his prolific career, but some of his fundamental beliefs reveal the lasting influence of his early, Chicago-based experiments in domestic architecture and design.

By the turn of the century, the Arts and Crafts Movement in the United States was spreading further afield. There were Arts and Crafts Societies in both metropolises – New York, Minneapolis, Detroit – and smaller towns. Such was the enthusiasm in Helena, Montana, that Ashbee was mobbed after giving a lecture to the Arts and Crafts Society there. 'Holy shade of Plato', he recalled, 'I don't quite know what happened after that, but Janet tells me I hid under a palm tree that was growing in a pot.'[22] Rural craft communities also appeared, in some cases moving out of cities in search of some rustic Utopia: the Handicraft Shop of the Boston Society of Arts and Crafts, for example, moved to the Wellesley Hills, inspired by the romantic exodus of Ashbee's Guild of Handicraft to Chipping Campden. Others began life in rural environments, such as the Rose Valley Association which the architect William Price (1861–1916) set up in an abandoned mill south-west of Philadelphia in 1901. Inspired by Morris's *News from Nowhere*, the Association included pottery, furniture and bookbinding workshops and a private press which published the journal *The Artsman* from 1903 to 1907. In 1902, Ralph Radcliffe Whitehead (1854–1929), an eccentric Englishman and friend of Ruskin, also established a rural community, the Byrdcliffe colony in Woodstock, New York, where craftsmen could escape 'the slavery of our too artificial and too complex life'.[23] Both communities explored the ideal of a pre-industrial work ethic centred on communal, rural living: but neither was a lasting success, echoing the fate of Ashbee's Guild of Handicraft, to which they were often compared. Rose Valley, despite influential backers, a Philadelphia showroom and about a hundred employees in its heyday, went bankrupt in 1909, while the Byrdcliffe colony suffered an exodus of craftsmen each winter, and its products never realized prices high enough to cover the labour which they entailed. In 1915 Ashbee found it reduced to 'the shell of a great life, and all empty but for two or three lonely spinsters, one metal worker, one weaver, and two potters. It was tragic'.

232. Roycroft Shops (designed and executed by Karl Kipp)

Roycroft Stein, c.1910

Copper, silver and jade, 16.5 x 11.7 cm (6 ½ x 4 ⁵/₈ in)

Roycroft Art Museum, East Aurora, NY

231. Roycroft Shops (designed and executed by Dard Hunter)

Hall Chair, c.1904

Oak, paint, leather and iron tacks

130 x 50.8 x 47 cm (51 ¼ x 20 x 18 ½ in)

Collection of Mr and Mrs Christopher Forbes

233. Elbert Hubbard, 1904

Private collection

234. Roycroft Shops (designed by Dard Hunter and Karl Kipp)
Hanging Lantern from the Roycroft Chapel, c.1908–10
Copper, leaded glass, copper chains and beam straps (replaced)
21.6 x 37.5 x 22.2 cm (8 1/2 x 14 3/4 x 8 3/4 in)
Los Angeles County Museum of Art, CA

235. Page from *The Craftsman*, August 1906

Not all rural communities were doomed to failure though. In 1894 Elbert Hubbard (1856–1915), a wealthy but footloose soap salesman who had sold his partnership in the Larkin Soap Company in 1893, travelled to Britain where he claimed to have met Morris at the Kelmscott Press. The encounter is now thought to be a characteristic Hubbard fabrication, but Hubbard was nevertheless inspired on his return to acquire and develop the Roycroft Press in East Aurora, near Buffalo, New York. The Press, which published artistic books and a monthly magazine called *The Philistine*, led to a bookbindery and then a leather shop, and gradually Hubbard's venture expanded until a quasi-religious community of craftsmen, the Roycrofters, were busily producing furniture, ceramics, and work in leather, metal and glass. Their output ranged from sturdy furniture in native oak (a favourite Roycroft material) (fig. 231) to more decorative items such as hammered copper boxes, humidors, hatpins and bookends, all of which manifested the simplicity and honesty of the Arts and Crafts (fig. 232). Ornamentation was kept to a minimum, and often came from exposed methods of construction alone.

Elbert Hubbard (fig. 233), the guiding light of all this activity, was an oddball by any standards. Liberated from the world of big business, he grew his hair, acquired a painter's smock and a velvet tam-o'-shanter, and delighted in his new incarnation as a paternalistic craft impresario. Janet Ashbee, who traipsed through snow to the Roycroft Workshops one night, described his entry into a room as 'like having a Holbein picture uncovered before you.'[24] An incorrigible name-dropper, Hubbard claimed to know Ashbee before he realized who Janet was, which did not get their meeting off to an auspicious start, but the two soon found common ground. Janet admired the way in which the Roycrofters lived close to their workshops 'as the medieval folks did, and in the intervals of book-making lend a hand to spread mortar or adjust a cornerstone,'[25] while Hubbard shared the Ashbees' holistic approach to creative, intellectual and physical pursuits: Roycrofters worked an eight-hour day, could enrol in an apprentice system, and had access to libraries, lectures, concerts and organized sports. Hubbard, a consummate showman, also opened the community to the public: visitors came in their thousands to ogle the craftsmen and Hubbard's outlandish behaviour, while he himself fraternized with celebrities at the Roycroft-furnished Roycroft Inn. For Janet Ashbee, 'The nicest part is that Hubbard has a fine sense of humour, and sees the joke of the whole thing as much as anyone.'[26]

236. 'A Craftsman House', from *The Craftsman*, March 1904

237. Living Room, from *The Craftsman*, October 1905

238. Will Bradley
Drawing for a Library, 1901
Watercolour on paper, mounted on linen, 64.8 x 95.3 cm (25 ¹/₂ x 37 ¹/₂ in)
Henry E Huntington Library and Art Gallery, San Marino, CA

But Hubbard did not see the project as an amusing diversion for long. 'The Roycroft began as a joke,' he wrote in 1903, 'but did not stay one: it soon resolved itself into a Commercial institution.'[27] Having experienced professional success in manufacturing and marketing, Hubbard had none of the hang-ups about commercial practice which plagued the British Arts and Crafts. Indeed, he saw the world of commerce as 'just as honorable as the World of Art and a trifle more necessary. Art exists on the surplus that Business Men accumulate.'[28] The Roycroft enterprises accordingly became both a tourist attraction and a thriving business, making use of the latest machinery to meet production targets, advertising widely in magazines, and boasting 400 employees by 1906. Hubbard was clever enough to appreciate that many customers had preconceptions of what good craftsmanship entailed, and was careful not to disillusion them. Thus his relentless publicity machine claimed (erroneously) that every piece of Roycroft furniture was handmade. The products were available through mail-order catalogues and directly from the workshops, disseminating the craft ideal to a huge middle-class audience, and small souvenirs were developed to tempt even those with little

money to spend. So it was that a soap salesman with no artistic training whatsoever succeeded in commercializing the Arts and Crafts.

One of Hubbard's most influential designer-craftsmen was Dard Hunter (1883–1966), who found 'monthly inspiration'[29] in German magazines such as *Deutsche Kunst und Dekoration* and *Dekorative Kunst*. The influence of Mackintosh, perhaps, and more probably that of the Viennese Secession and the Wiener Werkstätte is evident in Hunter's lanterns, in which the brio of the metalwork is tempered by the simple geometry of the stained glass (fig. 234). In 1908 and 1910 Hunter visited Europe to study its design at first hand, and on his return left the Roycrofters to manage his own craft enterprises, including the Dard Hunter School of Handicraft and the Mountain House Press. He became famous for his 'one-man' books which took integrated production to an extreme, with Hunter doing everything from making the paper and writing the text to designing the layout and setting the type. Others also spread their wings beyond Hubbard's empire – the banker-turned-coppersmith Karl Kipp (1882–1954), for example, left in 1912 to launch the Tookay Shop, though he later returned – and Hubbard himself met a dramatic end, drowning when the *Lusitania* sank in 1915. The Roycroft enterprises nevertheless continued under his son, who set up Roycroft franchises in department stores. Hit by the Depression in the 1930s, the business collapsed in 1938, but its happy collusion with key aspects of modernity – mass marketing, mechanized production and major retail outlets – demonstrated conclusively that the Arts and Crafts need not be shackled to a moneyed elite.

Hubbard was not the only American to succeed in democratizing the Arts and Crafts. His contemporary Gustav Stickley (1858–1942) developed a furniture empire so successful that, for many Americans in the early twentieth century, the name Stickley became synonymous with the craft ideal. The oldest of six brothers, Gustav first trained with his father as a stonemason, but found his vocation learning the art of furniture-making from an uncle in Pennsylvania. Following a trip to Europe in 1898, during which he met Ashbee, Voysey, Lethaby and Cobden-Sanderson, he began to espouse many Arts and Crafts ideas, not least the belief that creative satisfaction and artistic control were integral to a successful design. 'If the chair is to be valued as an individual piece of work,' he enthused, 'the man who makes it must have known the joy and enthusiasm of carrying out an idea that is his own, or with which he is in such perfect sympathy that the work becomes a delight'.[30] Inspired, he set up the United Crafts (later the Craftsman Workshops) in Eastwood, a suburb of Syracuse, New York, and began to develop his Craftsman furniture range. 'The United Crafts', he explained, 'endeavor to promote and extend the principles established by Morris, in both the artistic and the socialistic sense. In the interests of art, they seek to substitute the luxury of taste for the luxury of costliness; to teach that beauty does not imply elaboration or ornament; to employ only those forms and materials which make for simplicity, individuality and dignity of effect.'[31]

Craftsman furniture reveals the influence of British designers. Stickley copied a Baillie Scott table for his own house, and there were a total of seven Craftsman versions of the Morris chair. But there were American precedents for the Craftsman aesthetic as well, notably the furniture of the Shaker religious communities, with their plain, utilitarian bedsteads, tables and ladder-back chairs. Stickley had seen Shaker furniture at the Philadelphia Centennial, admiring its evocation of a pre-industrial vernacular, and acknowledged that his early work was 'after the "Shaker" model'.[32] Sturdy, affordable, and with an unmistakably national pedigree, Craftsman furniture held great appeal for the expanding

239. Lucia Mathews
Covered Jar, c.1906
Painted and gilded wood, 31.7 x 25.4 cm (12 ¹/₂ x 10 in)
Virginia Museum of Fine Arts, Richmond

middle classes, and became a regular feature of the American suburban home: it was comfortable, practical, stylish and safe – a tried and tested index of unadventurous good taste.

Key to this success was *The Craftsman*, the monthly periodical which Stickley published from 1901 to 1916. *The Craftsman* explored British developments, with its first two issues devoted to Morris and Ruskin; it published articles on social debates, from the efficacy of the garden suburb to 'Social Work in British Factories'; and it served as a mouthpiece for Stickley's theoretical views. The magazine also promoted the Craftsman aesthetic as being capable of raising standards of taste, playing on the insecurities of those who felt they lacked sophistication and skill in matters of craft and design (fig. 235). Gradually, the Craftsman rubric expanded, and the magazine began to feature houses and bungalows by various designers, complete with plans and descriptions of how they were built (fig. 236). Known as 'Craftsman Homes', these designs satisfied patriotic sentiment by evoking American building types, from the rustic log cabin to the colonial house; they met different budgets by using materials of varying quality and price: and, while they were pictured in attractive settings, the text emphasized that

240. Charles and Henry Greene
The Gamble House, 1908–9
Pasadena, CA

241. Main Entrance, The Gamble House

they could be modified to suit any site. Interior renditions, for their part, exuded homely comfort, cultural accomplishment and tasteful restraint. Thus a design for a living room of 1905 (fig. 237) includes an elegant lamp and runner and some well-chosen ceramics, while cultural pursuits are suggested by the piano and the books, which the inhabitant might read in the enticing Craftsman chair. *The Craftsman* published over 220 of these designs, complete sets of which were sold by mail order for do-it-yourself enthusiasts, and Stickley later issued them in book form as well. Accessible, adaptable and affordable, with Stickley setting their price range 'between two and fifteen thousand dollars',[33] they initiated a vogue for unpretentious houses and bungalows, and in the process changed the face of American domestic design.

Until the First World War, the Craftsman empire appeared to be impregnable, with showrooms across the country, and Stickley seemed an invincible populariser of the Craftsman ideal. In 1908, he began an ambitious, self-sufficient co-operative near Morris Plains in New Jersey. He also moved the editorial and administrative part of his business to prestigious offices in New York, expanding into the twelve-storey Craftsman Building in Manhattan, complete with showroom and restaurant, in 1913. Sadly, he had overextended his business, and financial rot set in, but such was the popularity of the Craftsman aesthetic that even Stickley's brothers emulated his success. As early as 1900 Leopold (1869–1957) and John George (1871–1921) set up a rival enterprise, the L & J G Stickley Company in Fayetteville, New York, which mass produced versions of their brother's furniture. In a galling move, they also took over Gustav's Eastwood workshops after he filed for bankruptcy in 1915. Stickley's empire therefore came to a humiliating end: but his furniture, houses and *The Craftsman* had made simple, honest design accessible to a vast public, in the process establishing comfort and convenience as key to the modern American home.

The Craftsman was one of several periodicals which disseminated Arts and Crafts ideals. *The Studio* had been published in America as *The International Studio* since 1897, and the *Ladies' Home Journal*, with its plans for reasonably priced houses, was an important conduit of domestic architecture and design. Its contributors included Prairie School architects, Cram from Boston, and Will Bradley, who from 1901 to 1902 published a series of furniture designs and interiors known as the 'Bradley House' which featured

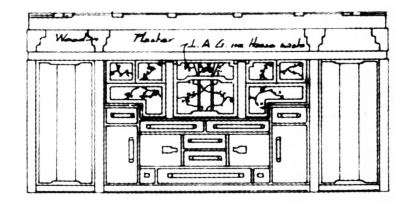

242. (following page) Staircase, The Gamble House

243. (above) Charles Greene
Detail from *Interior Detail Sheet No. 7* for The Gamble House, 19 February 1908
Ink on linen contract drawings
Avery Architectural and Fine Arts Library, Columbia University

244. Charles Greene
Dining Room Sideboard, The Gamble House, 1908–9
Honduras mahogany with art glass and light sconces approx. 125.5 x 287 x 73.5 cm (49 1/2 x 113 x 29 in)
The Gamble House, Pasadena, CA

inglenooks, window seats, leaded windows, decorative friezes, and exposed beams, rivets and mortise-and-tenon joints (fig. 238). Few of Bradley's furniture designs were actually realized, but the interior renditions were so popular that Edward Bok (1863–1930), the editor, commissioned a second series in 1905.

These publications expedited the transmission of Arts and Crafts ideas as far as California, which in the early twentieth century joined Boston and Chicago as the third great regional movement in the American Arts and Crafts. There were notable craft workshops in the Bay Area, such as the Copper Shop which Dirk Van Erp (1859–1933) opened in Oakland in 1908. Van Erp, a Dutch immigrant, used to tinker shell cases into vases while working in the shipyards near San Francisco, and eventually left his day job to launch a successful range of copperware. His fulgent lamps with their exposed rivets and tinted mica shades match the best of Benson's metalwork in Britain, though Van Erp, unlike Benson, believed in doing everything by hand. The artists and designers Arthur (1860–1945) and Lucia Mathews (1870–1955) also worked in the Bay Area, employing wood-carvers, cabinet-makers and decorators in their Furniture Shop to cater for the surge of building which followed the San Francisco earthquake of 1906. The Furniture Shop provided anything from a mural to a custom-made interior, furnished perhaps with medievalist furniture similar to that of the British Arts and Crafts, or with Lucia's beautifully crafted accessories, such as the jar which she painted and gilded for her sister's wedding in c.1906 (fig. 239). The most important developments on the West Coast, however, lay in architecture, in particular that of the Greene brothers, whose response to the natural beauty of the Golden State became one of the most distinctive features of the Californian Arts and Crafts.

Charles Sumner Greene (1868–1957) and Henry Mather Greene (1870–1954) were born in Cincinnati, and both graduated from the Massachusetts Institute of Technology before starting work in Boston. In 1893 they moved to California, setting up practice in the resort community of Pasadena the following year. They first worked in a range of styles, from American Shingle to British Georgian, but became interested in the Arts and Crafts following Charles's honeymoon in England in 1901. They also read *The International Studio* and subscribed to *The Craftsman*, with its mantra of explicit and appropriate construction. Their response to these influences is seen most fully in the 'ultimate bungalows' of 1907–9, in which the brothers developed an architectural idiom perfectly suited to the Californian climate and site.

The most expressive of the 'ultimate bungalows' is the Gamble House (1908–9), which was designed by Charles for a member of one of the families behind the Cincinnati soap conglomerate Procter & Gamble. Significantly, it was a winter retreat, built for the Ohio-based family to escape the icy months of the Midwest and make the most of the Californian sunshine. With this in mind, Charles designed a three-dimensional puzzle of balconies, verandas, porches and patios to extend the architecture into the landscape, enabling the Gambles to eat, socialize and even sleep outside (fig. 240). Exposed beams and rafters make a startling bid for freedom, fingering their way out from the body of the house, while overhangs provide shelter from the glare of the Californian sun. The building was deliberately oriented to catch prevalent breezes (the Greenes' father, a doctor specializing in respiratory problems, having impressed upon his sons the benefits of fresh air), while stained-glass windows, wood-frame fixtures and the low-wattage bulbs of the time helped to keep the interiors cool and dim. To the architectural visitor who associates the landscape of southern California with the light-filled houses of later architects, this darkness comes as a surprise. Stylistically, the house draws on various timber-based architectural models: it is shingle-clad in an echo of the Shingle style, while the bungalow form, the exposed joinery and construction, and the landscaping, with its trellises, pergolas and terraces, emulate the architectural and landscape traditions of the Far East. The brothers had studied Asian exhibits in the Museum of Fine Arts, Boston and, possibly, at the Columbian Exhibition in Chicago, but it was the St Louis World's Fair in 1904, with its displays from India, Ceylon, China and Japan, which cemented their love of Asian artefacts and design.

Inside the Gamble House there are rugs and runners, lights and latches, and stained-glass windows looking on to landscaped vistas, all designed by the Greenes. The front door provides one of many references to the local environment, depicting a California oak modelled in art glass by the craftsman Emil Lange (fig. 241). Most striking of all is the epicurean celebration of wood, which here includes native redwood, honey-coloured teak, mahogany, maple, cedar and oak. Both brothers had become accomplished woodworkers at the Washington University Manual Training School, and their woodwork was once compared to 'fresh butter or paste squeezed out of a tube',[34] so mellifluously does it bend and mesh in the joints of cabinets, the treads of stairs (fig. 242). The comprehensiveness of their vision is apparent in an

245. (previous page) Bernard Maybeck
Interior of the First Church of Christ Scientist, Berkeley, CA, 1910

246. Detail of the Ceiling, First Church of Christ Scientist

interior detail sheet, in which even handles and tiles are marked (fig. 243). These designs were executed exactly as planned by a team of gifted craftsmen which the Greenes cultivated: thus the built-in sideboard in the dining room (fig. 244), with its mahogany sheen set off by limpid art glass, corresponds exactly to the drawing on the detail sheet. So high was the priority accorded to good joinery and cabinet-making that the local brothers John and Peter Hall worked almost exclusively for the Greenes at the time, turning and shaving and joining and planing to create the tight connections and tactile inflexions which the dreamy Charles designed. Ashbee, who met Charles in Pasadena in 1909, found it 'the best and most characteristic furniture' he had seen in America, its 'supreme feeling for the material'[35] matching the finest craftsmanship in England at the time. Charles even designed cabinets for the kitchen and butler's pantry, including one to house the leaves of the dining table which were not in use, despite the fact that Mrs Gamble apparently never set foot in that part of the house. Published regularly in *The Craftsman*, *Architectural Record* and *Western Architect*, their designs exemplified how the Arts and Crafts idiom could be reworked to suit an entirely different clime.

While the Greene brothers were responding to geography and climate, others in California were concerned with the state's history and heritage. Their inspiration came from Charles Fletcher Lummis (1859–1928), a Harvard dropout who moved to Los Angeles in 1884 and took it upon himself to save what he could of the region's Spanish and Native American past. As city librarian, Lummis amassed an important collection of documents relating to the Spanish occupation; in 1894 he founded the California Landmarks Club, one of America's first preservation societies, to rescue derelict Spanish missions in southern California; and he campaigned tirelessly on behalf of the Native Americans, eventually setting up the Southwest Museum outside Los Angeles as a beacon to their cause. Lummis failed to appreciate the irony of trumpeting both the heritage of the Native Americans and that of the Spanish settlers who had oppressed them as part of one, harmonious, pre-modern idyll. But his work was significant for both cultures, not least in fuelling the Mission Revival style. This drew on architectural features of the Spanish missions and on their adobe method of building with sun-dried bricks, and came to be seen as something to which California could lay particular claim. In San Diego, for example, Irving Gill (1870–1936) employed the simple surfaces and regular geometry of adobe buildings to create a white, cubic architecture which prefigured the Modern style. Gill aimed to build simple, affordable and hygienic housing, explaining in *The Craftsman* that he rounded the joints between walls and floors so that there was no space for dust or 'for vermin of any kind'.[36] Moreover, he welcomed advances in technology, buying machinery which the US Army had used to produce prefabricated barracks, and promoting concrete as the most appropriate material for a modern house.

In the Bay Area, Bernard Maybeck (1862–1957) also incorporated new materials and technologies in his buildings. In the First Church of Christ Scientist (1910) in the university town of Berkeley, he used asbestos panels as cladding, and stock steel factory sash windows: the manufacturers of both products were horrified, thinking them far from suitable for a church. Inside, four massive, hollow columns serve as heating ducts and as exhausts for stale air, allying form with function in a manner typical of the Arts and Crafts. But in contrast to Gill's minimalism, Maybeck, who had served an apprenticeship in his father's furniture and wood-carving shop, believed that new technology should coexist with good craftsmanship. The church is therefore richly decorated, from the trefoil designs of the hammered-metal light fittings to the stencilling and tracery of the trusses, windows and walls (fig. 245). Even the capitals of the cast-concrete piers are painted in bright, primary colours, as if some mischievous child has coloured in the gaps (fig. 246).

Maybeck had trained at the École des Beaux-Arts in Paris, but was one of the least hidebound of architects: in his dress code of smock and beard, his career encompassed an eclectic range of styles. The vernacular German buildings which he encountered while studying in Europe, for example, inspired a range of rustic wooden chalets and bungalows in the Berkeley hills, with gables, shingles and crafted wooden details to suit the lulling topography of the site. The first of these houses was built for the poet and naturalist Charles Keeler, who joined Maybeck in proselytizing the suitability of Arts and Crafts architecture for the suburban development of the region. Keeler expounded its honest construction, craftsmanship and restraint in his book *The Simple Home* of 1904, and persuaded a bevy of clients to employ Maybeck to design them folksy wooden houses to complement Keeler's own. Unlike Wright and the Greenes, Maybeck did not design all the furnishings, but he insisted that each house suit its owner, making unannounced calls to study his clients' lifestyle, and even encouraging them to give parties so that he could see how they socialized and entertained. The result was a distinctive suburban architecture, based on a German vernacular but inflected by the needs of a Californian client on a Californian site.

The work of the Greenes, Gill, Maybeck and their peers gave the Californian Arts and Crafts Movement a style indelibly its own. It was about making the most of California's sunshine and scenery and embracing the lifestyle of its inhabitants. At times, it was also about responding to California's Spanish and Native American past. But the contrast between the Greenes' nest-like structures of slips and rafters, Gill's abnegation of ornamentation, and Maybeck's chalets underlines the diversity and the diversions from theory which we have come to expect of the Arts and Crafts. American designers were less anxious to find an alternative social order to capitalism than Ruskin, Morris and Ashbee had been. American architects also moved away from the British practice of looking to medieval influences. Instead, they turned to local landscape, native architectural forms and rural archaeology, from Spanish Mission to pre-Columbian, reminding us that the Movement is one of attitudes, not one of styles.

Perhaps most importantly, American designers realized that the great flaw in the British Movement lay in its disavowal of machinery. Thus in 1908 the American tile-maker Ernest Batchelder (1875–1957), who had studied at the Birmingham Municipal School of Art and worked at the Guild of Handicraft in Chipping Campden, published an article in *The Craftsman* entitled 'Why the Handicraft Guild at Chipping Campden has not been a Business Success', in which he argued that British designers were greatly hindered by their hostility towards the machine. American designers, in contrast, demonstrated that the use of machinery could be compatible with worker-conscious ideals, and that in the modern world it was essential in establishing a viable relationship between commerce and craft. This willingness to design for mechanized production was emblematic of a new mentality which wanted to engage with the incontrovertible advances of modernism, rather than look continually to the past.

Sam Maloof
Rocking Chair, 1997 (fig. 250)

EPILOGUE

THE ARTS AND CRAFTS MOVEMENT DID NOT LONG SURVIVE THE FIRST WORLD WAR, CONTINUING ONLY IN THE WORK OF ISOLATED ARCHITECTS AND DESIGNERS.

In Britain, the promotion of hand craftsmanship as a critique of industrial society and modernity had run its course. Neither was the idea of the crafts rising like a phoenix from the fertile ashes of medieval decorative art to play much part in later-twentieth-century design. Yet other elements of the Arts and Crafts Movement anticipated or inspired many later architects and designers, and in 1936 the architectural historian Nikolaus Pevsner (1902–83) famously identified Morris and his peers as critical to the development of Modernism in his book *Pioneers of the Modern Movement: from William Morris to Walter Gropius*. There is no doubt that aspects of the Arts and Crafts did tune into a key moment in Modernism: the concern with expressed construction, function and propriety, for example, sits happily with the Modernist emphasis on medium and method rather than subject. But just as the Arts and Crafts Movement was an organism of visual and intellectual complexity, so its influence has been more varied and nuanced than that exerted on Modernism alone.

To start with the more tangible legacies of the Arts and Crafts, some of its most influential guilds and societies continue to operate. The Arts and Crafts Exhibition Society still exists as the Society of Designer-Craftsmen, which has in recent years reverted to the practice of holding an annual members' exhibition. And the Art Workers' Guild continues to hold fortnightly meetings, except during the summer, at 6 Queen Square (its home since 1914). Many workshops also lasted well into the twentieth century. Production at Sapperton continued until the Barnsley brothers died in 1926; the Haslemere workshops operated until 1930; and the Ruskin Pottery lasted until 1934, to cite just three. While the practices of some of these workshops died with them (the founder of the Ruskin Pottery, William Howson Taylor, vowed that he would take its trade secrets to the grave), other ventures have emulated the honest workmanship which the Arts and Crafts workshops espoused. Some of the earliest – and most unusual – were the communities which Eric Gill set up to combine craft production with the Simple Life, most memorably in the Guild of SS Joseph and Dominic at Ditchling Common in Sussex. Gill, a devout convert to Catholicism, combined the seeming contradictions of a Dominican religious order, a strong sense of family, and a sexual appetite which encompassed adultery, incest and even bestiality. He also came to see the Arts and Crafts as an affectation, ridiculing its advocates as pious bores – 'you can *see* the boys don't drink'. But his Guild, part religious order and part craft workshop, owed a clear debt to those Arts and Crafts communities which aimed to recreate a pre-industrial way of life and work, Gill himself striving 'to make a cell of good living in the chaos of our world'.[2]

Ditchling became a retreat for other craftsmen and women who were vital in maintaining momentum in their respective crafts. They included the calligrapher Edward Johnston, who after the First World War enthralled a younger generation of calligraphy students at the Royal College of Art; the potter Bernard Leach (1887–1979), who later set up his renowned pottery at St Ives in Cornwall; and the weaver Ethel Mairet (1872–1952), who had been associated with Ashbee's Guild of Handicraft at Chipping Campden. Mairet was Modernist in her tastes and enthusiastic about relationships between handwork and industry, particularly after visiting the German Werkstätten exhibitions in the 1930s, and she and others at her weaving workshop in Ditchling designed for industry, believing it the duty of small craft workshops to improve industrial design. But equally, Mairet carried on hand-weaving all her life, and kept the Arts and Crafts faith that craft must be part of a building, and must involve the ordinary preoccupations of life. The concern with the handicrafts continued elsewhere, not least in the Cotswolds, where there was if anything more craft activity in the 1920s and 1930s than had been the case before the war. As well as new workshops, such as the pottery which Leach's pupil Michael Cardew set up in Winchcombe in 1926, descendants of Ashbee's Guildsmen and of other Arts and Crafts practitioners continued to work in the Cotswolds, and there are plans to open a museum in Chipping Campden which will document its ongoing relationship with craftsmanship and design. This is not to suggest that the craft movement in Britain became one of family members and pupils fanning the embers of moribund initiatives. On the contrary, there is a vital new growth of guilds and workshops and, since 1964, the state-subsidized Crafts Council, whose aims include preserving traditional skills and promoting the work of artist-craftsmen. The Arts and Crafts Movement in Britain can therefore be seen both as a distinct episode which came to an end in the interwar period, and as one phase in a much longer – and continuing – history of revived craft, the richness and variety of which are recounted in Tanya Harrod's masterful *The Crafts in Britain in the 20th Century* of 1999.

The craft tradition is just as buoyant abroad. There are thousands of workshops in the United States, and Europe has a vibrant network of practitioners and communities working in the Arts and Crafts tradition. To mention just one example which emphasises the resilience of the craft workshop culture: a new Gödöllő Applied Art Workshop was founded in Hungary in 1998, its works such as Erzsébet Szekeres's *Equestrians* tapestry of 2001 (fig. 247) illustrating the continuing interest in echoing folk traditions in vibrant, modern designs. Arts and Crafts ideals even travelled as far as Japan, where from the 1920s the Mingei or Folk Craft Movement advocated the revival of handmade folk crafts by anonymous craftsmen who worked not for personal glory or wealth, but simply to earn a living. Yanagi Sōetsu (1889–1961), the leader of the Movement, stressed the originality of Mingei theory, which prioritized natural materials, traditional methods and simple, functional forms, and aimed to elevate common household objects (*getemono*) to the status of art. Research has nevertheless highlighted the importance of Arts and Crafts ideas, which enjoyed wide currency in Japan at the time. Ruskin had been introduced in Japan in the late 1880s, with a substantial translation of his writing on architecture in 1911, and translations of *The Seven Lamps of Architecture* in 1930 and *The Stones of Venice* in 1931–2. Morris was first discussed in detail in an article of 1912 by Tomimoto Kenkichi (1886–1963), a young potter who had studied at London's Central School of Arts and Crafts, and who was active in the early Mingei Movement. Yanagi himself subscribed to *The Studio*, established a guild of craftsmen comparable to Morris & Co. in 1927, and founded the Japan Folk Crafts Museum inspired by the Nordic Museum in Stockholm in 1936. The Mingei Movement apart, the artist and educationalist Yamamoto Kanae (1882–1946) was inspired by visits to *kustar* museums in Russia to launch courses in 'peasant art' in 1919. These led to the Japan Peasant Art Institute (1923–35), which aimed to alleviate the financial hardship of peasants during the quiet months of the agricultural year, raise the artistic standard of their environment, and enable greater self-sufficiency by teaching craft skills. From 1925, Yamamoto's project was subsidized by a government grant and expanded to include forty peasant art co-operatives by 1931, some of which still exist, confirming the success with which Arts and Crafts ideas were transplanted on Japanese soil.

In architecture, the influence of the Arts and Crafts Movement has been just as compelling as in craft practices. Drive through the outskirts of any major city in Britain, as well as many suburbs in continental Europe, and you will pass detached, semi-detached and terraced houses whose gables, tiled roofs and bay windows owe a debt to the Arts and Crafts.

247. Erzsébet Szekeres
Equestrians, 2001
4-warp Gobelin tapestry, wool, 100 x 130 cm (39 ¹/₂ x 51 in)
Private collection

248. Charles Morris
The Orchard Room at Highgrove House, Gloucestershire, 1997

250. Sam Maloof
Rocking Chair, 1997
Cherry and ebony, 116.8 x 81.3 x 66 cm (46 x 32 x 26 in)
Los Angeles County Museum of Art, CA

There are also more idiosyncratic echoes of Arts and Crafts practices; for example, in the Orchard Room which the Norfolk architect Charles Morris designed in 1997 for Highgrove House in Gloucestershire, the home of the Prince of Wales. The Orchard Room was built with local materials by workmen who either lived locally or came from Norfolk, while its stubby Tuscan columns were inspired by those which appear both in an old piggery in the Highgrove farmyard, and in a seventeenth-century building in the nearby town of Tetbury (fig. 248).

In America, there is still a market for Stickley-style houses and for bungalows in California which mould themselves to the state's climate and scenery, while aspects of the Prairie idiom – the hovering volumes and banded windows of the Robie House, for example – have influenced the work of architects as seminal as Gropius, Mies van de Rohe and Le Corbusier. National Romantic developments in Europe have had a more problematic history, partly as they were harnessed to the National Socialist agenda in Nazi Germany. Nevertheless, the building styles which appeared as Finland, Hungary and Poland negotiated the path to independence in the late nineteenth and early twentieth

century still resurface. Since the 1970s, for example, various suburbs of Poland have witnessed a wave of villas in the Zakopane style. On a more global scale, the so-called New Vernacular has seen architects in many countries building with new materials and methods but echoing regional styles in a modern way, while the Garden City Movement has extended as far as Canberra and New Delhi, making a lasting impact on twentieth-century town planning and design.

If we move to the more abstract principles of the Arts and Crafts Movement, we find that many have become so ingrained in the modern artistic consciousness that we take them for granted. The insistence of the Society for the Protection of Ancient Buildings on minimal intervention in restoration work is now standard policy. The desire to use materials honestly and to use them well has also had unflagging appeal, even if the materials in question have changed. In the 1930s, for example, the Finnish designer Alvar Aalto created furniture out of laminated birch plywood which was moulded to the contours of the human form (fig. 249). While the material of plywood was new, Aalto's use of it recalls the way in which Arts and Crafts designers embraced other materials to meet a functional need (Prior's use of concrete at St Andrew's

249. Alvar Aalto
Paimio Chair, 1931–2
Bent plywood, bent laminated birch, and solid birch
66 x 60.3 x 87.6 cm (26 x 23 ³⁄₄ x 34 ¹⁄₂ in)
Private collection

GENESIS

In the beginning when God created[1] the heavens and the earth, 2 the earth was a formless void and darkness covered the face of the deep, while a wind from God[2] swept over the face of the waters. 3 Then God said, "Let there be light"; and there was light. 4 And God saw that the light was good; and God separated the light from the darkness. 5 God called the light Day, and the darkness he called Night. And there was evening and there was morning, the first day.

6 And God said, "Let there be a dome in the midst of the waters, and let it separate the waters from the waters." 7 So God made the dome and separated the waters that were under the dome from the waters that were above the dome. And it was so. 8 God called the dome Sky. And there was evening and there was morning, the second day.

9 And God said, "Let the waters under the sky be gathered together into one place, and let the dry land appear." And it was so. 10 God called the dry land Earth, and the waters that were gathered together he called Seas. And God saw that it was good. 11 Then God said, "Let the earth put forth vegetation: plants yielding seed, and fruit trees of every kind on earth that bear fruit with the seed in it." And it was so. 12 The earth brought forth vegetation: plants yielding seed of every kind, and trees of every kind bearing fruit with the seed in it. And God saw that it was good. 13 And there was evening and there was morning, the third day.

14 And God said, "Let there be lights in the dome of the sky to separate the day from the night; and let them be for signs and for seasons and for days and years, 15 and let them be lights in the dome of the sky to give light upon the earth." And it was so. 16 God made the two great lights – the greater light to rule the day and the lesser light to rule the night – and the stars. 17 God set them in the dome of the sky to give light upon the earth, 18 to rule over the day and over the night, and to separate the light from the darkness. And God saw that it was good. 19 And there was evening and there was morning, the fourth day.

20 And God said, "Let the waters bring forth swarms of living creatures, and let birds fly above the earth across the dome of the sky." 21 So God created the great sea monsters and every living creature that moves, of every kind, with which the waters swarm, and every winged bird of every kind. And God saw that it was good. 22 God blessed them, saying, "Be fruitful and multiply and fill the waters in the seas, and let birds multiply on the earth." 23 And there was evening and there was morning, the fifth day.

24 And God said, "Let the earth bring forth living creatures of every kind: cattle and creeping things and wild animals of the earth of every kind." And it was so. 25 God made the wild animals of the earth of every kind, and the cattle of every kind, and everything that creeps upon the ground of every kind. And God saw that it was good.

26 Then God said, "Let us make humankind[3] in our image, according to our likeness; and let them have dominion over the fish of the sea, and over the birds of the air, and over the cattle, and over all the wild animals of the earth,[4] and over every creeping thing that creeps upon the earth."

27 So God created humankind[5] in his image,
in the image of God he created them;[a]
male and female he created them.

28 God blessed them, and God said to them, "Be fruitful and multiply, and fill the earth and subdue it; and have dominion over the fish of the sea and over the birds of the air and over every living thing that moves upon the earth." 29 God said, "See, I have given you every plant yielding seed that is upon the face of all the

1 Or when God began to create or In the beginning God created
2 Or while the spirit of God or while a mighty wind
3 Heb adam
4 Syr: Heb and over all the earth
5 Heb him

251. The Arion Press Bible, 2000
45.7 x 33 cm (18 x 13 in)
Arion Press, San Francisco, CA

Church in Roker being one example which springs to mind). Aalto went on to co-found the firm Artek in 1933, which aimed to produce inexpensive, well-designed textiles, light fittings and furnishings: when these were exhibited at the exclusive London store of Fortnum & Mason later that year, figures as diverse as Voysey and Gropius admired the craftsmanship and functionalism of the work. One can see later designers working in the same mould, such as the American Sam Maloof, whose furniture is rooted in the twin constructs of fitness for purpose and superlative craftsmanship. Maloof's rocking chairs are so comfortable that to sit in them brings the same pleasure as sinking into a much-loved bed, despite the fact that the chairs are made of wood alone (fig. 250). The Private Press Movement too continues to thrive, maintaining the crafts of typecasting, letterpress printing and bookbinding in fine presses such as the Whittington Press in Herefordshire, the Rampant Lions Press in Cambridge, and the Arion Press in San Francisco. For its lavish folio Bible, issued in 2000, the Arion Press composed and cast 1,350 pages of Monotype that were printed by letterpress on all-cotton English mould-made paper (fig. 251). Typesetting and printing required two years, and binding by hand of the 400-copy edition is on-going. Some private presses now also employ non-traditional methods, including computer-generated typography and digital printing. Certain designers involved in the Private Press Movement even design digital type and new fonts, often for major conglomerates, leading to the dramatic improvement of computer typesetting over recent years.

Here, we encounter more subtle ways in which Arts and Crafts ideals continue to infiltrate our lives. Today it is not the horrors of industrialized production in the Western world which compel people to reassess the way in which they live and work. It is evils on a global scale, such as pollution, terrorism, or the exploitation of workers in certain areas of the Third World. Key attempts to address some of these problems – the practice of fair trade, for example – echo the Arts and Crafts identification of quality products with healthy lifestyles in localized communities. Thus the British-based chocolate manufacturer Green & Black's is committed to using only the finest of organic cocoa beans, and to sustaining the local industries in Belize which produce these. On a more domestic level, there has been a resurgence of the Simple Life ethos in the actions of those who choose to leave the rat race of high-paid and high-profile careers to seek a better quality of life in the country. Such changes often involve abandoning desk-bound occupations which use the head, in favour of making things by hand, echoing the anti-Cartesian approach which has underpinned so many ventures in this book. There is a whiff of the Arts and Crafts behind many of these attempts at the simplification of life, attempts that go further than the banker or celebrity who abandons his or her profession to run a ranch in Wyoming, or renovate a house in France. Thus the teleology of the Arts and Crafts – that a better environment can lead to better products and a better way of life – continues to have an impact on the way in which we manage our world and run our lives. For all the vibrant afterlife of specific Arts and Crafts designs – the continuing craze for Morris wallpapers, for example, or the renewed taste for simple, countrified furniture – it is the ongoing relevance of this key theoretical premise which is so striking. What began as an intellectual movement to reinvent the crafts as activities of social and moral relevance now lingers on in issues as supranational as Third World policy and environmental debates. The resilience of the Movement's theoretical and practical legacy in a world unrecognizable from that in which it originally evolved speaks volumes for its complex balance of flexibility and integrity, and is perhaps a portent that the values which informed the Arts and Crafts Movement will survive.

NOTES

INTRODUCTION
1. Ashbee, 1908, p. 5.
2. Naylor, 1990, p. 108.
3. Lee, 1884, vol. 2, p. 29.

ESCAPING THE 'INEXHAUSTIBLE MINES OF BAD TASTE'
1. Children's Employment Commission, 1842, p. 16.
2. Cole, 1953, p. 56.
3. Thomas Carlyle, 'Signs of the Times', *Edinburgh Review* (June 1829): in Tennyson (ed.), 1984, p. 34.
4. Ibid., p. 37.
5. Carlyle, 1858, p. 12.
6. *Economist* (May 1848): quoted in Trevelyan, 1968, p. 132.
7. Thomas Carlyle, *Latter-Day Pamphlets* (1850), no. 1, *The Present Time*: in Symons (ed.), 1955, p. 430.
8. Trevelyan, 1968, p. 43.
9. Atterbury and Wainwright (eds), 1994, p. 5.
10. Pugin, 1969, n.p.
11. Naylor, 1990, p. 17.
12. Klingender, 1947, p. 130.
13. 'History of the Great Exhibition', *Art Journal Illustrated Catalogue*, 1851, p. xi.
14. *Journal of Design and Manufactures*, 5 (1851), p. 158.
15. Ralph Nicholson Wornum, 'The Exhibition as a Lesson in Taste', *Art Journal Illustrated Catalogue*, 1851, p. v.
16. Ibid.
17. 'History of the Great Exhibition', *Art Journal Illustrated Catalogue*, 1851, p. xiv.
18. 'Preface', *Art Journal Illustrated Catalogue*, 1851, n.p.
19. Society of Arts, 1853, p. 256.
20. Denvir, 1986, p. 6.
21. Naylor, 1990, p. 18.
22. Ibid., p. 19.
23. *Journal of Design and Manufactures*, 1 (March–August 1849), p. 86.
24. Jones, 1856, p. 2.
25. Cook and Wedderburn (eds), 1903, vol. 8, p. 141.
26. Ibid., vol. 9, p. 70.
27. Ibid., vol. 8, p. 60.
28. Naylor, 1990, p. 14.
29. Ibid., p. 15.
30. Cook and Wedderburn (eds), 1904, vol. 10, p. 193.
31. Ibid., p. 196.
32. Ibid., p. 201.
33. Marx, 1971, p. 21.
34. Cook and Wedderburn (eds), 1903, vol. 8, p. 218.

FIRST EXPLORATIONS: WILLIAM MORRIS AND HIS CIRCLE
1. Mackail, 1901, vol. 1, p. 186.
2. Ibid., p. 33.
3. Thompson, 1991, p. 6.
4. MacCarthy, 1994, p. 261.
5. George Edmund Street, 'On the Future of Art in England', *Ecclesiologist*, 19 (1858), p. 240.
6. Lethaby, 1979, p. 11.
7. Ibid., p. 266.
8. *Architectural Review* (1897–8), p. 239: quoted in Skipworth, 2002, pp. 15–16.
9. Thompson, 1991, p. 7.
10. Mackail, 1901, vol. 1, pp. 106–7.
11. MacCarthy, 1994, p. 133.
12. Mackail, 1901, vol. 1, p. 121.
13. Letter from William Morris to J R Thursfield, undated: quoted in Mackail, 1901, vol. 1, p. 125.
14. William Morris, 'Preface' to Kelmscott edition of 'The Nature of Gothic': quoted in Mackail, 1901, vol. 2, p. 275.
15. Lethaby, 1979, p. 27.
16. Naylor (ed.), 2000, p. 37.
17. Sewter, 1974, vol. 1, p. 66.
18. Mackail, 1901, vol. 1, p. 161.
19. Ibid., p. 164.
20. *The Northern Counties Magazine*, I (1900–1), p. 326: quoted in Saint et al., 1992, p. 9.
21. Saint et al., 1992, p. 5.
22. Letter reproduced in Robinson and Wildman, 1980, p. 43.
23. MacCarthy, 1994, p. 378.
24. Ibid., p. 401.
25. Emma Lazarus, 'A Day in Surrey with William Morris', *Century Magazine*, XXXII [new series vol. X], no. 3 (July 1886), pp. 390–1.
26. Naylor, 1990, p. 9.
27. Lethaby, 1979, pp. 94–5.
28. Stansky, 1985, p. 52.
29. *Commonwealth* (6 August 1887), pp. 4, 252.
30. Harvey and Press, 1996, p. 58.

CRAFT AND COMRADESHIP IN THE METROPOLIS
1. Morris, 1913, pp. 36–7.
2. Letter from George Frederick Watts of 25 June 1894: George Frederick Watts Archive, Watts Gallery, Compton, Surrey.
3. Century Guild Prospectus, Century Guild Archive, William Morris Gallery, Walthamstow, London.
4. Arthur Heygate Mackmurdo, 'The Guild Flag's Unfurling', *Century Guild Hobby Horse*, 1 (April 1884), p. 2.
5. Rothenstein, 1931, vol. 1, p. 332.
6. MacCarthy, 1979, p. 29.
7. Farr, 1984, p. 58.
8. *Pall Mall Gazette*, 44, no. 6679 (12 August 1886), p. 1.
9. Charles Robert Ashbee, Journals, vol. 5, 9 May 1899, folio 9/40: Archive Centre, King's College, Cambridge.
10. MacCarthy, 1994, p. 600.
11. George Bernard Shaw, 'In the Picture Galleries', *The Studio*, 116 (November 1938), p. 229.
12. *Pall Mall Gazette*, 48, no. 7344 (29 September 1888), p. 6.
13. Sedding, 1893, p. 165.
14. MacCarthy, 1994, p. 594.
15. Stansky, 1985, p. 125.
16. Mackail, 1901, vol. 2, p. 202.
17. MacCarthy, 1994, p. 612.
18. William Morris, 'Preface' to Kelmscott edition of 'The Nature of Gothic': quoted in Mackail, 1901, vol. 2, p. 275.
19. MacCarthy, 1994, p. 648.
20. Ibid., pp. 591–2.
21. Ibid., p. 592.
22. Thompson, 1991, p. 156.
23. Ibid., p. 164.
24. Crawford, 2005, p. 116.
25. Ibid., p. 28.
26. *The Times* (25 June 1888), p. 13: quoted in Crawford, 2005, p. 30. Crawford notes that *The Times* misquoted both Ruskin and, probably, the beam. Crawford, 2005, p. 435, note 43.
27. Letter from Arthur Heygate Mackmurdo to Charles Robert Ashbee, 1888: quoted in MacCarthy, 1981, p. 24.
28. Crawford, 2005, p. 29.
29. Ashbee, 2002, p. 46.
30. Ibid., p. 70.
31. Crawford, 2005, p. 348.
32. Ibid., p. 356.
33. Ibid., p. 72.
34. Mackail, 1901, vol. 2, p. 349.
35. Rothenstein, 1932, vol. 2, p. 191.
36. Walter Crane, *Transactions of the National Association for the Advancement of Art and its Application to Industry* (1888), p. 216: quoted in Farr, 1984, p. 137.
37. Stansky, 1985, p. 71.
38. William Morris, 'How we live and how we might live', 1887: quoted in Naylor (ed.), 2000, p. 222.
39. Ashbee, 1911, p. 2.

EXPANSION ACROSS THE BRITISH ISLES
1. Letter from Mary Seton Watts to Mr Nicol, 17 December 1900: Mary Seton Watts Archive, Watts Gallery, Compton, Surrey.
2. Gould, 1993, p. 38.
3. Ashbee, 1974, p. 3.
4. Letter from Edward Barnsley to Olga Barnsley, 25 November 1968, Edward Barnsley Educational Trust Archive: quoted in Greensted et al., 1993, p. 26.
5. Garnett, 1993, p. 22.
6. Ibid., p. 23.
7. Ibid.
8. Lethaby, 1979, p. 136.
9. Garnett, 1993, p. 27.
10. May Morris, *Journal of the Royal Institute of British Architects*, 39 (20 February 1932), p. 303.
11. Charles Francis Annesley Voysey, *Individuality* (London, 1915), p. 111: quoted in Davey, 1995, p. 92.
12. Charles Francis Annesley Voysey, 'The English Home', *British Architect*, 75 (1911), p. 70: quoted in Davey, 1995, p. 92.
13. 'An Interview with Mr Charles F Annesley Voysey, Architect and Designer', *The Studio*, 1 (1893), p. 233.
14. Voysey, 'The English Home', p. 60: quoted in Davey, 1995, p. 97.
15. Ashbee, 2002, p. 102.
16. Bowe (ed.), 1993, p. 184.
17. Jones, 1990, p. 19.
18. See, for example, Helland, 1994.
19. Morris (ed.), 1992, vol. 22, p. 91.
20. Sedding, 1891, p. 113.
21. Letter from Mrs Parker to Walter Creese, 25 March 1960, Parker Papers: quoted in Davey, 1995, p. 181.
22. Ashbee, 1908, p. 9.
23. Lethaby, 1922, pp. 46–7.

'A CRY OF DELIGHT': AUSTRIA, GERMANY AND THE LOW COUNTRIES

1. 'L'Art Décoratif', *L'Art Moderne*, 32 (12 August 1883), p. 253: quoted in Ogata, 2001, p. 18.
2. 'Le Salon de la Libre Esthétique, L'Art Appliqué', *L'Art Moderne*, 11 (18 March 1894), p. 85: quoted in Ogata, 2001, p. 36.
3. *Le Soir* (18 February 1894): quoted in Ogata, 2001, p. 38.
4. MacCarthy, 1979, p. 33.
5. *Ver Sacrum*, 1 (1898), p. 6.
6. Royal Academy of Arts, 1971, p. 15.
7. Ulmer, 1997, p. 180.
8. *Künstlerkolonie Mathildenhöhe Darmstadt 1899–1914*, 1999, p. 72.
9. 'An die deutschen Kunstler und Kunstfreunde', *Deutsche Kunst und Dekoration* (1897–8), p. 1: quoted in Ulmer, 1997, p. 50.
10. *Entscheidung des Wettbewerbes zur Erlangung von Entwürfen für ein herrschaftliches Wohnhaus eines Kunstfreundes* (1901), p. 111: quoted in Kornwolf, 1972, p. 216.
11. Kornwolf, 1972, p. 223.
12. *Entscheidung des Wettbewerbes* (1901), p. 110: quoted in Kornwolf, 1972, p. 222.
13. Josef Hoffmann and Koloman Moser, 'The Work-Programme of the Wiener Werkstätte', 1905: in Benton, Benton and Sharp (eds), 1975, p. 36.
14. Ibid.
15. Ibid.
16. Muthesius, 1979, p. 11.
17. Hermann Muthesius, 'Die Bedeutung des Kunstgewerbes: Eröffnungsrede zu den Vorlesungen über modernes Kunstgewerbe an der Handelshochschule in Berlin', *Dekorative Kunst*, 10, no. 5 (1907), p. 181: quoted in Schwartz, 1996, p. 38.
18. Fritz Schumacher, 'Die Wiedereroberung harmonischer Kultur', *Der Kunstwart*, 21, no. 8 (1908), pp. 137–8: quoted in Schwartz, 1996, pp. 48–9.
19. Muthesius, 'Die Bedeutung des Kunstgewerbes' (1907), p. 181: quoted in Schwartz, 1996, p. 42.
20. Schwartz, 1996, pp. 122–5.
21. Conrads (ed.), 1970, pp. 29–30.
22. Bayer, Gropius and Gropius (eds), 1938, p. 18.
23. Gillian Naylor, 'Domesticity and Design Reform: the European Context', in Snodin and Stavenow-Hidemark (eds), 1997, p. 83.

A NATIONALIST MANIFESTO: HUNGARY AND POLAND

1. Crowley, 1995, p. 4.
2. Alfoldy, 2003, p. 149.
3. Charles Robert Ashbee, Journals, vol. 5, August–September 1899, folio 9/127: Archive Centre, King's College, Cambridge.
4. Charles Robert Ashbee, Journals, vol. 16, June–July 1905, folio 5/173: Archive Centre, King's College, Cambridge.
5. Gellér, 1990, p. 161.
6. Crowley, 1995, pp. 24–5.
7. Ibid., p. 25.
8. Crowley, 1992, p. 33.
9. Ibid., p. 45.
10. Ibid., p. 64.
11. Kallestrup, 2002, p. 151.
12. Kallestrup, 2001.

ARTISANS AND ARISTOCRATS: THE RUSSIAN EQUATION

1. Fedor Solntsev, 'Moya zhizn' i khudozhestvenno-arkheologicheskie trudy', *Russkaya starina*, 3 (1876), p. 634: quoted in Kirichenko, 1991, p. 78.
2. Butovsky, 1870, vol. 1, p. 1.
3. Mamontov, 1950, p. 64.
4. Viktor Vasnetsov, 'Rech' na sobranii Abramtsevskogo khudozhestvennogo kruzhka. Yanvar' 1893': in Sternin (ed.), 1988, p. 258.
5. Arzumanova et al., 1988, p. 177.
6. Viktor Vasnetsov, 'Vospominaniya o S. I. Mamontove': in Paston, 2003, p. 300.
7. Ibid.
8. Letter from Elena Dmitrievna Polenova to Vladimir Vasilievich Stasov, 1 October 1895: in Sakharova (ed.), 1964, p. 536.
9. N Sultanov, 'Vozrozhdenie russkogo iskusstva', *Zodchii*, 2 (1881), p. 11: quoted in Bowlt, 1973, p. 448.
10. [Nikolai Bartram], 'Pamyati N. Ya. Davydovoi', *Izvestiya* (20 April 1926): quoted in Salmond, 1996, p. 56.
11. Salmond, 1996, p. 96.
12. Ibid., p. 14.
13. Mikhail Bykovsky, speech to the first annual meeting of the Moscow Architectural Society, 24 November 1868: quoted in Cooke, 1995, p. 8.
14. For the history of Viollet-le-Duc's Russian project, see O'Connell, 1993.
15. Kirichenko, 1987, pp. 25–6.
16. 'Avant-propos', *Iskusstvo i khudozhestvennaya promyshlennost'*, 1 (October–November 1898), p. vii: quoted in Salmond, 1996, p. 70.
17. For Shekhtel's work in Glasgow, see Cooke, 1988.

NORDIC IDENTITIES: SCANDINAVIA AND FINLAND

1. Tuomi, 1979, pp. 69–70.
2. Pekka Korvenmaa, 'Who are we? Where do we come from? Where are we going? The Finnish Pavilion at the 1900 World Exhibition in Paris': in Becker (ed.), 2002, p. 70.
3. Janne Gallen-Kallela-Sirén, 'Akseli Gallen-Kallela and the Pursuit of New History and New Art: Inventing Finnish Art Nouveau': in Becker (ed.), 2002, p. 50.
4. Wäre, 2000, p. 22.
5. Kaplan (ed.), 1989, p. 57.
6. Snodin and Stavenow-Hidemark (eds), 1997, p. 30.
7. Ibid., p. 7.
8. Ragnar Östberg, *Stockholm Town Hall* (Stockholm, 1929), pp. 28–30: quoted in Davey, 1995, p. 226.
9. Tarja Halonen (President of the Republic of Finland), 'Greeting': in Becker (ed.), 2002, p. 8.

ACROSS THE ATLANTIC: TRANSFORMATIONS IN THE UNITED STATES

1. Callen, 1979, p. 129.
2. Wheeler, 1921, p. 121.
3. 'Cincinnati', *Crockery and Glass Journal* (28 August 1879), p. 19: quoted in Kaplan, Boris et al., 1987, p. 65.
4. 'Mary Louise McLaughlin', *American Ceramic Bulletin*, 17 (May 1938), p. 222: quoted in Kaplan, Boris et al., 1987, p. 250.
5. Kaplan, Boris et al., 1987, p. 252.
6. Mary G Sheerer, 'Newcomb Pottery', *Keramic Studio*, 1 (November 1899), p. 151: quoted in Kaplan, Boris et al., 1987, p. 325.
7. Thomas A Larremore and Amy Hopkins Larremore, *Marion Press* (Jamaica, 1943), p. 171: quoted in Thompson, 1996, p. 84.
8. Joseph M Bowles, 'Mr Updike's Altar Book', *Modern Art*, 4 (1896), pp. 124–5: quoted in Thompson, 1996, p. 85.
9. Cormack, 1999, p. 47.
10. Ashbee, 2002, p. 56.
11. Ibid., pp. 56–7.
12. Thomas E Tallmadge, 'The "Chicago School"', *Architectural Review*, (1908), p. 4.
13. Wright, 1970, p. 4.
14. Eaton, 1969, p. 31.
15. Fred C Robie Jr, 'Mr. Robie Knew What He Wanted', *Architectural Forum*, 109 (October 1958), p. 126.
16. Clark (ed.), 1972, p. 77.
17. Hildebrand, 1991, p. 51.
18. Meehan (ed.), 1987, p. 101.
19. Frank Lloyd Wright, 'In The Cause of Architecture', 1908, in Pfeiffer (ed.), 1992, vol. 1, p. 88.
20. Frank Lloyd Wright, 'In The Cause of Architecture: The Third Dimension', 1925: in Pfeiffer (ed.), 1992, vol. 1, p. 209.
21. Bowman, 1990, p. 92.
22. Ashbee, 2002, p. 122.
23. Ralph Radcliffe Whitehead, 'A Plea for Manual Work', *Handicraft*, 2 (June 1903), p. 69: quoted in Kaplan, Boris et al., 1987, p. 313.
24. Ashbee, 2002, p. 62.
25. Ibid., p. 64.
26. Ibid.
27. Clark (ed.), 1972, p. 48.
28. Shay, 1926, p. 201.
29. Hunter, 1958, pp. 43–4.
30. Gustav Stickley, 'Als Ik Kan', *Craftsman*, 8 (1905), p. 835.
31. 'Foreword', *Craftsman*, 1 (October 1901), p. i.
32. Smith, 1983, p. 3.
33. Davey, 1995, p. 193.
34. Bosley, 2000, p. 134.
35. Ibid., p. 140.
36. Irving J Gill, 'The Home of the Future: The New Architecture of the West: Small Homes for a Great Country. Number Four', *Craftsman*, 30 (1916), p. 147.

EPILOGUE

1. MacCarthy, 1989, p. 93.
2. Ibid., p. 22.

CHRONOLOGY

1845 Foundation of Swedish Society of Crafts and Design

1847 Henry Cole establishes Felix Summerly's Art-Manufacturers

1849 Fedor Solntsev, *Antiquities of the Russian State* (6 vols, 1849–56)

1852 William Morris and Edward Burne-Jones matriculate at Exeter College, University of Oxford

1856 Nikolai Nikitin, Pogodin's hut, Moscow

1857 Dante Gabriel Rossetti, Burne-Jones, Morris and others begin to decorate Debating Chamber of Oxford Union, Oxford

1859 Marriage of Morris and Jane Burden
Philip Webb begins work on Red House, Morris's first marital home

1861 Foundation of Morris, Marshall, Faulkner & Co. at 8 (later 26) Red Lion Square, London
George Frederick Bodley commissions stained glass from the firm for his first church, St Michael and All Angels in Brighton, leading to many commissions for stained glass

1862 William Morris designs his first wallpaper, the *Trellis* pattern, with birds by Philip Webb

1865 Morris, Marshall, Faulkner & Co. decorates Green Dining Room, South Kensington Museum
William Morris and family leave Red House to live in London, firm moves to larger premises in Queen Square

1867 Richard Norman Shaw, Leys Wood, Groombridge, Kent

1869 Richard Norman Shaw begins work at Cragside, Rothbury, Northumberland

1870 Savva and Elizaveta Mamontov purchase country estate of Abramtsevo, near Moscow

1871 William Morris and Dante Gabriel Rossetti take out joint tenancy on Kelmscott Manor

1872 William de Morgan, who has been designing for Morris, Marshall, Faulkner & Co. since early 1860s, establishes own pottery in Chelsea
Vladimir Stasov, *Russian Folk Ornament*
Nikolai Shokhin, *Traditional Russian Buildings*
Foundation of National Museum of Applied Arts in Budapest

1873 Savva Mamontov first invites young Russian artists to spend their summers at Abramtsevo

1874 Foundation of Association of Friends of Textile Art, Sweden

1875 Morris, Marshall, Faulkner & Co. reorganized under Morris's sole ownership as Morris & Co.
Construction starts on Vladimir Shervud's Historical Museum, Moscow
Foundation of Finnish Society of Crafts and Design, Helsinki

1876 School of Carpentry set up by Tatra Society, Zakopane, Poland
Elizaveta Mamontova establishes joinery and carpentry workshops at Abramtsevo

1877 William Morris gives his first public lecture, entitled 'The Decorative Arts' and later published as *The Lesser Arts*
Foundation of Society for the Protection of Ancient Buildings (SPAB, or 'Anti-Scrape')
Foundation of New York Society of Decorative Art
Mary Louise McLaughlin develops faïence known as 'Cincinnati Limoges'

1878 William Morris and family move to Kelmscott House, Hammersmith, London

1879 William Morris begins first tapestry, *Vine and Acanthus*
Elizabeth Wardle establishes School of Embroidery in Leek, Staffordshire
First amateur dramatics at Abramtsevo
Foundation of Friends of Finnish Handicraft, Helsinki
Candace Wheeler and Louis Comfort Tiffany set up Tiffany & Wheeler
Women's Art Museum Association, Cincinnati, begins tuition in embroidery and other crafts
Mary Louise McLaughlin founds Cincinnati Pottery Club

1880 Maria Longworth Nichols establishes Rookwood Pottery, Cincinnati

1881 Morris & Co. moves to Merton Abbey. William de Morgan sets up a pottery nearby
Viktor Vasnetsov and others, Church of the Saviour Not Made by Hands, Abramtsevo
First artefacts collected for the museum of folk art, Abramtsevo
Tiffany & Wheeler absorbed into Louis C Tiffany & Co., Associated Artists

1882 Foundation of Century Guild of Artists
Lewis F Day, Walter Crane and others found The Fifteen
Abramtsevo artists stage *Snegurochka* in Savva Mamontov's Moscow residence, with stage and costume designs by Viktor Vasnetsov
Henry Hobson Richardson visits William Morris at Merton Abbey and Kelmscott House

1883 Ernest Newton, Edward S Prior, Gerald C Horsley, Mervyn Macartney and William Richard Lethaby found St George's Art Society
Foundation of Brussels exhibition society Les Vingt
Sofia Davydova establishes Mariinsky Lace School in St Petersburg, Russia
Morris & Co. exhibit at Boston Foreign Fair

1884 Foundation of Home Arts and Industries Association
Foundation of *The Century Guild Hobby Horse*
The Fifteen and the St George's Art Society amalgamate as the Art Workers' Guild
Birmingham School of Art moves to new premises and becomes Birmingham Municipal School of Arts and Crafts
Alice Hart founds Donegal Industrial Fund
First exhibition of Les Vingt

1885 Phoebe Anna Traquair begins to decorate mortuary chapel in the Royal Hospital for Sick Children, Edinburgh
Foundation of Hungarian Society of Applied Arts
Launch of *Művészi Ipar* (Artistic Crafts), Budapest
József Huszka, *The Hungarian Decorative Style*
Etelka Gyarmathy sets up home industry association in Kalotaszeg, Hungary
Performance of Nikolai Rimsky-Korsakov's operatic version of *Snegurochka* at Abramtsevo
Elena Polenova is employed to direct the Abramtsevo workshops, and designs her famous column cupboard for the workshops to produce
Foundation of Moscow Kustar Museum

1886 Century Guild commissioned to work at Pownall Hall, Cheshire
Stanisław Witkiewicz first visits Zakopane, Poland
Elizaveta Mamontova opens first of two shops in Moscow to market products of Abramtsevo workshops

1887 Foundation of Arts and Crafts Exhibition Society, for which Thomas Cobden-Sanderson coins the term 'Arts and Crafts'
Frank Lloyd Wright starts work in architectural office of Dankmar Adler and Louis H Sullivan, Chicago

1888 First Arts and Crafts Exhibition held in the New Gallery, Regent Street, London
John Dando Sedding begins work on Holy Trinity Church, Sloane Street, London
Charles Robert Ashbee founds Guild of Handicraft, Whitechapel, London
Foundation of National Association for the Advancement of Art and its Application to Industry, Liverpool
Carl and Karin Larsson given house of Lilla Hyttnäs, Sundborn, Sweden

1889 Edward S Prior develops 'Early English' method of making glass

Phoebe Anna Traquair begins work in the Song School of St Mary's Cathedral, Edinburgh
Frank Lloyd Wright moves to Chicago suburb of Oak Park and begins to design own house

1890 Edward Burne-Jones begins *Holy Grail* tapestries
Arthur Heygate Mackmurdo moves to 20 Fitzroy Street, which becomes new headquarters for Century Guild of Artists
Ernest Gimson, Sidney Barnsley, Mervyn Macartney, William Richard Lethaby and Reginald Blomfield establish furniture company Kenton & Co.
Arthur Dixon establishes Birmingham Guild of Handicraft
Foundation of Kelmscott Press
Alfred Finch works at Kéramis ceramics factory in La Louvière
Stanisław Witkiewicz moves permanently to Zakopane
Louis Sparre, Eva Mannerheim-Sparre and Akseli Gallen-Kallela first visit Karelia
Foundation of Abramtsevo Ceramics Studio
Rookwood Pottery commissions new premises

1891 School and Guild of Handicraft move to Essex House, Mile End Road, London
Philip Webb, Standen, West Sussex
John Dando Sedding, *Garden Craft Old and New*
Maria Yakunchikova opens embroidery workshop on her estate of Solomenko, Tambov province, Russia
Sergei Malyutin first designs *matrioshka* dolls
Louis Sparre moves to Finland
Foundation of Norwegian Society for Home Crafts
Walter Crane lectures and exhibits in the United States

1892 Mackay Hugh Baillie Scott, Red House, Isle of Man
Munich Secession
Ministry of Agriculture opens St Petersburg Kustar Museum, Russia
Work begins on Martin Nyrop's Town Hall, Copenhagen
Frida Hansen founds tapestry weaving studio in Norway
Ralph Adams Cram launches *The Knight Errant* in Boston

1893 Thomas Cobden-Sanderson sets up Doves Bindery, Hammersmith, London
Charles Robert Ashbee, Magpie and Stump, Chelsea, London
Launch of art magazine *The Studio*
Foundation of Belgian artistic society La Libre Esthétique
Van de Velde begins to teach course in decorative art at Antwerp Academy
Launch of Flemish journal *Van Nu en Straks*, modelled on *The Century Guild Hobby Horse*
Elena Polenova leaves Abramtsevo workshops
Kataro Shirayamadani sent by Rookwood Pottery

to study in Japan
Frank Lloyd Wright establishes own architectural practice in Chicago
Charles Sumner Greene and Henry Mather Greene move to California, setting up practice in Pasadena in early 1894
Daniel Berkeley Updike founds Merrymount Press, Boston

1894   Lucien and Esther Pissarro set up Eragny Press, Hammersmith, London
C H St John Hornby sets up Ashendene Press, Hertfordshire
Maude and Joseph King establish Haslemere Weaving Industry, Haslemere, Surrey
Harold Rathbone establishes Della Robbia pottery, Birkenhead
Foundation of Arts and Crafts Society of Ireland
Gustave Serrurier-Bovy exhibits a study at first exhibition of La Libre Esthétique
Yrjö Blomstedt, Victor Sucksdorff and Lars Sonck win grant from Finnish Antiquarian Society to study Karelian architecture

1895   Samuel Bing opens La Maison de L'Art Nouveau, Paris
Gustave Serrurier-Bovy organizes exhibition of decorative arts in Liège
Henry van de Velde designs his family home, Bloemenwerf, in Uccle, Belgium
Walter Crane has solo show at Museum of Applied Arts, Budapest
Akseli Gallen-Kallela completes Kalela, his wilderness studio in Ruovesi, central Finland
Foundation of Newcomb Pottery at the H Sophie Newcomb Memorial College, the women's affiliate of Tulane University, New Orleans
Will Bradley sets up Wayside Press in Springfield, Massachusetts
Elbert Hubbard takes over Roycroft Press in East Aurora, near Buffalo, New York
Foundation of Chalk and Chisel Club in Minneapolis, which in 1899 becomes the Minneapolis Arts and Crafts Society

1896   Kelmscott Press publishes *The Works of Geoffrey Chaucer*
Charles Ricketts sets up Vale Press, Chelsea, London
Central School of Arts and Crafts opens, with W R Lethaby and George Frampton as co-principals
Godfrey and Ethel Blount set up Peasant Arts Society, Haslemere, Surrey
Mary Seton Watts begins work on mortuary chapel, Compton, Surrey
Edward S Prior, The Barn, Devon
Edwin Lutyens, Munstead Wood, Surrey
Hermann Muthesius appointed architectural attaché to German Embassy in London
Viktor Vasnetsov designs menus for feasts commemorating accession of Tsar Nicholas II
Louis Sparre and Eva Mannerheim-Sparre study

modern design during tour of Europe
Herman Gesellius, Armas Lindgren and Eliel Saarinen form architectural partnership
Charles Robert Ashbee's first lecture tour to the United States
Merrymount Press, Boston, publishes *The Altar Book*
Launch of *Bradley, His Book*
Publication of *The Song of Songs*, the first book of the Roycroft Press
First issue of *House Beautiful* in Chicago

1897   Foundation of Edinburgh Arts and Crafts Club
Charles Rennie Mackintosh begins work on Glasgow School of Art
Foundation of Vereinigte Werkstätten für Kunst im Handwerk, Munich
Vienna Secession
Grand Duke of Hesse commissions Baillie Scott, Ashbee and Guild of Handicraft to carry out work for his palace in Darmstadt
Aladár Körösfői-Kriesch and Sándor Nagy undertake first sketching trip to Carpathian mountains
Launch of *Magyar Iparművészet* (Hungarian Applied Arts)
Stanisław Witkiewicz, Dom pod Jedlami (House under the Firs), Zakopane, Poland
Elena Polenova designs dining room for Maria Yakunchikova's house of Nara, near Moscow
Louis Sparre and Eva Mannerheim-Sparre set up Iris Workshops, Porvoo, Finland
Lars Sonck designs Church (later Cathedral) of St John, Tampere, Finland
Carl Larsson exhibits watercolours of Lilla Hyttnäs at Stockholm Exhibition of Art and Industry
Foundation of Boston Society of Arts and Crafts
Foundation of Chicago Society of Arts and Crafts at Hull House
The Studio begins publication in the United States as *The International Studio*

1898   Charles Robert Ashbee sets up Essex House Press
Foundation of Ruskin Pottery, near Birmingham
William Richard Lethaby, Melsetter House, island of Hoy, Orkney
Charles Francis Annesley Voysey, Broadleys, Cumbria
Foundation of Dresdner Werkstätten für Handwerkskunst, Dresden
Hendrik Petrus Berlage begins work on Amsterdam Stock Exchange
József Huszka, *Hungarian Ornamentation*
Maria Tenisheva establishes Museum of Russian Antiquities and Folk Art at Talashkino, near Smolensk
First exhibition of Chicago Society of Arts and Crafts includes work by Charles Robert Ashbee
Gustav Stickley travels to Europe, meeting, among others, C F A Voysey, C R Ashbee, and Samuel Bing

1899 Art Workers' Guild stages *Beauty's Awakening* masque, Guildhall, London
Foundation of Compton Potters' Arts Guild, Compton, Surrey
Mackay Hugh Baillie Scott, Blackwell, Cumbria
Foundation of artists' colony at Darmstadt
Foundation of Association of Swedish Handicrafts
Carl Larsson publishes twenty-four watercolours of Lilla Hyttnäs as *Ett hem*
Gustav Stickley founds United Crafts in suburb of Eastwood, Syracuse, New York

1900 Thomas Cobden-Sanderson and Emery Walker set up Doves Press, Hammersmith, London
Foundation of Aldourie Pottery, Scotland
Hoffmann designs houses for artists' colony on the Hohe Warte outside Vienna
Walter Crane has second solo show at Museum of Applied Arts, Budapest
Abramtsevo Ceramics Studio moves to Moscow
Maria Tenisheva employs Sergei Malyutin to direct carpentry workshop at Talashkino
Viktor Vasnetsov designs new main entrance and facade of Tretyakov Gallery, Moscow
Arts and Crafts work dominates Russian submission to Exposition Universelle, Paris
Sparre resigns as creative director of Iris Workshops, Porvoo, Finland
Gesellius, Lindgren and Saarinen design Finnish Pavilion for Exposition Universelle, Paris
Carl Westman and Lars Israel Wahlman study recent architectural design during trip to Britain
Clara Barck Welles establishes Kalo Shops, Chicago
Foundation of Guild of Arts and Crafts of New York
Charles Robert Ashbee and Frank Lloyd Wright first meet at Hull House, Chicago
Leopold and John George Stickley establish L & J G Stickley Company, Fayetteville, New York

1901 Staff at Central School of Art and Design begin to publish specialist craft manuals
William Richard Lethaby, All Saints Church, Brockhampton, Herefordshire
Robert Lorimer, Wayside, St Andrews, Scotland
Mackintosh, Baillie Scott and others submit designs to 'House for an Art Lover' competition launched by *Innendekoration* in 1900
First exhibition, 'Ein Dokument Deutscher Kunst', at Darmstadt artists' colony
Aladár Körösfői-Kriesch buys house in Gödöllő, leading to artists' colony there
Foundation of Polish Applied Art Society
Sergei Malyutin, Teremok, Talashkino, near Smolensk
Fedor Shekhtel designs Russian village for Glasgow International Exhibition
Gesellius, Lindgren and Saarinen produce first design for National Museum of Finland, begin work on Suur-Merijoki outside Vyborg, and design their own house-studio of Hvitträsk, near Helsinki
The Larssons make Lilla Hyttnäs in Sundborn their permanent home

Carl Westman, Press House, Stockholm
Frank Lloyd Wright publishes 'A Home in a Prairie Town' in *Ladies' Home Journal*, and gives lecture on 'The Art and Craft of the Machine' to the Chicago Arts and Crafts Society at Hull House
William Price sets up Rose Valley Association, near Philadelphia
Gustav Stickley launches journal *The Craftsman*, Syracuse, New York
Will Bradley begins to publish 'Bradley House' interior and furniture designs in *Ladies' Home Journal*

1902 Guild of Handicraft moves to Chipping Campden, Cotswolds
Edwin Lutyens remodels Lindisfarne Castle
Evelyn Gleeson and Elizabeth and Lily Yeats set up Dun Emer workshops, Dundrum, near Dublin
Josef Hoffmann and Fritz Wärndorfer travel to Britain to study contemporary design
Foundation of Deutsche Gartenstadtgesellschaft
First exhibition of Polish Applied Art Society in Cracow and Warsaw
Launch of *Records of Polish Applied Art*
First All-Russian Kustar Exhibition, St Petersburg
Carl Larsson, *Larssons*
Boston Society of Arts and Crafts begins monthly journal *Handicraft*
Ralph Radcliffe Whitehead sets up Byrdcliffe colony, Woodstock, New York
Tobey Furniture Company, Chicago, establishes William Morris Memorial Room

1903 Ernest Gimson and Ernest Barnsley set up new workshops in Sapperton, Gloucestershire
Edward S Prior, St Andrew's Church, Roker, Sunderland
First Garden City, Letchworth, Hertfordshire
Sarah Purser sets up An Túr Gloine (the Tower of Glass), Dublin
Foundation of Wiener Werkstätte
Peter Behrens appointed director of Düsseldorf Kunstgewerbeschule
Launch of *Le Cottage* in Belgium
Maria Tenisheva opens shop Rodnik in Moscow to sell products of Talashkino workshops

1904 Foundation of Association des Cités-jardins, Belgium
Hermann Muthesius, *Das englische Haus* (3 vols, 1904–5)
Henry van de Velde appointed director of Weimar Kunstgewerbeschule
István Medgyaszay designs first studio house at Gödöllő
Carl Westman, Tallom, Stocksund
Charles Keeler, *The Simple Home*

1905 Riemerschmid designs *Maschinenmöbel* for Dresdner Werkstätten
Sergei Malyutin and N K Zhukov, Dom Pertsova, Moscow

1906 Schmidt, Muthesius and others hold major arts and crafts exhibition in Dresden
Gödöllő artists exhibit 'The Home of an Artist' at International Exhibition, Milan
Arthur and Lucia Mathews set up Furniture Shop in San Francisco

1907 Guild of Handicraft goes into liquidation
Mackintosh adds east stairwell, west range and west wing to Glasgow School of Art
Hermann Muthesius, Freudenberg House, Nikolassee, Berlin
Start of Germany's first Garden City at Hellerau, near Dresden
Hermann Muthesius appointed to first chair of applied arts, Berlin Business School
Foundation of Deutscher Werkbund
Peter Behrens appointed artistic adviser to Allgemeine Elektricitäts-Gesellschaft (AEG)
Bruno Paul appointed director of education at Kunstgewerbemuseum, Berlin
Dezső Malonyay (ed.), *Art of the Hungarian People* (5 vols, 1907–22)
Ede Toroczkai-Vigand publishes *Az én falum* (My Village), a series of architectural designs
Charles Sumner Greene and Henry Mather Greene begin 'ultimate bungalows' in California

1908 Elizabeth and Lily Yeats set up Cuala workshops, Dundrum, near Dublin
Bruno Paul launches *Typenmöbel* furniture range
Frank Lloyd Wright, Robie House, Chicago
Dirk Van Erp opens Copper Shop in Oakland, California, moving to San Francisco in 1910
Charles Sumner Greene and Henry Mather Greene, Gamble House, Pasadena, California

1909 Foundation of Society of Podhale Art, Poland
New crafts workshops open in Museum of Industry, Cracow
Lars Israel Wahlman, Engelbrekt Church, Stockholm
Ragnar Östberg begins Stockholm City Hall
Edward J Lewis founds University City Pottery, Missouri
Christopher Whall begins clerestory windows for Church of the Advent, Boston
Gustav Stickley, *Craftsman Homes*
Charles Robert Ashbee and Charles Sumner Greene meet in Pasadena, California

1910 Carl Larsson, *Åt solsidan* (On the Sunny Side)
Bernard Maybeck, First Church of Christ Scientist, Berkeley, California

1911 *The Studio* publishes *Peasant Art in Austria and Hungary*
Akseli Gallen-Kallela begins second studio house at Tarvaspää, near Helsinki
Adelaide Alsop Robineau wins Grand Prix at International Exposition of Decorative Arts, Turin, for *Scarab Vase*

1912 4th Marquess of Bute founds Dovecot tapestry studio, Corstorphine, Scotland
Charles J Connick sets up stained glass studio in Boston
William Drummond, Charles Barr House, River Forest, Chicago
Karl Kipp founds Tookay Shop, East Aurora, New York
Gustav Stickley, *More Craftsman Homes*

1913 Richard Riemerschmid appointed director of Munich Kunstgewerbeschule
Gödöllő artists design murals, mosaics, sculpture and stained glass for Palace of Culture in Marosvásárhely, Transylvania
Foundation of Cracow Workshops, Cracow
Second All-Russian Kustar Exhibition, St Petersburg
Gustav Stickley moves business to Craftsman Building in Manhattan, New York

1914 Major Deutscher Werkbund exhibition in Cologne: conflict between Muthesius, Van de Velde and their respective supporters over principle of *Typisierung*
Art Workers' Guild moves to its current home of 6 Queen Square, London

1915 Gustav Stickley's business declared bankrupt
Elbert and Alice Hubbard perish aboard the *Lusitania*

1916 Elizabeth E Copeland wins Boston Society of Arts and Crafts' Medal of Excellence
Final issue of *The Craftsman*

1919 Foundation of Bauhaus
Yamamoto Kanae inspired by *kustar* museums in Russia to launch courses in 'peasant art'

1923 Foundation of Japan Peasant Art Institute
Completion of Stockholm City Hall by Ragnar Östberg

1925 Cracow Workshops mount acclaimed display at Exposition Internationale des Arts Décoratifs, Paris

1926 Foundation of LAD ('Harmony') artistic co-operative in Warsaw
Michael Cardew founds pottery in Winchcombe, Gloucestershire
Start of Mingei or Folk Craft Movement in Japan

1933 Alvar Aalto founds furnishing firm Artek, Finland

1936 Nikolaus Pevsner, *Pioneers of the Modern Movement: from William Morris to Walter Gropius*
Yanagi Sōetsu establishes Japan Folk Crafts Museum

1998 Foundation of new Applied Art Workshop, Gödöllő, Hungary

A CONTEXT OF EVENTS

1809 Finland becomes a Grand Duchy of Russia

1812 Helsinki replaces Turku as capital of Finland

1815 Act of Union binds Norway and Sweden, with the latter controlling foreign policy

1823 Foundation of Mechanics' Institutes

1835 Select Committee of Arts and their connection with Manufactures, London
Elias Lönnrot publishes first version of the Finnish epic *The Kalevala*, followed by a longer version in 1849

1836 A W N Pugin, *Contrasts; Or a Parallel between the Noble Edifices of the Fourteenth and Fifteenth Centuries, and Similar Buildings of the Present Day; Shewing the Present Decay of Taste*

1837 Foundation of first School of Design, London
Queen Victoria ascends the British throne

1841 A W N Pugin, *The True Principles of Pointed or Christian Architecture*

1843 John Ruskin, *Modern Painters* (3 vols, 1843–60)

1845 Foundation of Glasgow School of Art
Start of Great Famine, Ireland

1846 Foundation of Finnish Art Society

1847 Introduction of ten-hour working day for women and children in factories

1848 Foundation of Pre-Raphaelite Brotherhood
Outbreak of cholera in Britain
Revolutions in Europe
Foundation of Finland's first official art school
John Stuart Mill, *Principles of Political Economy*
Karl Marx and Friedrich Engels, *Communist Manifesto*

1849 John Ruskin, *The Seven Lamps of Architecture*
Henry Cole launches *Journal of Design and Manufactures*

1851 The Great Exhibition of the Works of Industry of All Nations, London
John Ruskin, *The Stones of Venice* (3 vols, 1851–3)

1852 Foundation of Museum of Manufactures, Marlborough House, London
Henry Cole appointed general superintendent of new Department of Practical Art
Death of Augustus Welby Northmore Pugin
Charles Dickens, *Bleak House*
Ford Madox Brown, *Work*

1853 Pierre Joseph Proudhon, *Philosophie du progrès*

1854 Foundation of Working Men's College, London, by F D Maurice
John Ruskin's marriage annulled on grounds of non-consummation (his wife, Effie Gray, marries the Pre-Raphaelite painter John Everett Millais the following year)
Start of Crimean War (to 1856)
Charles Dickens, *Hard Times*

1856 Owen Jones, *The Grammar of Ornament*

1857 Opening of South Kensington Museum (now Victoria and Albert Museum)

1859 Charles Darwin, *On the Origin of Species*

1860 Foundation of Central Imperial Stroganov School of Technical Design, Moscow
Launch of official Finnish currency

1861 Emancipation of the serfs, Russia
Outbreak of American Civil War (to 1865)

1862 International Exhibition, South Kensington, London
Foundation of School of the Society for the Encouragement of Artists, St Petersburg

1863 Polish uprising in Russian partition of Poland
Russian authorities recognize Finnish as well as Swedish as the official languages of Finland

1864 Metropolitan railway, part of which is underground, opens in London
Denmark cedes Schleswig-Holstein to Germany
Opening of Österreichisches Museum für Kunst und Industrie, Vienna

1867 First permanent women's suffrage societies founded in London, Manchester and Edinburgh
Austro-Hungarian Compromise leads to Dual Monarchy (1867–1918), during which Hungary considered a separate state with control over internal affairs
Exposition Universelle, Paris
Foundation of Moscow Architectural Society

1869 Ruskin appointed first Slade Professor of Fine Art at University of Oxford
Foundation of Moscow Archaeological Society
East and west coasts of the United States linked by American Pacific Railway

1870 Foundation of *Women's Suffrage Journal*
Viktor Butovsky publishes first volume of *Histoire de l'ornement russe du Xe au XVIe siècle d'après les manuscrits*

1871 Ruskin founds his Guild of St George, and begins social experiments including street-sweeping in London and road-mending outside Oxford
Introduction of Bank Holidays in Britain

Wilhelm I crowned first Emperor of a united Germany
Minister for Galician Affairs appointed to represent Polish concerns in Vienna
Foundation of Central School of Applied Arts, Helsinki
Both the Ministry of Finance and the Imperial Russian Geographical Society form commissions to study the state of Russia's *kustar* industries
Great fire of Chicago

1872 Launch of Russian journal *Zodchii* (The Architect)

1873 Tytus Chałubiński arrives in Zakopane, Podhale, and establishes Tatra Society to preserve local traditions and improve education and local employment
Foundation of Finnish Museum of Art and Design, Helsinki
Artur Hazelius founds Nordic Museum, Stockholm

1874 Thomas Hardy, *Far from the Madding Crowd*
First Impressionist exhibition in Paris
Populist movement known as 'going to the people' in Russia
Imperial Russian Geographical Society publishes sixteen-volume report on state of *kustar* industries in Russia

1875 Public Health Act, Trade Union Act and Artisans' Dwelling Act passed in Britain
Foundation of Liberty's, which later stocked many goods inspired by the Arts and Crafts

1876 Philadelphia Centennial Exhibition
Foundation of Baron Stieglitz School, St Petersburg

1877 Viollet-le-Duc, *L'Art Russe. Ses origins, ses éléments constitutifs, son apogée, son avenir*
Whistler sues Ruskin for libel, and is awarded damages of one farthing in 1878

1878 London University admits women to degrees, and University College London becomes co-educational
Ruskin resigns Slade Professorship, suffers first of seven attacks of madness over next decade
Foundation of Salvation Army
Carbon-filament, gas-filled light bulb invented by the American Thomas Edison and the Briton Joseph Swan

1880 Fiftieth anniversary of Belgian independence

1881 Assassination of Tsar Alexander II of Russia
Death of Thomas Carlyle

1882 Fine Art and Industrial Exhibition, Manchester
Married Women's Property Act

1883 Andrew Mearn, *The Bitter Cry of Outcast London*
Launch of the *Ladies' Home Journal* in the United States
Boston Foreign Fair

1885 International Inventions Exhibition, London
Patrick Geddes and others found Edinburgh Social Union
First publication of *Oxford English Dictionary*

1886 Exhibition of Navigation and Manufacture, Liverpool
Edinburgh International Exhibition

1887 Queen Victoria's Golden Jubilee
Royal Jubilee Exhibition, Manchester
The New Gallery opens in London

1888 First murders by Jack the Ripper in London's East End
Ministry of State Domains appointed to oversee *kustar* industries in Russia

1889 Charles Booth, *Life and Labour of the People in London* (17 vols, 1889–1903)
Foundation of Hungarian Ethnographic Society
Jane Addams and Ellen Gates Starr found Hull House

1890 William Morris begins to publish *News from Nowhere* in *Commonweal*
Alexander Koch launches *Innendekoration*
Oscar Wilde, *The Picture of Dorian Gray*

1891 Skansen, open-air architectural museum, opens in Stockholm

1892 Pavel Tretyakov donates collection of Russian art to city of Moscow
Arthur Conan Doyle, *The Adventures of Sherlock Holmes*

1893 World's Columbian Exhibition, Chicago
First line of the Elevated Rapid Transport System opens in Chicago
Douglas Hyde sets up Gaelic League to revive Irish language
Vilho Penttilä begins to publicize merits of Finnish wooden building traditions in *Suomen Teollisuuslehti* (The Industrial Magazine of Finland)
Edvard Munch, *The Scream*

1894 Charles Fletcher Lummis founds California Landmarks Club
Rudyard Kipling, *The Jungle Book*

1896 Hungary celebrates millennium of Magyar settlement in the Carpathian basin
Nicholas II ascends the Russian throne
All-Russian Arts and Industries Exhibition,

Nizhny Novgorod
Ruskin's *The Stones of Venice* translated into
Hungarian (1896–8)

1897 Tate Gallery opens in London
Foundation of National Union of Women's
Suffrage Societies
Launch of *Country Life*
Alexander Koch launches *Deutsche Kunst und
Dekoration*
Work of John Ruskin begins to be translated into
Swedish
Stockholm Exhibition of Art and Industry

1898 Ebenezer Howard, *Tomorrow: A Peaceful Path to Real
Reform*
Joseph Maria Olbrich designs Secession Building
in Vienna
Launch of *Mir Iskusstva* (The World of Art) and
Iskusstvo i khudozhestvennaya promyshlennost (Art and
Industrial Design) in Russia
Launch of *Ateneum*, Finland's first colour-
illustrated art journal

1899 Foundation of Garden City Association
Savva Mamontov is declared bankrupt, charged
with embezzlement and imprisoned
February Manifesto establishes Russian as official
language in Grand Duchy of Finland, and
increases Russian control of Finnish affairs.
European statesmen and intellectuals respond
with the 'Pro-Finlandia' petition, and Jean Sibelius
writes *Finlandia*
Ellen Key, *Skönhet för alla* (Beauty for All)
Exhibition of furnishings for low-income families
opens in Stockholm
Foundation of Industrial Art League, Chicago

1900 Exposition Universelle, Paris
Eighth Secession Exhibition, Vienna, includes
work by Ashbee, the Guild of Handicraft and the
Glasgow Four
Deaths of John Ruskin and Oscar Wilde

1901 Death of Queen Victoria, accession of Edward VII
to the British throne
First Nobel prizes given on principles laid down

by Alfred Bernhard Nobel, the Swedish inventor
of dynamite

1902 Royal Scottish Academy starts to include applied
art in its exhibitions
Van de Velde founds Weimar Kunstgewerbeschule

1903 Georg Simmel, *Die Grosstädte und das Geistesleben*
The Wright brothers complete the first sustained,
powered flight in the United States

1904 St Louis World's Fair

1905 Union between Norway and Sweden unilaterally
dissolved by Norway: after threat of war, Swedish
parliament accepts dissolution of the union, giving
Norway full independence
Albert Einstein expounds his theory of relativity
Russia loses the Russo-Japanese War

1906 San Francisco earthquake and fire

1911 Ebenezer Howard's *Tomorrow: A Peaceful Path to Real
Reform* translated into Russian
International Exposition of Decorative Arts, Turin

1913 Roger Fry establishes Omega workshops in
Bloomsbury, London, in which painters
endeavour to earn an income by turning their
hand to the applied arts and interior design

1914 Outbreak First World War (to 1918)

1915 Foundation of Design and Industries Association
(DIA), whose members include Selwyn Image,
W A S Benson and W R Lethaby

1917 Russian Revolution
Finland declares unilateral independence from
Russia: P E Svinhufvud becomes first head of state

1928 Foundation of National Party of Scotland

1930 John Ruskin's *The Seven Lamps of Architecture*
translated into Japanese

1964 Foundation of Crafts Council in Great Britain

SELECTED BIBLIOGRAPHY

Steven Adams, *The Arts and Crafts Movement* (London 1992)

Sandra Alfoldy, 'Laura Nagy: Magyar muse', in Bridget Elliott and Janice Helland (eds), *Women Artists and the Decorative Arts, 1980–1935: The Gender of Ornament* (Aldershot 2003), pp. 138–49

Anthony M Alofsin (ed.), *Frank Lloyd Wright: Europe and Beyond* (Berkeley, CA 1999)

Stanford Anderson, *Peter Behrens and a New Architecture for the Twentieth Century* (Cambridge, MA 2000)

Isabelle Anscombe and Charlotte Gere, *Arts and Crafts in Britain and America* (New York 1978)

The Art Journal Illustrated Catalogue (London 1851)

L'Art Moderne (Paris 1875–6, Brussels 1881–7)

Arts & Crafts Metalwork (exh. cat., Blackwell, Kendal 2003)

Olga I Arzumanova, Anna G Kuznetsova, Tatyana N Makarova and Vilyams A Nevskii, *Muzei-zapovednik 'Abramtsevo'* (2nd edn, Moscow 1988)

Charles Robert Ashbee, *Craftsmanship in Competitive Industry* (Chipping Campden and London 1908)

Charles Robert Ashbee, *Modern English Silverwork* (London 1974; first published London 1909)

Charles Robert Ashbee, *Should We Stop Teaching Art?* (London 1911)

Felicity Ashbee, *Janet Ashbee: Love, Marriage and the Arts and Crafts Movement* (Syracuse, NY 2002)

Paul Atterbury (ed.), *A W N Pugin: Master of Gothic Revival* (New Haven, CT and London 1995)

Paul Atterbury and John Henson, *Ruskin Pottery: The Pottery of Edward*

Richard Taylor and William Howson Taylor, 1898–1935 (Yeovil 1993)

Paul Atterbury and Clive Wainwright (eds), *Pugin: A Gothic Passion* (exh. cat., London 1994)

Jeffrey A Auerbach, *The Great Exhibition of 1851: A Nation on Display* (New Haven, CT and London 1999)

Dianne Ayres et al. (eds), *American Arts and Crafts Textiles* (New York 2002)

Sylvia Backemeyer (ed.), *Making their Mark: Art, Craft and Design at the Central School, 1896–1966* (London 2000)

Sylvia Backemeyer and Theresa Gronberg (eds), *WR Lethaby, 1857–1931: Architecture, Design and Education* (London 1984)

Mackay Hugh Baillie Scott, *Houses and Gardens: Arts and Crafts Interiors* (Woodbridge 1995; first published London 1906)

Joanna Banham and Jennifer Harris (eds), *William Morris and the Middle Ages* (Manchester 1984)

John Batchelor, *John Ruskin: No Wealth But Life* (London 2000)

Herbert Bayer, Walter Gropius and Ise Gropius (eds), *Bauhaus 1919–1928* (New York 1938)

Elizabeth Beazley, 'The Watts Chapel', *The Architectural Review* (September 1961), pp. 167–72

Ingeborg Becker (ed.), *Now the Light Comes from the North: Art Nouveau in Finland* (Bröhan 2002)

Quentin Bell, *The Schools of Design* (London 1963)

Charlotte Benton, Tim Benton and Dennis Sharp (eds), *Form and Function: A Source Book for the History of Architecture and Design 1890–1939* (London 1975)

Patricia G Berman, 'Norwegian Craft Theory and National Revival

in the 1890s', in Nicola Gordon Bowe (ed.), *Art and the National Dream: The Search for Vernacular Expression in Turn-of-the-Century Design* (Dublin 1993), pp. 155–68

Dinah Birch (ed.), *Ruskin and the Dawn of the Modern* (Oxford 1999)

Dinah Birch (ed.), *John Ruskin: Selected Writings* (Oxford 2004)

Eileen Boris, *Art and Labor: Ruskin, Morris and the Craftsman Ideal in America* (Philadelphia, PA 1986)

Franco Borsi, *Vienna 1900: Architecture and Design* (New York 1986)

Edward R Bosley, *Gamble House: Greene & Greene* (London 1992)

Edward R Bosley, *Greene & Greene* (London 2000)

Nicola Gordon Bowe (ed.), *Art and the National Dream: the Search for Vernacular Expression in Turn-of-the-Century Design* (Dublin 1993)

Nicola Gordon Bowe, 'A Contextual Introduction to Romantic Nationalism and Vernacular Expression in the Irish Arts and Crafts Movement c.1886–1925', in Nicola Gordon Bowe (ed.), *Art and the National Dream: the Search for Vernacular Expression in Turn-of-the-Century Design* (Dublin 1993), pp. 181–200

Nicola Gordon Bowe, 'Wilhelmina Geddes, Harry Clarke and Their Part in the Arts and Crafts Movement in Ireland', *Journal of Decorative and Propaganda Arts*, 8 (Spring 1988), pp. 58–79

Nicola Gordon Bowe, *The Life and Work of Harry Clarke* (Dublin 1989)

John E Bowlt, 'Two Russian Maecenases: Savva Mamontov and Princess Tenisheva', *Apollo* (December 1973), pp. 444–53

Leslie Greene Bowman, *American Arts and Crafts: Virtue in Design* (exh. cat., Los Angeles, CA 1990)

John Brandon-Jones et al., *C F A Voysey: Architect and Designer 1857–1941* (London 1978)

David Brett, *C R Mackintosh, the Poetics of Workmanship* (London 1992)

Harold Allen Brooks, *The Prairie School: Frank Lloyd Wright and his Midwest Contemporaries* (Toronto 1972)

William Craft Brumfield, 'The Decorative Arts in Russian Architecture: 1900–1907', *Journal of Decorative and Propaganda Arts*, 5 (Summer 1987), pp. 12–27

William Craft Brumfield (ed.), *Reshaping Russian Architecture: Western Technology, Utopian Dreams* (Cambridge 1990)

William Craft Brumfield, *The Origins of Modernism in Russian Architecture* (Berkeley, CA 1991)

William Craft Brumfield and Blair A Ruble (eds), *Russian Housing in the Modern Age* (Cambridge 1993)

Jennie Brunton, *The Arts and Crafts Movement in the Lake District* (Lancaster 2001)

Lucius Burckhardt (ed.), *The Werkbund: Studies in the History and Ideology of the Deutscher Werkbund 1907–1933* (London 1980)

Jude Burkhauser (ed.), *Glasgow Girls: Women in Art and Design, 1880–1920* (Edinburgh 1990)

Georgiana Burne-Jones, *Memorials of Edward Burne-Jones*, 2 vols (London 1904)

Viktor Butovsky, *Histoire de l'ornement russe du Xe au XVIe siècle d'après les manuscrits*, 2 vols (Paris 1870–3)

Anthea Callen, *Angel in the Studio: Women in the Arts and Crafts Movement, 1870–1914* (London 1979)

Joan Campbell, *The German Werkbund: the Politics of Reform in the Applied Arts* (Princeton, NJ 1978)

Thomas Carlyle, *Chartism and Past and Present* (London 1858)

Annette Carruthers, *Edward Barnsley and his Workshop: Arts and Crafts in the Twentieth Century* (Wendlebury 1992)

Annette Carruthers and Mary Greensted, *Good Citizen's Furniture: The Arts and Crafts Collections at Cheltenham* (Cheltenham 1994)

Annette Carruthers and Mary Greensted (eds), *Simplicity or Splendour: Arts and Crafts Living. Objects from the Cheltenham Collections* (Cheltenham 1999)

David Cathers, *Furniture of the Arts and Crafts Movement* (New York 1981)

David Cathers, *Gustav Stickley* (London 2003)

David Cathers and Alexander Vertikoff, *Stickley Style: Arts and Crafts Homes in the Craftsman Tradition* (New York 1999)

Jon Catleugh, *William De Morgan Tiles* (London 1983)

Freeman Champney, *Art & Glory: the Story of Elbert Hubbard* (Kent, OH 1983)

Children's Employment Commission, *First Report of the Commissioners: Mines* (London 1842)

Garth Clark, *The Mad Potter of Biloxi: The Art & Life of George E Ohr* (New York 1989)

Robert Judson Clark (ed.), *The Arts and Crafts Movement in America, 1876–1916* (exh. cat., Princeton, NJ 1972)

Margot Coatts and Elizabeth Lewis (eds), *Heywood Sumner: Artist and Archaeologist, 1853–1940* (exh. cat., Winchester 1986)

Margaret Cole, *Robert Owen of New Lanark* (London 1953)

Mary Comino, *Gimson and the Barnsleys: 'Wonderful Furniture of a Commonplace Kind'* (London 1980)

Ulrich Conrads (ed.), *Programmes and Manifestoes on 20th-Century Architecture* (trans. Michael Bullock: London 1970)

Edward Tyas Cook and Alexander Wedderburn (eds), *The Works of John Ruskin*, 39 vols (London 1903–12)

Catherine Cooke, 'Shekhtel in Kelvingrove and Mackintosh on the Petrovka: Two Russo-Scottish Exhibitions at the Turn of the Century', *Scottish Slavonic Review*, 10 (Spring 1988), pp. 177–203

Catherine Cooke, *Russian Avant-Garde: Theories of Art, Architecture and the City* (London 1995)

Peter Cormack, *Christopher Whall, 1849–1924: Arts & Crafts Stained Glass Worker* (exh. cat., London 1979)

Peter Cormack, 'Recreating a Tradition: Christopher Whall (1849–1924) and the Arts and Crafts Renaissance of English Stained Glass', in Nicola Gordon Bowe (ed.), *Art and the National Dream: The Search for Vernacular Expression in Turn-of-the-Century Design* (Dublin 1993), pp. 15–42

Peter Cormack, *The Stained Glass Work of Christopher Whall, 1849–1924: 'Aglow with Brave Resplendent Colour'* (Boston, MA 1999)

Peter Cormack, 'Decorative and Applied Arts', in *Pre-Raphaelite and Other Masters: The Andrew Lloyd Webber Collection* (exh. cat., London 2003), pp. 229–75

Alan Crawford (ed.), *By Hammer and Hand: The Arts and Crafts Movement in Birmingham* (Birmingham 1984)

Alan Crawford, *C R Ashbee: Architect, Designer and Romantic Socialist* (2nd edn, New Haven, CT and London 2005; first published New Haven, CT and London 1985)

Alan Crawford, *Charles Rennie Mackintosh* (London 1995)

Alan Crawford, 'W A S Benson, Machinery, and the Arts and Crafts Movement in Britain', *Journal of Decorative and Propaganda Arts*, 24 (2002), pp. 94–117

Alan Crawford and Fiona MacCarthy (eds), *C R Ashbee & the Guild of Handicraft* (exh. cat., Cheltenham 1981)

David Crowley, *National Style and Nation-State: Design in Poland from the Vernacular Revival to the International Style* (Manchester and New York 1992)

David Crowley, 'The Uses of Peasant Design in Austria-Hungary in the Late Nineteenth and Early Twentieth Centuries', *Studies in the Decorative Arts*, 2, no. 2 (1995), pp. 2–28

David Crowley, 'Finding Poland in the Margins: the Case of the Zakopane Style', *Journal of Design History*, 14, no. 2 (2001), pp. 105–16

Elizabeth Cumming, *Phoebe Anna Traquair, 1852–1936* (exh. cat., Edinburgh 1993)

Elizabeth Cumming and Nicola Gordon Bowe, *The Arts and Crafts Movements in Dublin and Edinburgh, 1885–1925* (Dublin 1998)

Elizabeth Cumming and Wendy Kaplan, *The Arts and Crafts Movement* (London 1991)

Peter Davey, *Arts and Crafts Architecture* (London 1995; first published London 1980)

John R Davis, *The Great Exhibition* (Stroud 1999)

Bert R Denker (ed.), *Substance of Style: Perspectives on the American Arts and Crafts Movement* (Winterthur, DE 1996)

Bernard Denvir, *The Late Victorians: Art, Design and Society 1852–1910* (London 1986)

Michael Drury, *Wandering Architects: In Pursuit of an Arts and Crafts Ideal* (Stamford 2000)

Leonard K Eaton, *Two Chicago Architects and Their Clients: Frank Lloyd Wright and Howard Van Doren Shaw* (Cambridge, MA 1969)

Bridget Elliott and Janice Helland (eds), *Women Artists and the Decorative Arts, 1880–1935: The Gender of Ornament* (Aldershot 2003)

Anita J Ellis, *Rookwood Pottery: The Glorious Gamble* (New York 1992)

Gyula Ernyey (ed.), *Britain and Hungary: Contacts in Architecture and Design during the Nineteenth and Twentieth Century. Essays and Studies* (Budapest 1999)

Gyula Ernyey (ed.), *Britain and Hungary 2: Contacts in Architecture, Design, Art and Theory during the Nineteenth and Twentieth Centuries* (Budapest 2003)

Stuart Evans, 'The Century Guild Connection', in J H G Archer (ed.), *Art and Architecture in Victorian Manchester* (Manchester 1985), pp. 250–68

Michelle Facos, 'The Ideal Swedish Home: Carl Larsson's Lilla Hyttnäs', in Christopher Reed (ed.), *Not at Home: The Suppression of Domesticity in Modern Art and Architecture* (London 1996), pp. 81–91

Michelle Facos, *Nationalism and the Nordic Imagination* (Berkeley, CA 1998)

Gabriele Fahr-Becker, *Wiener Werkstätte, 1903–1932* (Cologne 1995)

Dennis Farr, *English Art 1870–1940* (Oxford 1984)

Charlotte and Peter Fiell, *William Morris (1834–1896)* (Cologne 1999)

Ian Fletcher, *Rediscovering Herbert Horne: Poet, Architect, Typographer, Art Historian* (Greensboro, NC 1990)

Barbara Floyd and Julia Baldwin, *The Noble Craftsman We Promote: The Arts and Crafts Movement in the American Midwest* (exh. cat., Toledo, OH 1999)

John Crosby Freeman, *The Forgotten Rebel: Gustav Stickley and his Craftsman Mission Furniture* (New York 1966)

Oliver Garnett, *Standen, West Sussex* (London 1993)

Trevor Garnham, James Macaulay and Edward R Bosley, *Arts and Crafts Masterpieces* (St Andrews Church, Roker, Glasgow School of Art and First Church of Christ Scientist, Berkeley) (London 1999)

Katalin Gellér, 'Eléments symbolistes dans l'œuvre des artistes de la colonie de Gödöllő', *Acta Historiae Artium*, 28 (1982), pp. 131–74

Katalin Gellér, 'Hungarian Art Nouveau and its English Sources', *Hungarian Studies*, 6, no. II (1990), pp. 155–65

Katalin Gellér, 'Romantic Elements in Hungarian Art Nouveau', in Nicola Gordon Bowe (ed.), *Art and the National Dream: The Search for Vernacular Expression in Turn-of-the-Century Design* (Dublin 1993), pp. 117–26

Charlotte Gere, *Nineteenth-Century Decoration. The Art of the Interior* (London 1989)

Charlotte Gere and Michael Whiteway, *Nineteenth-Century Design: From Pugin to Mackintosh* (London 1993)

David Gilson de Long (ed.), *Frank Lloyd Wright and the Living City* (London 1998)

Mark Girouard, *The Victorian Country House* (Oxford 1971)

Veronica Franklin Gould, *The Watts Chapel, an Arts and Crafts Memorial* (Compton 1993)

Veronica Franklin Gould, *Mary Seton Watts, 1849–1938: Unsung Heroine of the Art Nouveau* (London 1998)

Rosalind P Gray (later Blakesley), 'Questions of Identity at Abramtsevo', in Laura Morowitz and William Vaughan (eds), *Artistic*

Brotherhoods in the Nineteenth Century (Aldershot 2000), pp. 103–21

Nancy E Green and Jessie Poesch, *Arthur Wesley Dow and American Arts and Crafts* (New York 1999)

Paul Greenhalgh, *Ephemeral Vistas: The Expositions Universelles, Great Exhibitions and World's Fairs, 1851–1939* (Manchester 1988)

Paul Greenhalgh, 'Education, Entertainment and Politics: Lessons from the Great Exhibitions', in Peter Vergo (ed.), *The New Museology* (London 1989), pp. 74–98

Paul Greenhalgh (ed.), *Quotations and Sources on Design and the Decorative Arts* (Manchester 1993)

Paul Greenhalgh (ed.), *Art Nouveau, 1890–1914* (exh. cat., London 2000)

Mary Greensted (ed.), *An Anthology of the Arts and Crafts Movement: Writings by Ashbee, Lethaby, Gimson and their Contemporaries* (London 2005)

Mary Greensted et al., *The Arts and Crafts Movement in the Cotswolds* (Stroud 1993)

Mary Greensted and Sophia Wilson (eds), *Originality and Initiative: The Arts and Crafts Archives at Cheltenham* (London 2003)

Martin Greenwood, *The Designs of William De Morgan: A Catalogue* (Shepton Beauchamp 1989)

Diane Haigh, *Baillie Scott: The Artistic House* (London 1995)

Ian Hamerton (ed.), *W A S Benson: Arts and Crafts Luminary and Pioneer of Modern Design* (Woodbridge 2005)

Mark Hamilton, *Rare Spirit: A Life of William De Morgan, 1839–1917* (London 1997)

David A Hanks, *The Decorative Designs of Frank Lloyd Wright* (exh. cat., Washington, DC 1979)

Martin Harrison, *Victorian Stained Glass* (London 1980)

Tanya Harrod, *The Crafts in Britain in the 20th Century* (New Haven, CT and London 1999)

Charles Harvey and Jon Press, *William Morris: Design and Enterprise in Victorian Britain* (Manchester 1991)

Charles Harvey and Jon Press, *Art, Enterprise and Ethics: The Life and Works of William Morris* (London 1996)

Dean Hawkes (ed.), *Modern Country Homes in England: The Arts and Crafts Architecture of Barry Parker* (Cambridge 1986)

Janice Helland, 'The Critics and the Arts and Crafts: The Instance of Margaret Macdonald and Charles Rennie Mackintosh', *Art History*, 17, no. 2 (June 1994), pp. 209–27

Janice Helland, *The Studios of Frances and Margaret Macdonald* (Manchester 1996)

Janice Helland, 'A Sense of Extravagance: Margaret Macdonald's Gesso Panels, 1900–1903', *Visual Culture in Britain*, 2:1 (Spring 2001), pp. 1–15

John Heskett, *Design in Germany, 1870–1918* (London 1986)

Robert Hewison, *John Ruskin: The Argument of the Eye* (London 1976)

Robert Hewison, *Ruskin and Oxford: The Art of Education* (Oxford 1996)

Robert Hewison (ed.), *Ruskin's Artists: Studies in the Victorian Visual Economy* (London 2000)

Grant Hildebrand, *The Wright Space: Pattern and Meaning in Frank Lloyd Wright's Houses* (Seattle, WA 1991)

Alison Hilton, 'The Peasant House and its Furnishing: Decorative Principles in Russian Folk Art', *Journal of Decorative and Propaganda Arts*, 11 (Winter 1989), pp. 10–29

Alison Hilton, *Russian Folk Art* (Bloomington, IN 1995)

Tim Hilton, *John Ruskin: The Early Years 1819–1859* (New Haven, CT and London 1985)

Tim Hilton, *John Ruskin: The Later Years* (New Haven, CT and London 2000)

Wendy Hitchmough, *C F A Voysey* (London 1995)

Wendy Hitchmough, *Arts and Crafts Gardens* (London 1997)

Wendy Hitchmough, *The Arts and Crafts Home* (London 2000)

Edward Hollamby, Trevor Garnham and Brian Edwards, *Arts and Crafts Houses I* (Red House, Melsetter House and Goddards) (London 1999)

Dard Hunter, *My Life With Paper: An Autobiography* (New York 1958)

Michael Jacobs, *The Good and Simple Life: Artist Colonies in Europe and America* (Oxford 1985)

Gertrude Jekyll and Lawrence Weaver, *Arts and Crafts Gardens* (Woodbridge 1997; revised edn of *Gardens for Small Country Houses*, London 1913)

Anthony Jones, *Charles Rennie Mackintosh* (London 1990)

Owen Jones, *The Grammar of Ornament* (London 1856)

Journal of Design and Manufactures (London 1849–52)

Shona Kallestrup, *Eclectic and Neo-National Aspects in Romanian Art and Design 1878–1930* (PhD thesis, University of St Andrews 2001)

Shona Kallestrup, 'Romanian "National Style" and the 1906 Bucharest Jubilee Exhibition', *Journal of Design History*, 15, no. 3 (2002), pp. 147–62

Wendy Kaplan (ed.), *Encyclopedia of Arts and Crafts: The International Arts Movement, 1850–1920* (London 1989)

Wendy Kaplan (ed.), *Designing Modernity: The Arts of Reform and Persuasion, 1885–1945* (London 1995)

Wendy Kaplan (ed.), *Charles Rennie Mackintosh* (exh. cat., Glasgow, London and New York 1996)

Wendy Kaplan (ed.), *The Arts and Crafts Movement in Europe and America: Design for the Modern World* (exh. cat., Los Angeles, CA 2004)

Wendy Kaplan, Eileen Boris et al., *'The Art that is Life': The Arts and Crafts Movement in America, 1875–1920* (Boston, MA 1987)

Edgar Kaufman Jr and Ben Raeburn (eds), *Frank Lloyd Wright: Writings and Buildings* (New York 1960)

Norman Kelvin (ed.), *The Collected Letters of William Morris*, 4 vols (Princeton, NJ 1984)

Katalin Keserü, 'Vernacularism and its Special Characteristics in Hungarian Art', in Nicola Gordon Bowe (ed.), *Art and the National Dream: the Search for Vernacular Expression in Turn-of-the-Century Design* (Dublin 1993), pp. 127–42

Katalin Keserü, 'The Workshops of Gödöllő: Transformations of a Morrisian Theme', *Journal of Design History*, I, no. 1 (1998), pp. 1–23

Evgenia Kirichenko, 'The Historical Museum: A Moscow Design Competition 1875–83', *Architectural Design*, 7/8 (1987), pp. 24–6

Evgenia Kirichenko, *Russian Design and the Fine Arts, 1750–1917* (New York 1991)

Francis D Klingender, *Art and the Industrial Revolution* (London 1947)

James D Kornwolf, *M H Baillie Scott and the Arts and Crafts Movement:*

Pioneers of Modern Design (Baltimore, MD and London 1972)

Künstlerkolonie Mathildenhöhe Darmstadt 1899–1914: Das Buch zum Museum/The Museum Book (Darmstadt 1999)

Natasha Kuzmanovic, *John Paul Cooper. Designer and Craftsman of the Arts and Crafts Movements* (Stroud 1999)

Lionel Lambourne, *Utopian Craftsmen: The Arts and Crafts Movement from the Cotswolds to Chicago* (London 1980)

George P Landow, *The Aesthetic and Critical Theories of John Ruskin* (Princeton, NJ 1971)

Barbara Miller Lane, *National Romanticism and Modern Architecture in Germany and the Scandinavian Countries* (Cambridge 2000)

Paul Larmour, *The Arts and Crafts Movement in Ireland* (Belfast 1992)

Vernon Lee, *Miss Brown*, 3 vols (London 1884)

William Richard Lethaby, 'Design and Industry', in *Form in Civilisation: Collected Papers on Art and Labour* (London 1922)

William Richard Lethaby, *Philip Webb and his Work* (London 1979; first published Oxford 1935)

Neil Levine, *The Architecture of Frank Lloyd Wright* (Princeton, NJ 1996)

Elisabeth Lichtenberger, *Vienna: Bridge between Cultures* (London and New York 1993)

Karen Livingstone and Linda Parry (eds), *International Arts and Crafts* (exh. cat., London 2005)

Coy L Ludwig, *The Arts and Crafts Movement in the New York State 1890s–1920s* (Hamilton, NY 1983)

James Macauley, Wendy Hitchmough and Edward R Bosley, *Arts and Crafts Houses II* (Hill House,

the Homestead and the Gamble House) (London 1999)

Fiona MacCarthy, *A History of British Design, 1830–1970* (London 1979)

Fiona MacCarthy, *The Simple Life: C R Ashbee in the Cotswolds* (London 1981)

Fiona MacCarthy, *British Design since 1880: A Visual History* (London 1982)

Fiona MacCarthy, *Eric Gill* (London 1989)

Fiona MacCarthy, *William Morris: A Life for our Time* (London 1994)

John William Mackail, *The Life of William Morris*, 2 vols (new edn, London 1901; first published London 1899)

Randell L Makinson, *Greene & Greene: Architecture as a Fine Art* (Salt Lake City, UT 1977)

Randell L Makinson, *Greene & Greene: Furniture and Related Designs* (Salt Lake City, UT 1979)

V Mamontov, *Vospominaniya o russkikh khudozhnikakh* (Moscow 1950)

Jan Marsh, *Jane and May Morris, a Biographical Story 1839–1938* (London 1986)

Karl Marx, *A Contribution to the Critique of Political Economy* (London 1971; first published Berlin 1859)

Henri Jean Louis Joseph Massé, *The Art Workers' Guild 1884–1934* (Oxford 1935)

Roberta A Mayer and Carolyn K Lane, 'Disassociating the "Associated Artists": The Early Business Ventures of Louis C Tiffany, Candace T Wheeler, and Lockwood de Forest', *Studies in the Decorative Arts*, 8, no. 2 (Spring–Summer 2001), pp. 2–36

Joseph McBrinn, 'The Peasant and Folk Art Revival in Ireland, 1890–1920: With Special Reference to Ulster', *Ulster Folklife*, 48 (2002), pp. 14–61

Standish Meacham, *Regaining Paradise: Englishness and the Garden City Movement* (New Haven, CT and London 1998)

Patrick J Meehan (ed.), *Truth Against the World: Frank Lloyd Wright Speaks for an Organic Architecture* (New York and Toronto 1987)

Christopher Menz, *Morris & Company, Pre-Raphaelites and the Arts and Crafts Movement in South Australia* (exh. cat., Adelaide 1994)

Marilee Boyd Meyer (ed.), *Inspiring Reform: Boston's Arts and Crafts Movement* (New York 1997)

Mervyn Miller, *Raymond Unwin: Garden Cities and Town Planning* (Leicester 1992)

May Morris (ed.), *The Collected Works of William Morris*, 24 vols (London 1992; first published London 1910–15)

William Morris, *A Dream of John Ball and A King's Lesson* (Pocket Edition, London 1913; first published London 1888)

Hermann Muthesius, *The English House* (trans. Janet Seligman, London 1979; first published Berlin 1904–5)

Gillian Naylor, *The Arts and Crafts Movement: A study of its sources, ideals and influence on design theory* (London 1990; first published London 1971)

Gillian Naylor, *The Bauhaus Reassessed: Sources and Design Theory* (London 1985)

Gillian Naylor (ed.), *William Morris by Himself: Designs and Writings* (London 2000; first published London 1988)

Zsófia Németh (ed.), *Women at the Gödöllő Artists' Colony* (exh. cat., Glasgow 2004)

Riitta Nikula, *Armas Lindgren 1874–1929* (Helsinki 1988)

Lauren M O'Connell, 'A Rational, National Architecture: Viollet-le-

Duc's Modest Proposal for Russia', *Journal of the Society of Architectural Historians*, 52 (December 1993), pp. 436–52

Amy F Ogata, *Art Nouveau and the Social Vision of Modern Living: Belgian Artists in a European Context* (Cambridge 2001)

M Omilanowska, 'Searching for a National Style in Polish Architecture at the End of the 19th and Beginning of the 20th Century', in Nicola Gordon Bowe (ed.), *Art and the National Dream: The Search for Vernacular Expression in Turn-of-the-Century Design* (Dublin 1993), pp. 99–116

Nancy E Owen, *Rookwood and the Industry of Art: Women, Culture, and Commerce, 1880–1913* (Athens, OH 2001)

Linda Parry, *Textiles of the Arts and Crafts Movement* (London 1988)

Linda Parry (ed.), *William Morris: Art and Kelmscott* (Woodbridge 1996)

Linda Parry (ed.), *William Morris* (exh. cat., London 1996)

Eleanora Paston (ed.), *Stil' zhizni - stil' iskusstva* (Moscow 2000)

Eleanora Paston, *Abramtsevo: iskusstvo i zhizn'* (Moscow 2003)

Netta Peacock, 'A Log House Dining Room in Russia', *The Artist*, 24 (January–April 1899), pp. 1–7

Netta Peacock, 'The New Movement in Russian Decorative Art', *The Studio*, 22 (1901), pp. 268–76

Amelia Peck and Carol Irish, *Candace Wheeler: the Art and Enterprise of American Design, 1875–1900* (exh. cat., New York 2001)

Nikolaus Pevsner, *Pioneers of Modern Design: From William Morris to Walter Gropius* (London 1936)

Bruce Brooks Pfeiffer (ed.), *Frank*

Lloyd Wright: Collected Writings, 5 vols (New York 1992–1995)

Stephen Pudney, 'Alexander Fisher: Pioneer of Arts and Crafts Enamelling', *The Decorative Arts Society Journal*, 23 (1999), pp. 71–85.

Augustus Welby Northmore Pugin, *Contrasts* (London 1969; first published London 1836)

Louise Purbrick, 'South Kensington Museum: The building of the house of Henry Cole', in Marcia Pointon (ed.), *Art Apart. Art Institutions and Ideology across England and North America* (Manchester 1994), pp. 69–86

Louise Purbrick (ed.), *The Great Exhibition of 1851: New Interdisciplinary Essays* (Manchester and New York 2001)

Michael Raeburn (ed.), *The Twilight of the Tsars: Russian Art at the Turn of the Century* (exh. cat., London 1991)

Aileen Reid, *Brentham: A History of the Pioneer Garden Suburb 1901–2001* (London 2000)

Maria Rennhofer, *Koloman Moser: Master of Viennese Modernism* (London 2002)

Margaret Richardson, *Architects of the Arts and Crafts Movement* (London 1983)

Margaret Richardson, *Sketches by Edwin Lutyens* (London 1994)

Duncan Robinson, *William Morris, Edward Burne-Jones and the Kelmscott Chaucer* (London 1982)

Duncan Robinson and Stephen Wildman, *Morris & Company in Cambridge* (exh. cat., Cambridge 1980)

William Rothenstein, *Men and Memories: Recollections of William Rothenstein*, 2 vols (London 1931–2)

Royal Academy of Arts, *Vienna Secession: Art Nouveau to 1970* (London 1971)

Godfrey Rubens, *William Richard Lethaby: His Life and Work 1857–1931* (London 1986)

John Ruskin, *The Lamp of Beauty: Writings on Art* (3rd edn, ed. Joan Evans, London 1995)

Andrew Saint, *Richard Norman Shaw* (New Haven, CT and London 1976)

Andrew Saint et al., *Cragside, Northumberland* (London 1992)

Andrew Saint et al., *London Suburbs* (London 1999)

Ekaterina V Sakharova (ed.), *Vasilii Dmitrievich Polenov, Elena Dmitrievna Polenova: khronika sem'i khudozhnikov* (Moscow 1964)

Wendy Salmond, 'The Solomenko Embroidery Workshops', *Journal of Decorative and Propaganda Arts*, 5 (Summer 1987), pp. 126–43

Wendy Salmond, 'Reviving Folk Art in Russia: The Moscow Zemstvo and the Kustar Art Industries', in Nicola Gordon Bowe (ed.), *Art and the National Dream: The Search for Vernacular Expression in Turn-of-the-Century Design* (Dublin 1993), pp. 81–98

Wendy Salmond, 'Design Education and the Quest for National Identity in Late Imperial Russia: The Case of the Stroganov School', *Studies in the Decorative Arts*, 1, II (Spring 1994), pp. 2–24

Wendy Salmond, *The Arts and Crafts in Late Imperial Russia: Reviving the Kustar Art Industries, 1870–1917* (Cambridge 1996)

Ilona Sármány-Parson, 'The Influence of the British Arts and Crafts Movement in Budapest and Vienna', *Acta Historiae Artium*, 33 (1987–8), pp. 179–98

Peter Savage, *Lorimer and the Edinburgh Craft Designers* (Edinburgh 1980)

Daniel Schaffer, *Garden Cities for America: The Radburn Experience* (Philadelphia, PA 1982)

Roberto Schezen, *Vienna 1850–1930, Architecture* (New York 1992)

Carl E Schorske, *Fin-de-Siècle Vienna: Politics and Culture* (New York 1981)

Frederic J Schwartz, *The Werkbund* (New Haven, CT and London 1996)

Werner J Schweiger, *Wiener Werkstätte: Design in Vienna, 1903–1932* (London 1984)

John Dando Sedding, *Garden Craft Old and New* (London 1891)

John Dando Sedding, *Art and Handicraft* (London 1893)

A Charles Sewter, *The Stained Glass of William Morris and his Circle*, 2 vols (New Haven, CT and London 1974–5)

Douglass Shand-Tucci, *Boston Bohemia, 1881–1900: Ralph Adams Cram, Life and Architecture* (Amherst, MA 1995)

Felix Shay, *Elbert Hubbard of East Aurora* (New York 1926)

Duncan Simpson, *C F A Voysey, an Architect of Individuality* (London 1979)

Peyton Skipworth, *Holy Trinity, Sloane Street* (London 2002)

Helen Sloan, *May Morris 1862–1938* (exh. cat., London 1989)

Bruce Smith and Alexander Vertikoff, *Greene and Greene: Master Builders of the American Arts and Crafts Movement* (London 1998)

John Boulton Smith, 'Art Nouveau and National Romanticism in Finland', *Apollo*, CXV, no. 243 (1982), pp. 380–7

Mary Ann Smith, *Gustav Stickley: the Craftsman* (Syracuse, NY 1983)

Michael Snodin and Elisabet Stavenow-Hidemark (eds), *Carl and Karin Larsson, Creators of the Swedish Style* (exh. cat., London 1997)

Michael Snodin and John Styles, *Design and the Decorative Arts, Britain 1500–1900* (London 2001)

Society of Arts, *Lectures on the Results of the Great Exhibition of 1851*, 2 vols (London 1852–3)

Gavin Stamp, *Edwin Lutyens: Country Houses* (London 2001)

Peter Stansky, *Redesigning the World: William Morris, the 1880s and the Arts and Crafts* (Princeton, NJ 1985)

Elisabet Stavenow-Hidemark, 'Viking Revival and Art Nouveau: Traditions of Excellence', in D R McFadden (ed.), *Scandinavian Modern Design 1880–1980* (New York 1982)

L A Stein, 'German Design and National Identity 1890–1914', in Wendy Kaplan (ed.), *Designing Modernity: The Arts of Reform and Persuasion, 1885–1945* (London 1995), pp. 49–77

Grigory Yu Sternin (ed.), *Abramtsevo: khudozhestvennyi kruzhok, zhivopis', grafika, skul'ptura, teatr, masterskie* (Leningrad 1988)

Gustav Stickley, *Craftsman Homes: Architecture and Furnishings of the American Arts and Crafts Movement* (London 1979; first published New York 1909)

Gustav Stickley, *More Craftsman Homes: Floor Plans and Illustrations for 78 Mission Style Dwellings* (London 1982; first published New York 1912)

Julian Symons, *Thomas Carlyle: The Life and Ideas of a Prophet* (London 1952)

Julian Symons (ed.), *Carlyle: Selected Works, Reminiscences and Letters* (London 1955)

Lou Taylor and David Crowley (eds), *The Lost Arts of Europe: The Haslemere Museum Collection of European Peasant Art* (Haslemere 2000)

George Bernhard Tennyson (ed.), *A Carlyle Reader: Selections from the Writings of Thomas Carlyle* (Cambridge 1984)

Edward Palmer Thompson, *William Morris: Romantic to Revolutionary* (London 1997; first published London 1955)

Paul Thompson, *The Work of William Morris* (3rd edn, Oxford and New York 1991; first published London 1967)

Susan Otis Thompson, *American Book Design and William Morris* (revised edn, London 1996; first published New York 1977)

Adrian Tinniswood, *The Arts and Crafts House* (London 1999)

Pamela Todd, *The Arts and Crafts Companion* (London 2004)

Kenneth R. Trapp (ed.), *The Arts and Crafts Movement in California: Living the Good Life* (New York 1993)

George Macaulay Trevelyan, *Illustrated English Social History, vol. 4. The Nineteenth Century* (6th edn, Harmondsworth 1968)

Ritva Tuomi (later Wäre), 'On the Search for a National Style', *Abacus: Museum of Finnish Architecture Yearbook* (Helsinki 1979)

Robert C Twombly, *Frank Lloyd Wright: His Life and His Architecture* (New York 1979)

Renate Ulmer, *Jügendstil in Darmstadt* (Darmstadt 1997)

Kirk Varnedoe (ed.), *Vienna 1900: Art, Architecture and Design* (exh. cat., New York 1986)

Peter Vergo, *Art in Vienna 1898–1918* (3rd edn, London 1993; first published London 1975)

Marie Via and Marjorie Searl (eds), *Head, Heart and Hand: Elbert Hubbard and the Roycrofters* (Rochester, NY 1994)

Angela Volker, *Textiles of the Wiener Werkstatte 1910–1932* (London 1994)

Tod M. Volpe and Beth Cathers (eds), *Treasures of the American Arts and Crafts Movement, 1890–1920* (New York 1988)

Diane Waggoner (ed.), *'The Beauty of Life': William Morris and the Art of Design* (exh. cat., San Marino, CA 2003)

Robert Waissenberger et al. (eds), *Vienna, 1890–1920* (New York 1984)

Ritva Wäre, 'How Nationalism was Expressed in Finnish Architecture at the Turn of the Last Century', in Nicola Gordon Bowe (ed.), *Art and the National Dream: The Search for Vernacular Expression in Turn-of-the-Century Design* (Dublin 1993), pp. 169–80

Ritva Wäre, 'The National Context' in Anne Stenros (ed.), *Visions of Modern Finnish Design* (Keuruu 1999)

Ritva Wäre, 'From Historicist Architecture to Early Modernism', in Marja-Riitta Norri, Elina Standertskjöld and Wilfried Want (eds), *20th-Century Architecture: Finland* (Helsinki 2000), pp. 17–37

Toshio Watanabe (ed.), *Ruskin in Japan 1890–1940: Nature for Art, Art for Life* (exh. cat., Sheffield 1997)

Ray Watkinson, *William Morris as Designer* (2nd edn, London 1990; first published London 1967)

Lawrence Weaver, *Houses and Gardens by E. L. Lutyens* (London 1913; republished Woodbridge 1981)

Uwe Westphal, *The Bauhaus* (London, 1991)

Candace Wheeler, *The Development of Embroidery in America* (New York and London 1921)

Frank Whitford, *The Bauhaus* (London 1984)

Stephen Wildman and John Christian, *Edward Burne-Jones: Victorian Artist – Dreamer* (exh. cat., New York 1998)

Robert Winter (ed.), *Toward a Simpler Way of Life: the Arts and Crafts Architects of California* (Berkeley, CA 1997)

Christopher Wood, *The Life and Works of Sir Edward Burne-Jones* (London 1998)

Auke van der Woud, *The Art of Building from Classicism to Modernity: the Dutch Architectural Debate 1840–1900* (Aldershot 2002)

Frank Lloyd Wright, *An Organic Architecture: The Architecture of Democracy* (London 1970; facsimile of 1st edn, 1939)

Frank Lloyd Wright, *The Early Work of Frank Lloyd Wright, with a new introduction by Grant Carpenter Manson* (New York 1982; originally published as *Ausgefuhrte Bauten* with an introduction by Charles Robert Ashbee, Berlin 1911)

INDEX

263

PICTURE CREDITS

ACKNOWLEDGEMENTS

Any book of this nature draws on the work of experts in specialized fields, and I am indebted to David Crowley, Shona Kallestrup, Amy Ogata and Wendy Salmond for their pioneering work in Poland, Romania, Belgium and Russia. Shona showed particular generosity in sending me her unpublished work. In Great Britain and Ireland, I would like to thank Annette Carruthers for organizing an excellent conference on the Arts and Crafts Movement, and Felicity Ashbee, Amy Clarke, Peter Cormack, Stuart Evans, Kathryn Ferry, Norah Gillow, Nicola Gordon Bowe, Mary Greensted, Diane Haigh, Carola Hicks, Richard Jefferies, Frank Johnson, Juliet Kinchin, Karen Livingstone, Stephen Lovell, Sandra McElroy, Andrew Saint, and David and Jonathan Stephenson for answering specific queries. I am also indebted to scholars abroad for their hospitality and expertise. Notable among them have been Edward Bosley, William Craft Brumfield, Alison Hilton, Sona Hoisington and Karen Kettering in the United States; Renate Ulmer and Wolfgang Glüber in Darmstadt; Ritva Wäre, Marianne Aav, Marjatta Levanto, Helmiriitta Sariola, Timo Huusko and Petja Hovinheimo in Helsinki; Marianne Nilsson in Sundborn; Jesco Oser, Galina Andreeva, Anna Grigorieva, Ella Paston, Irina Shumanova, Evgenia Ilyukhina, Lydia Torstensen, Evgenia Plotnikova and Natalia Ardashnikova in Moscow; Elena Nesterova and Tatiana Verizhnikova in St Petersburg; Lydia Kudryavzeva in Talashkino; and Edyta Supińska-Polit and Andrzej Szczerski in Poland. My research trip to Finland was facilitated by Timo Valjakka, Susanna Pettersson and Michael and Hannele Branch, to whom I extend my sincere thanks, while that in Russia was stimulated by lengthy debates with Catherine Cooke. I would like here to pay tribute to Catherine's groundbreaking research, and to her generosity in sharing her work. She is sorely missed following her tragic death in 2004. I would also like to acknowledge my gratitude to the following, among others who wish to remain anonymous, for opening the doors of their houses: Joe Federici in River Forest, Chicago; John and Jennifer Talbot in Cambridge; David Stemple in St Andrews; Fiero Messina, who found the keys to open Ashbee's house in Taormina; and the late Edward Hollamby and his wife Doris, who welcomed me on my first visit to William Morris's Red House.

I have received invaluable comments on early drafts from Sue Ashworth, Susanna Avery-Quash, Edward Bosley, Graham Clarke, David Crowley, Shona Kallestrup, Katalin Keserü, Sheila Kirk, Aleksandra Koutny, Marjatta Levanto, Gilly Macmillan, John Milner, Jesco Oser, Susanna Pettersson, Margaret Richardson, Wendy Salmond, Zoltan Sarnyai, Aya Soika and Ritva Wäre. I have also been blessed in working with Pat Barylski and Julia MacKenzie, editors so sensitive and intelligent that I always left their offices happy, even when they told me to rewrite the first half of the book. At Phaidon Press, I am grateful to Jane Ace, David Anfam and Beulah Davies for their support, and to Sophia Gibb and Emmanuelle Peri for their patience and persistence in assembling the images. Rosie Ibbotson, Lizzie Morgan and Margaret Outen were research assistants of the highest calibre, and innumerable librarians and archivists expedited my work, in particular Ann Scheid of the Gamble House, California and, in Cambridge, Pat Aske of Pembroke College, Patricia McGuire of King's College, and Madeleine Brown of the Faculty of Architecture and History of Art. The British Academy, the University of Newcastle, the University of Kent, the University of Cambridge, Pembroke College and the Scandinavian Studies Fund all generously funded aspects of my research, and I am deeply grateful to the fellows of Pembroke College and the staff of the History of Art Department at Cambridge for providing a congenial and stimulating atmosphere in which to complete this book.

Finally, I would like to acknowledge my greatest professional debt, which is to Alan Crawford, a scholar of remarkable distinction and wit for whom my respect knows no bounds. Alan has written so many pages of eloquent, incisive and often humorous advice that they rival this book in length, and themselves deserve to be published. On a personal note, I would like to thank Priscilla Chase, Philippa Haden, Tessa Harvey, John and Caitlin Kennedy, Fiona Rawes and Emma Widdis for their encouragement in the closing months of this project; Nigel and Clare Casey for their hospitality in Moscow; Simon Gray, Peter de Voisey, Peter Donaldson and John and Hilary Furlong for their unwavering enthusiasm; and my parents Mavis and Peter Gray, who read endless drafts of this book but still managed to get a pub quiz question on William Morris wrong. Most patient of all has been Patrick Blakesley, who from the Moscow ring-road to the shores of Swedish lakes has accompanied me in my quest to understand the Arts and Crafts. For someone who at heart prefers books about plants or pies, his support has been extraordinary. Everywhere I look in my life there are things which Patrick has done to enhance it, and this book is for him, with love.